A Shared Home Place
SEAMUS MALLON

To Orla, Lara and Mark

A Shared Home Place

SEAMUS MALLON

with ANDY POLLAK

THE LILLIPUT PRESS
DUBLIN

First published 2019 by
THE LILLIPUT PRESS
62–63 Sitric Road, Arbour Hill
Dublin 7, Ireland
www.lilliputpress.ie

ISBN 978 1 84351 7740

10 9 8 7 6 5 4 3

The Lilliput Press gratefully acknowledges the financial
support of the Arts Council/An Chomhairle Ealaíon.

Set in 11 pt on 15 pt Garamond with
Frutiger display by Marsha Swan
Printed in Dublin by ePrint

Contents

Illustrations between pages 114 and 115.

Acknowledgments

This book would not have happened without Tim O'Connor, who suggested to Seamus Mallon that he should ask Andy Pollak to collaborate with him on writing it. Particular thanks are also due to Tim for his detailed recall and wise interpretation of the Good Friday Agreement. Special thanks also go to Pat Hynes, who, along with Tim, acted as an informal editorial advisory team; Frank Sheridan, for his great help with archival material; and Dáithí Ó Ceallaigh, an invaluable source of advice and support throughout.

Other people who contributed their help and insights were: Orla Mallon, Marie Harte, Nuala Feehan, Brian Barrington, Alex Attwood, Noel Dorr, Cian Ferriter, David Donoghue, Eugene Reavey, John Redmond, Frank Feely, Anne Roper, Sean Farren, Brid Rodgers, Colm Larkin, Hugh Logue, Mike Nesbitt, Seán Ó hUiginn, Tony McCusker, Billy Gamble, Michael Lillis, Mary McNulty, Gary Ansbro, John Rogers, Peter Makem, Cormac McCarthy, Tom Kelly (*Irish News* columnist), Anne Cadwallader, Barry Cullen, Niall Gibbons and the helpful and efficient people at Rathmines Public Library; also Doireann Ní Bhriain, as always.

At Lilliput, particular thanks are due to publisher Antony Farrell, who took on the job of copy-editing our manuscript himself, and to his colleague Ruth Hallinan, for help in a multitude of ways.

Our grateful thanks go to all of them.

Introduction

Courage and generosity: those are the two words that come to mind when I think of Seamus Mallon. Courage because for twenty-five years between the 1970s and 1990s he spoke out ceaselessly against violence from whatever quarter it came, republican or loyalist or state forces. As a result he suffered constant threats (including death threats); physical attacks on him, his family and his home; intimidation and vilification. He vowed that he would attend every funeral in his Armagh and Newry constituency, whether the victim was civilian, IRA or security force member, and frequently took face-to-face abuse from victims' families for that brave stand. He publicly condemned every IRA and loyalist killing in the harshest terms. At the same time he denounced collusion, harassment and sectarian bias by the RUC and the Ulster Defence Regiment, and demanded their reform or abolition. In the face of British government and unionist resistance and hostility, he demanded justice and equality in the actions of the security forces and the courts for the nationalist people of Northern Ireland, who had long been treated as second-class citizens at best and dangerous subversives at worst in their home place.

It is also often forgotten what an important role he played in the extremely difficult negotiations leading to the Belfast or Good Friday Agreement. Garret FitzGerald, not his favourite Southern politician, said after the Agreement was signed that Mallon's 'will be amongst the names to which history will pay tribute. Throughout this negotiation his steadiness, clarity and rationality have won universal respect in complementing John Hume's long-sighted vision.' Senator George Mitchell noted that he was 'an important and influential figure' in those talks who was 'liked and respected on all sides for his intelligence and integrity'.

However, he was the opposite of a soft touch. The loyalist leader David Ervine described his negotiating *modus operandi*: 'He was skilful, incisive and brutal. He could take somebody's scrotum and slice off their balls – it would be over in a second; they wouldn't know it was done, such was his skill.' Former Secretary of State for Northern Ireland John Reid once said Mallon was the only politician he had ever met who could 'make "Good morning" sound like a threat'.

Seán Ó hUiginn, the senior Irish diplomat who was one of the architects of the 1990s peace process, summed up Mallon's importance:

> He personified the decent, put-upon strand of Northern nationalism in a wonderfully attractive way. People in the Republic would say that if this good, honourable man is complaining, there must be something to his complaints. He thus had a very important and under-appreciated role in keeping the benign elements in the South engaged to some extent with the North during the Troubles, rather than falling back into the easy distancing mechanism that all Northerners were as bad as each other and were impossible people who could not be talked to or reasoned with.

Another diplomat, one of the Department of Foreign Affairs' regular 'travellers' to the North, described Mallon in 1987 like this: 'A formidable personality. The "green" conscience of the SDLP, to whom many younger members gravitate, but who is basically a loner who has not really built up a "Mallon wing" as such.'

Despite Mallon's sometimes dour self-presentation, it is difficult to find a Northern politician of any stripe to say a bad word about him. Ulster Unionist deputy leader John Taylor called him 'a good friend who will work for the good of Northern Ireland'. For Rita O'Hare of Sinn Féin he was 'a tough negotiator, a formidable opponent, but always honest and honourable'. The surgeon and senator John Robb said his main strength was 'his simple, absolute, complete integrity'. 'I would trust Seamus Mallon with my life. I wouldn't say that about many other politicians on my side or the other side,' said Ulster Unionist security spokesman Ken Maginnis.[1]

Unlike John Hume, who was to some extent insulated from the surrounding violence as the uncrowned king of nationalist Derry, Mallon had to live in and represent an area in which the murderous activities of republican and loyalist paramilitaries, along with rogue elements of the security forces, pushed the inhabitants of both communities into a savage internecine war mindset. In Armagh he personally witnessed the Northern conflict at its most depraved and sectarian.

1. Quotes on pages ix–x from *For the record: Seamus Mallon*, RTÉ programme, 27 March 2014; George Mitchell, *Making Peace: The inside story of the making of the Good Friday Agreement* (London 1999); Department of Foreign Affairs papers 1998–2001.

Generosity because he has always been sensitive to the fears and needs of the unionist community among whom he grew up. Even today he sits comfortably sipping coffee in a Protestant-owned cafe in his native village of Markethill, surrounded by evangelical pamphlets and biblical verses on the wall. This makes him unique among Northern nationalist politicians, with the possible exception of Gerry Fitt (who never called himself a nationalist anyway). Mallon remains a proud nationalist who believes in the long run only Irish unity can solve the deep historical divisions that have blighted Northern Ireland. But he believes with equal passion that his unionist friends and neighbours around Markethill, personified by the farmer and murdered police reservist whom he calls 'Jack Adams', have as much right to live in peace and without fear in Ireland as the community he led with such distinction over the years. And he believes his nationalist community, now they are moving into the ascendant, must show the generosity to unionists that was sadly absent from the way in which they were treated by the unionists during fifty years of one-party rule at Stormont.

Courage and generosity are there in abundance in Seamus Mallon's central proposal in this book: that Irish unity must wait until there is a majority – or at least a substantial minority – in the Protestant and unionist community prepared to support it. This is what he calls 'Parallel Consent' for unity. He knows he will be damned from the heavens by most nationalists, who will say that just as the prospect of a numerical majority for unity – based largely on the demographic growth of the Northern Catholic community – is within sight, he has proposed moving the posts so that their long-dreamed-of goal of a united Ireland is pushed further into the future. Equally, he knows there will be little welcome for his proposal in the fearful and begrudging minds of many unionists, who will see it as an excuse to dig their heels in for another generation rather than as a new and nobler way to come to terms with the medium-term prospect of unity by genuine consent. However, he believes that there is another unionist constituency, those who voted for the Good Friday Agreement and against Brexit, who are open to looking at unity, or at least a greater accommodation with the South, in a new way after nearly a century of division and conflict.

Above all, he stresses the importance of generosity between the Northern communities. After several centuries of the United Kingdom being a 'cold house' for Irish nationalists, the independent Irish state being feared as a 'cold house' for unionists, and Northern Ireland being a 'cold house' for Northern nationalists, he hopes his own community will demonstrate a new generosity to their unionist neighbours as the prospect of Irish unity becomes visible on the horizon.

Thus he hopes (against hope, some might say) that unionists and nationalists can eventually be united, after centuries of fear and conflict, 'in all the diversity of their identities and traditions' in the 'harmony and friendship' of the post-Good Friday Agreement amendment to the Irish Constitution.

At this late stage in his life Mallon is proposing this dramatic reconfiguration of the traditional nationalist demand because he knows that a simple majority for unity in a Border Poll in the foreseeable future can only be a narrow one: probably little more than the bare numerical majority laid down as a blunt instrument in the otherwise marvellously nuanced 1998 Good Friday Agreement. Unusually among nationalist leaders, he knows his unionist neighbours intimately; he knows what they are capable of when they feel coerced or threatened, and he knows this will probably mean a return to, and possibly an intensification of, the intercommunal violence of the 1968 to 1998 period. He knows from his own experience of the darkest years of murder gangs and counter-murder gangs in Armagh in the 1970s and 1980s, and of being Deputy First Minister during the most terrifying Drumcree confrontation in 1998, that at times of political instability – and there can be no deeper instability than the period following a narrow vote for unity – Northern Ireland is always in danger of going over the edge into outright civil war. He has also seen the new and angry divisions opening up in Britain following a narrow Brexit referendum vote.

My own belief was summarized thirty-five years ago by Bernard Cullen (later professor of philosophy at Queen's University) who grew up as a Catholic in a Belfast working-class Protestant area. In response to a question at the 1984 New Ireland Forum about what would happen some day in the future if there was the threat of a demographic Catholic nationalist majority in the North for unity, he said the probability – given that there were loyalists willing to kill in order to resist what they saw as rampant Irish nationalism – was that there would be 'a most terrible and horrific outcome, much greater in carnage and loss of life than anything we have seen so far'.

Mallon is careful to position his proposal to require the Parallel Consent of the two Northern communities for unity firmly in the context of a pre-Border Poll Review of the Good Friday Agreement, insisting it should be seen as an evolution of that Agreement. He also proposes a new version of the 1992–3 Opsahl Commission to initiate a wider public discussion on whether and how Irish unity can be brought about as peacefully and consensually as possible. He believes this double process should lead to the redefinition of the simple majority consent principle contained in the Good Friday Agreement, so that an eventual referendum on unity can gain as wide a measure of consent as possible.

Such a deliberative process should also work to resolve the hard questions that will be raised in the event of such a vote for unity, and which are almost completely absent from political and public discourse in today's Republic of Ireland. How and over what period of time will the British element in the governance of Northern Ireland be replaced by an Irish one? Is some kind of joint authority or joint sovereignty feasible during a transitional period? What parliamentary, consultative, public administration and public finance structures will be put in place both during and after that transitional phase? How would justice, law and order be guaranteed during the probable breakdown of law and order that too precipitate a transition could cause, with the danger that revived loyalist paramilitaries would violently resist it and revived republican paramilitaries seek to enforce it? What guarantees will be put in place so that the proud British identity of the unionists will be protected, cherished and incorporated into the institutions, ethos and symbols of the new state? Would that identity be better protected under a separate Northern regional administration? What kind of continuing British government involvement will this require? Will it, for example, reverse the safeguard built into the 1985 Anglo-Irish Agreement to protect nationalists – that the Irish government would be consulted by the British government on key issues of concern to that community – so that in any future unity agreement, the interests of unionists would be protected by a legal clause giving the British government the equivalent right to intervene to protect their community?

All these issues need to be thrashed out in as mutually respectful and open-minded a manner as possible. It will take a considerable time. The peace process that started with the 1993 Downing Street Declaration, whose high point was the 1998 Good Friday Agreement, and which dragged on until the devolution of policing and justice in 2010, lasted almost seventeen years; or twenty-two years if one dates its beginning from the first Hume–Adams talks in 1988. Seamus Mallon suggests it could take even longer to prepare for the complex and potentially destabilizing consequences of a Border Poll that might lead to unity.

This book is an example of collaboration between the two traditions in Ireland. It is written by a former nationalist leader and Deputy First Minister of Northern Ireland from the Catholic tradition, with the help of a journalist from a Northern Presbyterian background (still a practising Unitarian) who is now proud to be an Irish citizen. Both politician and journalist believe that some form of Irish unity in the future – probably a medium- to long-term future – is the only way to resolve the centuries-old divisions in Ireland. But they also believe that if the journey to unity is mishandled, it could lead to civil war on this island that we love and which both traditions call home.

Because of the growth of the Catholic population in Northern Ireland, the theoretical possibility of a narrow majority for unity in a Border Poll is perhaps only twenty to thirty years away. Now is the time to begin thinking deeply about the consequences of this huge change for the happiness and harmony of the people of Ireland. Sinn Féin, fiercely dogmatic in their demand for 'accelerated reunification post-Brexit' – in party chairman Declan Kearney's words – are incapable of leading that thinking. We can only hope that wiser and more generous nationalist leaders in the Seamus Mallon mould will emerge to engage in meaningful and empathetic negotiation with unionism.

In the meantime the wisdom of Mallon's words about the two traditions learning to share their common home place, Northern Ireland, should be listened to. That is the only way forward to a new Ireland based on the twenty-first century challenge of how to bring together diverse peoples, with all the major complications that implies, rather than the nineteenth-century nationalist obsession with the unity of territory.

Andy Pollak
February 2019

A Shared Home Place
SEAMUS MALLON

1. *A Happy Upbringing in South Armagh*

Every day of the week I am fortunate to be within touching distance of places and moments that have helped to shape our country's history, and indeed have helped to shape me, both as a person and a politician. I was born in and have lived for nearly eighty-three years in the large village of Markethill, seven miles south of Armagh on the road to Newry. This was for many centuries up to the end of the sixteenth century part of Gaelic Ulster, whose chieftains were the O'Neill family. To the north I look across the rich lands of mid and north Armagh, settled largely by English 'planters' in the seventeenth century. To the south I can see Camlough Mountain and the brooding presence of Slieve Gullion, which marked the end of that good land, and towards the rugged, stony hill country of the Fews in south Armagh, settled in part by Scottish Presbyterians, but mainly the home of dispossessed Irish Catholics. Beyond that are the fertile lands of north Leinster, part of the 'Pale' under the control of the English from the twelfth century.

Both views are beautiful, and a reminder that this area is the Northern Ireland problem in microcosm. In simplistic terms one could say each of my kitchen windows looks at the symbols of four centuries of divided history: the fears, the prejudices, the ethnic hatred, the lack of understanding, the use and abuse of power that have fuelled life and tragic death in the county proclaiming it is the historic centre of Christianity in Ireland.

Markethill is a small and, to outsiders, an unremarkable place that these days is bypassed by the main Armagh–Newry road. Its houses line each side of a hill and appear almost to be clinging to each other to remain standing. On the brow of the hill are a few big, solid buildings, including an old courthouse and a Church of Ireland church. These solid hilltop buildings were put up by the Acheson family of nearby Gosford Castle. My childhood home was in Main Street, just a couple of hundred yards from where I now live on the edge of the village.

From my living room I can see across the main Armagh–Newry road to the Gosford Castle estate, the lands – 8000 acres at the time of Plantation, rising to 12,000 acres in the early nineteenth century – on which the Acheson family were 'planted' from their home in East Lothian in Scotland in 1610.[1] Running through my garden is part of the old Armagh–Dublin road along which Hugh O'Neill marched in 1598 after beating the English forces at the Battle of the Yellow Ford during the Nine Years War, a war that ended with his final defeat, his flight to the Continent and the seizure of his lands and their plantation by English and Scottish settlers. The two armies skirmished again as the English retreated at Mullaghbrack, north-west of Markethill. Most of that battle was fought in the place where 250 years later a school was built where I was to attend as a pupil and later become principal, and a church was constructed where I served Mass as a child. Both are close to the remains of a Mass Rock or Mass Garden, a constant reminder of the anti-Catholic Penal Laws.

The mainly Presbyterian retainers and labourers who came across from Scotland with Archibald Acheson were also, in a sense, displaced. They were taken from their home place to a foreign land, fearful and mistrustful of the native Irish, with their different language and religion. Because of their noncomformist religion, they too were second-class citizens and there was significant tension between them and their Anglican fellow planters, many of them from England.

This was especially so during the reign of Charles the First, who introduced legislation that the Presbyterians saw as discriminatory. He levied a harsh tithe tax, payable by Catholic and Presbyterian alike, for the upkeep of the established Church of Ireland. As a result some returned to Scotland while others some generations later sailed to America, where they joined their co-religionists from Scotland and England as a group that was to play a significant role in the

---

1. Acheson family details from Nick Kingsley, *Landed families in Britain and Ireland*. landedfamilies.blogspot.com/2013/03/10-acheson-of-gosford-castle-baronets.html

American War of Independence. They were, one might say, the original rebels against the British empire.

The Achesons were granted the hereditary titles of Baron Gosford in 1776, Viscount Gosford in 1785 and Earl of Gosford in 1806. The Gosford estate, a square mile of idyllic pasture and rich forest (with a unique arboretum), is reputedly where Jonathan Swift wrote part of *Gulliver's Travels* during a stay of several months in 1728–9. In 1862 the second earl completed a vast castle in the neo-Norman style, whose 197 rooms then made it the largest building in Ireland. His extravagance crippled the family's finances and in 1921 its contents were sold to pay his grandson's large gambling and other debts. During the 1968–98 Troubles the estate was sometimes used by loyalist paramilitary groups for training. It is now a beautiful public forest park.

From plantation times County Armagh, with its mixture of Irish natives and English and Scottish settlers, was a place where conflict was waiting to happen. The Plantation of Ulster, the Penal Laws and, much later, the Partition of Ireland, were based on the same flawed policy: to create a Protestant ascendancy in order to maintain Britain's rule over Ireland. The Protestant immigrants were enjoined 'to enforce the doctrines of the English Reformation' and 'Protestantise the Gaelic speaking papists' and to impose segregation, so that 'all Gaelic Irish inhabitants were to be cleared off the Plantation estates of the English and Scottish undertakers'.[2] One of the first things the Acheson family did when they arrived here was to build five defensive forts around their estate: nearly four centuries later the British army were once again erecting forts on nearly every hill in south Armagh.

Military and religious conflict usually coincided with economic conflict. At the end of the eighteenth century Protestants and Catholics increasingly competed for land and work in the growing cottage industry of handloom weaving of linen. Armagh was experiencing something of an economic boom in the 1780s and 1790s, based on the growth of that industry. A table of sales of unbleached linen in 1784 showed that the orchard county had the highest turnover in the province of Ulster, with weekly sales worth £5000 (over £300,000 today) in the markets at Armagh, Keady, Richhill, Tandragee and Lurgan.

The late 1780s and 1790s were particularly ferocious. Initially the problem was one of drinking and public brawling escalating into gang warfare, and sectarianism was less evident. Near my Markethill home is a small street known as Bunker Hill. In 1785 this had a gang known as the Bunker Hill Defenders, whose membership was mainly Catholic but whose leader was a Presbyterian. Only in

2. J. McCavitt, 'Rebels, Planters and Conspirators: Armagh 1504–1640', *Armagh: History and Society* (Dublin 2001), 255.

the following year did the strife take a sectarian turn, with gangs from the countryside around evolving into the Protestant Peep O'Day Boys to take on the Catholic Defenders, as gangs fought at fairs and markets and raided houses by night. An attempt to burn down Catholic homes in the Bunker Hill area on 1 January 1789 was thwarted by vigilant Defenders alerted by Protestant friends.

The Peep O'Day Boys were joined by the Volunteers – a Protestant-only militia originally formed to repel possible French invasion and later to defend Protestant Ireland's separate parliament in Dublin – in planned attacks against their Catholic neighbours. The Volunteers carried guns and were answerable to local landlords. They used this licence to raid Catholic homes (ostensibly to search for illegal arms) and brutalize, burn out and often kill their inhabitants. Catholic reprisals were equally savage, but greater access to firearms and force of numbers usually saw the Protestants winning. As the violence spread throughout the county in 1790, local authorities (the landed gentry backed by the military) took action, with six people executed and six more publicly whipped for crimes of murder, assault and robbery.

In the mid-1790s sectarian disturbances resumed in Armagh. These culminated in the Battle of the Diamond in Loughgall in 1795, leading to the formation of the Orange Order. Lord Gosford, as Governor of Armagh, was asked by the British authorities in Dublin for an explanation of the conflict. He said it was impossible to prevent an Orange parade of up to 1500 people marching through his estate. He neglected to disclose that he himself had taken the salute at the parade! This man, supposedly impartial, ruling the county of Armagh on behalf of the British crown, was giving explicit support to an organization which was directly involved in the killing of Catholics and the burning of their houses.

One Protestant couple from just outside Markethill wrote to relatives in the USA in 1796: 'The Orange Boys has not left a papist family in all the lower part of the County from Richhill downward but they have [them] driven away.'[3] In the following year an army officer serving near Keady wrote:

> I am informed, and it is generally understood by every one, that the depredations committed by what they call Orange boys is done by the sanction of government. Were I to enumerate the robberies, murders and shameful outrages committed on the Catholicks of this place by those Orange boys, headed by officers in full Yeomanry uniform, would be an endless business.[4]

---

3. C.F. McGleenon, *Views on the Speckled Summit: Mullaghbrack and the Church of St James of Jerusalem* (Armagh 2013), 50–3.

4. D. Miller, 'The Origins of the Orange Order in County Armagh', *Armagh History and Society* (Dublin 2001), 601.

It is alarming to think that nearly two centuries later more outrages were being committed by the Yeomanry's successors in the RUC and UDR with the apparent collusion of their superiors. These forces, whether in the eighteenth or twentieth centuries, were set up by the British in classic colonial mould: put one section of the population in uniform, let them police the other section, and they will fight our battles for us.

Many Catholics were forced to leave the area, around 800 migrating to Mayo. The statistics are revealing. In 1765, 5750 Catholics and 2875 Protestants lived in the parish of Mullaghbrack Ballymore, incorporating the village of Markethill and its surrounding areas. Over the next seventy years that Catholic population declined sharply while the Protestant population increased. By 1834 there were 2330 Catholics and 6481 Protestants in that parish: 3382 Church of Ireland, 2983 Presbyterians and 116 other Protestant Dissenters.[5] A small but significant number of Catholics 'took the soup', disavowed their religion and became Protestants, thus keeping their land. This displacement of Catholics by Protestants did little to heal the bitter hatred or lessen the memory of internecine conflict between the planter and the Gael in County Armagh. In my lifetime I was once again to experience forty years of sectarian murder, hatred and deep suspicion in this, my home area. William Faulkner's words were never more bleakly relevant: 'The past is not dead. It is not even past.'

However, Markethill was not all bad community relations and outbreaks of intercommunal violence. The Gosford family had a reputation for benevolence during the Great Famine. Lord Gosford was sympathetic to the plight of his poorer farmer tenants who depended so much on the potato, and in autumn 1846, as it failed, he instructed his agent that tenants with under twenty acres who were dependent on that crop should not be charged rent. His two youngest daughters, who later became Catholics, were founders and patrons of a local school for Catholic girls, and actively engaged in charitable works in the area, tending to the sick and the poor.[6]

I have lived all my life among Protestants. Today over 90 per cent of Markethill's inhabitants are Protestant, making it probably the most Protestant village in south Armagh. As so often in Irish villages, the Catholic church and school are not in the village at all, but a mile outside it at Mullaghbrack.

Despite its sometimes forbidding facade and often bloody history, Markethill in the nineteenth and early twentieth centuries developed into an outwardly prosperous place of commerce and worship. It had a town hall, a courthouse, a

---

5. McGleenon, 48 and 65.

6. *Ibid*, 69–70.

railway station, a bank, and in my childhood no fewer than six places of worship, all Protestant: two Presbyterian, Church of Ireland, Methodist, Baptist and Elim Pentecostal. It was, and remains, a church-going place, but the old adage was apt: 'the nearer the chapel the further from God'. Christians here were as deeply divided as in any small Northern Ireland town or village.

Yet when I grew up here in the 1930s, 40s and 50s it was a happy childhood, and I felt secure and well looked after. I grew up in a loving and comfortable home. Both my paternal grandparents had come to Markethill from rural south Armagh as jobseekers: my grandfather, Charles Mallon, from Doogary on the border with Monaghan to work as a baker; my grandmother, Mary McKinley, from Dorsey on the other side of Slieve Gullion, to the wealthy Catholic Cummings family to work as a childminder and tutor.

Mary McKinley was a remarkable woman. Her life was difficult, particularly after my grandfather died when she was only in her forties, leaving her with two small children (my father was just two at the time). But she had an innate dignity and charm, and a poetic sensibility that revealed itself in her beautiful use of language and her lyrical singing voice. There were no pensions then, so she had to make a living somehow, and she did it by opening a little huckster's shop in the front room of her tiny terraced house.

My grandmother was very near to the heart of the working people of Markethill, especially the 'shawlies': the women, Protestant and Catholic, who worked for twelve hours a day for a barely sufficient wage in its one linen mill, Spence and Bryson. The mill-horn used to sound twice every morning. There was a wake-up call at seven. A second, sounding half an hour later, saw huddles of shawled women hurrying to the mill, their dark figures morphing into larger blobs of black as they gathered around the factory gate. Once inside one could almost hear the sigh of relief from the assembled workers that once again there would be food on the table that night.

Few men worked full-time in the village then. The lucky ones, most of them Protestants, were part of Lord Gosford's retinue of coachmen, household attendants and gardeners. Others, both Protestant and Catholic, relied on odd jobs on farms or drove cattle to fairs and markets. Some were hired hands, 'bought' by wealthy farmers in Tyrone or Derry for one- or two-year terms. Some were paid a just wage and treated well; most were treated as indentured servants, working long hours for basic food and lodgings.

Many of these poor people came to Granny Mallon's shop. It was barely a shop: a single shelf held the plugs of War Horse tobacco, Woodbine cigarettes and other small items. Under the makeshift counter were the tea and sugar chests with their distinctive smells, lined with silver paper that crackled when the chests were moved, and the little funnel-shaped scoops used to measure their contents into brown paper bags. My occasional job was to fill those bags, mostly on a Thursday evening. I loved doing it. The smell of the tea leaves was addictive, the pay two clove rock sweets out of a big jar, and for a seven-year-old boy the sense of having a 'job' – even for an hour a week – was almost payment in itself.

Seldom did I see money changing hands in that little room. Eggs were bartered for tea and coffee. 'Luxury' items like a cut of home-cured bacon were exchanged for other 'luxury' items like War Horse plug tobacco. Occasionally a chicken came in as payment for groceries, but it was never sold: it was cooked for us, every scrap savoured in what for that time was a rare and veritable feast.

I never saw anybody turned away empty-handed. Often the small boy in the corner heard the whispered plea: 'Mary, I have nothing on me now. Can I pay you later?' And always a knowing smile and the same reply from my grand-mother: 'Take it with you, Mabel. Pay me when you can.'

Even the village shysters knew that tolerant smile. When they sidled into the shop seeking a half ounce of War Horse with the stuttered assurance that 'I'll pay you later when I get a day's driving with Doyle's cattle to the fair,' her reply never changed: 'Ah, of course you will George, sometime.'

Decades later, when I first stood for election to Stormont, a staunch unionist and Orangeman – and a celebrated Lambeg drummer – came to my house one night in an agitated state to say that voting for me would go against everything he had ever believed, but he would ensure that 'she' and 'some of them' would do so. I was touched by his good intentions, but not convinced that he had the neces-sary authority over his fearsome wife and two fighting sons, who were barred from every pub in the district. As he slipped away into the night, he volunteered the reason: 'Seamie, I don't much care for you, but your granny helped us out often when money was scarce. I want to say thanks to her.'

My father Frank, the principal of the Coolmillish Catholic primary school at Mullaghbrack, was the 'Master', a tall and broad-shouldered man who, when he wanted, could draw himself up to his full height in an almost imperious way. He always wore a waistcoat with a large watch on a chain strung from one pocket to the other. Daddy was a complex person: a devout Catholic who had no time for clericalism. He could be scathing about how some priests treated their schools as their petty fiefdoms. He had originally been supportive of the IRA's fight for Irish independence, but that changed when six Protestants were murdered in a very brutal way at Altnaveigh outside Newry in 1922. I used to listen to him talking about Hugh O'Neill's forgotten and unmourned foot soldiers who had died in our area three and a half centuries earlier. He would finish with a warning: 'The only weapons which should ever be used again in this country are words. Guns never solve problems; they make them. Always remember that, son.'

My mother, Jane O'Flaherty, who came from a strongly republican family in Castlefinn in Donegal, was even more disillusioned. Her three brothers had been active in the IRA in Donegal during the 1916–23 period. Her youngest brother Sam was the officer commanding the East Donegal Brigade and had been incarcerated along with Eamon de Valera in Lincoln jail. In 1919 Sam, a classics student, wrote a letter with instructions in Latin to those outside who were planning to spring de Valera in what was to become a celebrated break-out. But he was later interned by the new Free State government during the Civil War and died as a young man from ailments sustained during his years of guerrilla activities. I could see the pain in my mother's face when these matters were raised: 'Leave things be,' she would plead.

My father was a teetotaller all his life and went to bed each evening at 9 pm on the dot. He was also an avid GAA man. I remember the first time he took me to an All-Ireland final in Croke Park, Roscommon versus Kerry in 1946. To a ten-year-old boy who had never been out of his own village, there was a sense of awe: the bands playing, the bishop throwing the ball in, all that ceremonial stuff. It was a change from the Orange bands in the middle of our street. Even at that early age I got a sense that the GAA was something to hold onto.

Despite his stern visage and abstemious lifestyle, my father was not an intolerant man. He could smile his way through any heated argument or angry confrontation and inevitably won in the end. In those days teachers had no security of tenure and were subject to the whims of a parish priest who had the absolute right to hire and fire. Despite this, I remember one clash with a curate who liked to beat small children, whom my father ordered to leave his classroom or he would put him out. The priest left, shouting that he would have Mallon sacked. On another occasion he ejected a particularly obnoxious school attendance officer for being disrespectful to the children. He was not popular in some quarters for helping to organize a teachers' union, the Irish National Teachers Organization, in the area. That and his confrontations with authority ensured that he would not get promoted from his three-teacher primary school outside a south Armagh village.

He was a very good teacher. He had been picked out as a particularly bright pupil by his own teacher at Coolmillish school – James Cotter, a Cork man who was the first chairman of the Armagh GAA county board – initially to be a monitor and then to be sent on a scholarship to St Patrick's teacher training college in Dublin, where he was a student during the 1916 Rising. When we left his school, we knew some Latin and some Irish, neither of which he was supposed to teach. He was not supposed to teach Irish history either – only British – but that was another regulation he roundly ignored.

I started in the infant class of my father's school when I was four, with a new cap and 'sparable' boots, studded with metal so they would last longer. The classroom enthralled me, with its long desks and open fire blazing in the grate. I remember my first teacher, Mrs Butterfield, with great affection for her kindness and her attempts to teach us how to sing, including English folk songs like 'Bobby Shafto'. Every day I walked with my father the mile to the school, much of it along the wall of Gosford Castle. I was fascinated by that wall, trying to imagine the painful labours of the men who in the nineteenth century had to hoist its stone blocks onto a horse-drawn cart in a quarry beyond Newry and transport them here in a twenty-mile round journey in all weathers. I had listened to tales of carriages delivering famous visitors to its east door, including Jonathan Swift. But however much I quizzed my father, my mother, my sisters and both school and adult friends about life on the Gosford estate, I was never able to acquire much information about that unknown and inaccessible world so close to my home. That wall, I concluded with all the certainty of a small boy, was meant to keep the likes of me out.

The maternal warmth of the infants' class cooled somewhat when I moved up to the Master's room. There was a constant air of busyness there. There had to be. There were three classes in the room with one teacher, my father, overseeing them all. One at a time the classes were brought up to the blackboard and what was written on it was drilled into us without interruption. 'Effort' was the keyword in that classroom: the effort necessary to acquire the knowledge required for each pupil to make something of himself or herself in later life.

At the end of the day, the infants were the first to leave. Their chatter rose by decibels as the older children followed them into the hall, which acted as a cloakroom. As their voices blended with the tinsel tones of the younger children, the cows in the field opposite sometimes joined in. The Master came out, took a deep breath, and a smile crept onto his face. He often said that fusion of sounds, human and animal, was the moment he waited for every day. It was for him a celebration both of the children's freedom and that moment when man and nature joined to create what he called the 'Mullaghbrack Chorus'.

My father was known for his fairness, generosity and willingness to help others. As a child I often saw my mother making two or three extra packed lunches, which I assumed my father took to school to give to those poorer children who had none. He often acted as a counsellor to less educated neighbours. A knock would come at the door and it would be someone looking for a job reference, for example to join the British army, often the only place a young fellow, usually a Catholic, could get a job in those days. He wrote letters for people unable to read or write and made contacts for them with those in authority. He was particularly solicitous when a Protestant came to the door: they were always treated with friendship and respect, and often helped when their own unionist councillors could not.

My mother had arrived in Markethill along with her priest brother when he became curate in our parish. Tall and stately, she ran the house and everyone in it, including my father. I know that my mother felt a deep love for the complex man who was my father. She, like him, was generous to a fault, and only after her death did I become aware of the help she gave to local families who had fallen on hard times.

Often, when we were all there in the house, she would sing a traditional song in her beautiful Donegal Gaelic. Years later, in times of particular stress, I would hear echoes of that lovely lilting song in memories of walking with her along the bank of the river Finn that ran through her father's farm.

As the only boy with four sisters, I was used to being around strong women. My gregarious and adventurous eldest sister Maura, whom we still call 'the Duchess', was not made for village life. She was the first to leave home when she went to teach at a British army school in Germany. She later lived in Guyana and British Columbia in Canada before retiring back to Newry. Peggy and Jean were the next two; they were rather more reserved than the charismatic Maura, natural home-makers who made life very comfortable for my father and me after our mother's death. Peggy, a district nurse in the Bessbrook/Camlough area who radiated care and kindness to all, was the one I went to when I needed help or just to talk things over after a particularly harrowing experience. After our father had a stroke and became bedridden, it was Peggy who gave up her job to care for him. After leaving school Jean went to London to work in a bank, where she met and married the company secretary, John Povey, and has lived in England ever since, in the pleasant seaside town of Deal near Dover.

The baby of the family was Kate, whose blonde hair, pixie face and blue eyes belied a razor-sharp mind. She was my big pal when we were young, bossing me around but always standing up for me when I was caught up in some mischief, which was often. In later years I stayed with both Kate and Jean in their homes near each other at Beckenham in Kent when I was attending the House of Commons.

The most important place for me as a child was the house next door owned by the Binghams. Davy Bingham's yard was a veritable treasure house. The Binghams, a Protestant family, had a shop and a seed and grain business. There was a loft with stone steps up to it where local farmers collected bags of grass, seed, grain and fertilizer. Opposite was a large pigsty and, in a shed above it, a poultry-rearing unit. Sometimes there were day-old chicks under a heating lamp. They were soft, fluffy and beautiful and one day I could not resist the temptation to put one in each trouser pocket, bring them home and put them in a box at the side of our living-room fire. No one noticed for a while, but then the inevitable happened. 'What in the name of God is this? Where did these chicks come from?' exclaimed my mother. When I stuttered that I loved these little creatures and was going to rear them for Mr Bingham, she marched me with the chick box into Binghams' shop, which was half full of customers.

At the top of her voice, she announced: 'Seamie has something to tell you, Mrs Bingham.' Mortified, I put the little box on the counter and began to stutter: 'I'm sorry, Mrs Bingham, I didn't mean …' My mother cut me off sharply in mid-sentence: 'Did they fly into your pocket? He stole them from your loft, Mrs Bingham. What do you think of that?' Mrs Bingham, a kindly lady, smiled knowingly at me: 'No, no, Mrs Mallon, he did not steal them. I gave them to him as a wee present, didn't I, Seamie?' As I tried to stutter the word 'Yes,' my mother frogmarched me out of the shop. My public humiliation had purged any remains of guilt I felt about the theft of the chicks. That evening my father had a twinkle in his eye: 'I hear you're going into the poultry business, Seamie.'

I spent much of my young life with the Binghams, and particularly with my best friend Davy. As a baby my mother used to leave me with the Binghams when she went to Mass. Davy and I were never seen without each other, and also with two other friends who lived up the street, Sean Cassidy and John McConnell. We were known locally as the Main Street Gang and we were of mixed religion. We stayed good friends into our late teens and beyond.

There were, of course, tensions around the time of the Orange marching season. As every twelfth of July approached, a standing joke among the town's Catholics was that 'they [our Protestant neighbours] seem to have lost their voices', not greeting their Catholic fellow citizens with their usual cordiality for the days around the 'twelfth'. But that was very temporary. And I wouldn't under-emphasize the way in which Catholic farmers in the area would milk the cows and do other chores for their Protestant neighbours on the twelfth of July, with the Protestants reciprocating when the Catholics took the fifteenth of August off to go to local seaside resorts like Warrenpoint and Omeath.

There are some myths about the Orange marching season and one is that it has always been anathema to the nationalist community. In fact, as a child I liked the music of those parades, the pageantry, colour and sense of excitement. Even as a young man I didn't find the twelfth of July particularly threatening. I enjoyed watching the marches, and particularly wondering how some people I knew well would be marching in their full regalia, but would then be able to get to the first race at Dundalk before I did. Those people were mad into racing. It's like a lot of what happens everywhere in Ireland: the same happens at funerals – people wanted to be *seen* to be at the parade; that was the important thing.

Having said that, as a Catholic I had to watch the 'twelfth' parade from the window in our sitting room. It would have caused a row if I'd appeared on the street. I remember that on a Friday evening in July my mother used to say: 'Stay in the house, don't be on the street, there is going to be a parade and the streets will be taken over – it's no place for the like of us.' My sisters and I would peep out the window watching the drumming match right in front of our house, the sounds of war. The interesting thing is that the two men doing the drumming were among the most inoffensive people I have ever known and here they were beating the tom-toms in the middle of a packed street that people like me could not even set foot on. We knew there were occasional incidents, with Catholics being beaten up. We were sometimes told on the way to school: 'You're not wanted here.'

The Second World War brought the excitement of the great outside world to Markethill in the form of German prisoners of war in Gosford Castle; tidy Belgian soldiers who never got into trouble; and American GIs who were never out of it. The townsfolk gave the Belgians and the Americans a warm welcome, particularly the GIs, young men with all the bravado of soldiers on their way to the front. They drank heavily in the pubs, often offered heady brews that were concocted specially for them at an exorbitant price. When they piled out of the pubs onto the street, their raucous renditions of 'The Yanks are Coming' were quickly stilled by red-coated military police, who arrived on cue, batons drawn, to throw them, these young men who were going to die for their country and for ours, into the backs of jeeps, like cattle into trucks bound for the abattoir.

For me the thrilling highlight of this period was the arrival of four light US aeroplanes on to Terry McCone's field on the Mullaghbrack Road, where a runway of sorts had been constructed. The pilots had a real swagger about them and their officer came to our school to apologize for any inconvenience caused by their take-offs and landings and to give the Master, my father, a huge bag of goodies for distribution to the pupils (including delicious treats called American 'cookies').

I quickly decided that I wanted the Americans to win the war. Not everybody shared that view. Our local curate forbade any child of his flock to have any contact with these glamorous young pilots and, above all, banned anyone from getting into one of their aeroplanes. I decided I would do just that. Shortly after the priest's edict I spoke to one of the pilots, a young man called Travis, on the road into Markethill and indicated in a roundabout fashion that I would love a flight in his plane. 'OK, buddy, I'll see you tomorrow afternoon,' he said with a grin. I told no one of my forthcoming assignation. The next day on the way home from school I lagged behind my friends, complaining of a sore ankle. I then disappeared behind a large tree, and crawled carefully along a ditch to the aero-drome's gate until I heard Travis call out, 'Hey, buddy, are you ready to go up?'

It was an astounding experience for an eight-year-old boy. From the sky our school looked tiny and squat and ugly. I could see the wall of Gosford Castle looking insignificant and inoffensive from the sky. I looked down on a lone figure walking along the road from the school. I knew immediately from his brisk pace and the tilt of his shoulders that it was my father. When I arrived home that evening, my father was in his usual chair, having a cup of tea and a biscuit. There was the trace of a smile on his lips. After a long silence he asked in a conspiratorial voice: 'Hey, buddy, did you have a good day?'

Less impressive than the US airmen was the Markethill Home Guard. I remember our family, complete with gasmasks and overexcited children, responding to a call by loudhailer from the head of that mighty military unit to evacuate the village by nineteen hundred hours. After several hours lying in a midge-infested field my father announced: 'That's it, we're going home. Why the hell would Hitler want to bomb Markethill? We were bloody fools to listen to that self-important shorty with the white moustache.'

Things in Markethill used to become more polarized during elections. For example, I remember the Westminster election for the Armagh constituency in 1948. There were two candidates: O'Reilly, the nationalist, and Harden, the unionist, who lived in a big house at nearby Clare. I was, of course, shouting for O'Reilly. Coming home from school we had to shout those names at the other crowd and be shouted at in return.

In the immediate postwar period important changes were on the way. Water mains were laid down and running water in the home became available to all. We almost washed the skin off our faces as we enjoyed this new luxury. This was followed by the arrival of electricity. Overnight the brass lamps, water basins and pitchers were disposed of.

Then in 1948 I was successful in the eleven-plus exam, which allowed me to go on to a good secondary education in a grammar school. That was the first year of the exam in Northern Ireland, which opened the door to Catholic children who previously would never have dreamed of going on to higher education. John Hume also came from that first generation. I went to St Patrick's College in Armagh for a short time and then switched to Abbey CBS Grammar School in Newry. I enjoyed it there: I was a fairly good footballer and we went on in 1954 to become the first day school to win the MacRory Cup, the Ulster GAA's premier schools competition. It wasn't easy in those days. After school you had football training no matter what the weather was like and when that was finished you were covered in mud; you washed yourself as best you could at a freezing outside tap, and then rushed down to the town to catch the bus home. As soon as you arrived home you had to start into your homework. It was hard but enjoyable. I also played for the local team, Mullaghbrack, and on the Armagh minor team; my life was centred around football.

I also enjoyed dancing, although I was never particularly good at it. You would be really hitting the high spots if you could take a girl to the Thursday night hop at the City Hall in Armagh. If I hadn't a girlfriend to take I'd often cycle the fourteen miles to Armagh and back. There was also an occasional ceili at the parochial hall in Mullaghbrack. One of the good friends I met there was the musician Tommy Makem, who was from down the road in Keady; I always treasured his friendship.

Looking back, being a Catholic teenager in County Armagh was a mixed blessing. It was the era of the IRA's border campaign and road checks with B-Specials who knew me well asking: 'Good evening, Mr Mallon, what's your name?' It was fairly common when we were stopped on the road to Newry to be told to take our shoes off. Of course, I had nothing to show but my feet. Later, when a student in Belfast, I remember being taken off a bus back to college with another young Catholic man from the Markethill area and brought into Finaghy RUC station in the south of the city for questioning. The police there phoned the local station in Markethill and told them to search our house. To his credit the local constable, Bob Henry, who lived two doors from us, refused. We were let go after a considerable number of hours. It was my belief that it was a local bus driver who had fingered us. It was my first experience of being arrested and I didn't like it.

I worked hard at school and was good at English language and literature, Latin and Irish. In those days there was no such thing as career guidance, or any expectation of getting some important well-paid job. If you were a young Catholic with a bit of education, you were either going to be a teacher, a priest or a civil servant (if you could get in). Only if your family had money could you go into one of the professions. My family didn't so it was assumed that I would follow my father into teaching; there was no reason not to. I would have loved to go to Queen's University to study law and regret that I didn't at some stage of my life.

So I went to St Joseph's teacher training college on the outskirts of Andersonstown in west Belfast. There was hardly a house in those days beyond Casement Park, and St Joseph's, surrounded by fields, was known as 'the Ranch'. Belfast was something of a liberation: I was a young man about town, I lived in digs, I had no restraints on me, I could do almost anything I wanted. One problem was that my digs cost £2.50 per week and my allowance was £3. Luckily one of my best friends was Sean McLoughlin from Ahoghill in County Antrim, whose main interest in life was greyhound racing and who knew which dogs to put money on. We went regularly to Celtic Park and Dunmore Stadium (now both closed) and if I hadn't known Sean I simply wouldn't have survived financially.

At dances in places like Club Orchid in the city centre I was meeting people from my home area, both sides of it. I also met other kinds of people: I remember in particular the lectures on English literature, and particularly poetry and drama, given by a magnificent teacher called Sean Breslin; you would never dream of missing a single class of Sean's. He instilled in me a love of the First World War poets, Wilfred Owen and Siegfried Sassoon. I also used to hire a car and give members of the great Down football team – fellow St Joseph's students Kevin and Fintan Mussen and Oliver Donnelly – lifts down to training in Downpatrick, where I would train alongside them. I was absolutely delighted to be at Croke Park in 1960 the first time Down won the All-Ireland, and even more so to be in the crowd in Newry that welcomed them home with a stirring rendition of 'Little town in the old County Down'. I only wished that Armagh could have followed their example – it would be another forty-two years before they did so.

It was to Newry that I first went after graduation, to St Joseph's, a new, what used to be called 'secondary modern' school, with 800 boys, a lot of young fellows from the more disadvantaged areas of the town, the ones who had failed their eleven-plus. Newry was a hugely deprived town, with one of the highest unemployment rates in the UK. In its housing estates the moneylenders were a real menace, threatening poor people with violence and inflicting actual violence on them when they failed to pay up.

I spent four years at St Joseph's and it was a good experience. Because I was somebody who played football I was put in charge of the senior football team. I regarded it as an injustice that there was not one square yard of grass to play on at the school, so every time we had to play or train, I had to march the boys a mile and a half from the Armagh Road through the town centre to a football field called The Marches out on the Warrenpoint Road. In St Joseph's we looked across the fence to the neighbouring Catholic grammar school, St Colman's College, which had three beautifully manicured playing pitches. Discrimination was not the sole preserve of the unionist establishment.

Some of the boys there were involved in petty crime and when the Troubles started in the early 1970s several of them joined the IRA. I remember one poor boy, a real character whom I had managed to keep out of jail on a few occasions by pleading his case with the local police inspector. He and another lad went into a shop in Hill Street and poured petrol on the goods as they came in the door. Shortly afterwards they were seen at the window screaming to get out as the flames rose around them; they were both burned to death. Another lad in my class was shot dead on the street by the British army. A third was blown up by his own bomb on the road to the border.

I was a form master, and I suppose I was put in charge of a class that was supposedly difficult because I was on the big side. There were two big, quiet boys in that class – Pat Jennings and Dan McAlinden – and their presence really toned down the atmosphere. Pat Jennings was to become a star goalkeeper for Tottenham Hotspur and Northern Ireland. I remember inviting him and his wife to the House of Commons and watching, amazed, while officials – clearly Spurs fans – ushered him into a parking place in a strictly forbidden area, and inside at lunch a queue of old fellows, MPs and attendants alike queued up for his autograph. Dan McAlinden was later to become British and Commonwealth heavyweight boxing champion. I remember that, like a fool, I accepted his invitation to spar with him. Nobody, but nobody, sparred with Dan McAlinden, but I used to stay on after school for three days a week to get the face knocked off me by fifteen-year-old Dan.

Then, in my early twenties, I succeeded my father on his retirement as principal of Mullaghbrack primary school. It was a very pleasant place to work. One of the great advantages was that I knew not only the children, but also their parents, their grandparents and even their great-grandparents. I got to know the community very, very well in that job.

During this period, after coming out of college, I became involved in local theatre groups. Part of my studies at St Joseph's involved drama in schools, and I took part there in a show put on by an inspirational lecturer from Derry called Eithne McDermott. I was always attracted to the stage, and being able to suspend reality for two or three hours of an evening. When I started to teach in Newry, one of the subjects I taught was drama and of course the boys would object, saying 'that's a silly old thing, Seamie, that's a girl's thing', and I tried to persuade them it wasn't, with little success.

Then I became peripherally involved with the drama festival in Newry and with the Newpoint Players (made up of people from Newry and Warrenpoint), who were a famous amateur dramatic society that put on very professional productions. I took part in one George Bernard Shaw play and that convinced me I would never make a decent actor. But I was very interested in production, and in 1962 I got the opportunity to direct Thornton Wilder's *Our Town*. It is a marvellous play but a difficult one because there is nothing on the stage except chairs and people – you had to convey the whole emotion of the play, about two families in New Hampshire at the beginning of the last century, without any props. We entered the Newry Drama Festival but were well beaten by a group from Dundalk. We then went to a very good festival in Courtown in Wexford and won it, which gave us a passage to the Esso all-Ireland finals in Athlone.

I went down there two days beforehand to check the venues, what we needed for lights and other equipment. I found that a local pub was running a book on the festival, and all the plays were up on a board behind the bar, so I went in to have a look and we were at 9–4. A group from Sligo were favourites. I reckoned 9–4 was a decent price so I asked what about the rest and the barman shrugged and said the rest were nowhere. 'Are you having a bet?' he asked. I told him no but if he gave me 3–1, I would put a bet on. I had what for me at that time was a lot of money, £40, so I put that on, and that was more pressure. We were the last show in the programme. Tension was very high and there was a great audience. We got the lights right and that was important because any atmospheric effect in *Our Town* was going to come from the lighting. The cast put on a great performance and got a very good adjudication and we won the all-Ireland trophy.

Later I did some musical productions with the girls at St Catherine's College in Armagh. That was the old convent school before it became an all-ability school.

It really was a finishing school for young Catholic ladies. I was met at the door by a nun who took me in for tea with lovely china cups and then kept an eye on me the whole time. *Oklahoma!* was the first show and I enjoyed it immensely. I also did *The Student Prince* and *West Side Story* with them. The principal of St Catherine's, Sister Considine, was somebody I came to admire immensely. She was head of a very grandiose grammar school but she made the courageous decision, in the face of widespread opposition (including from the Church hierarchy, her own order and some of the staff), that the school should provide education for everybody. She had a vision of an all-ability, all-social background school and the courage and determination to implement it long before it became fashionable elsewhere.

A few years later a theatre group was formed in Armagh by Stanley Fitzgerald, Larry Ryan and myself. We started off with Brendan Behan's *The Hostage*, which I had seen in Joan Littlewood's original production in Wyndham's Theatre in London. The playwright himself was on the pavement outside the theatre saying hello to everybody and busking. That was a tremendous production with all sorts of musical items and extra characters added. But it was not what he wrote, which was about the catharsis of people talking about and acting out violent Irish republicanism. We in Armagh tried to get the heart of what Behan wrote without losing any of the excitement of the West End production and I think we just about succeeded.

That was followed by Jean Anouilh's *The Lark*, a very difficult play but with a good cast we got away with it; and after that John B. Keane's hilarious *Many Young Men of Twenty* as a bit of light relief. Then I decided that we would try to create a one-act play, *Adam's Children,* which we wrote and workshopped ourselves, using nursery rhymes as a commentary on the central theme of man's inhumanity to man. That was a great experience, but against my wishes they decided they would take it to Belfast Drama Festival. The adjudicators there said it was not a play at all so they would not even mark it.

I had first met my future wife Gertrude, who was from the Moy Road in Armagh, when we were both around fifteen. We used to go to dances in Armagh City Hall, where top bands like the Clipper Carlton used to play; or more occasionally to the Parochial Hall. In the latter big Bobby Carson, as the custodian of Catholic morality, would watch the dancers like a hawk and put anybody out who was dancing too close or jiving. Gertrude and I were evicted quite a few times. Despite that Bobby and I were friends until he died. At eighteen Gertrude went off to train as a nurse in Newcastle upon Tyne, where she had a sister. I could not afford to visit her there so it was another three years before I saw her again. We were very brave and used to meet in the Rainbow café in Armagh for coffee. I thought she was absolutely gorgeous.

In June 1964 we got married in Armagh Cathedral. It was a classic small-town Irish wedding between a teacher and a nurse. We went to Sorrento with Joe Walsh Tours for our honeymoon. When I got back I discovered that Gertrude's brother and a few friends had 'borrowed' the limousine we had hired for the wedding from a local undertaker and taken it to the races in Listowel, much to the undertaker's consternation. Luckily they had a number of winners, which enabled them to pay for the escapade.

Gertrude was marvellous in an understated way. She worked as a nurse in Armagh City Hospital until it closed down in the mid-1970s, when she switched, mainly to night duty, at Tower Hill, the town's geriatric hospital. I used to worry greatly about her travelling up and down between Markethill and Armagh in the middle of the night, with her friend May Rice, during the late 1970s and early 80s when all kinds of evildoers were out on the roads. It was precisely during that period, when I was an unemployed politician after the fall of the first power-sharing Assembly, that she was the family's main breadwinner. She never complained about it. We had built the bungalow where I still live on the outskirts of Markethill after our marriage and our daughter Orla was born in the summer of 1969.

The 1960s were when the rumblings and tensions were building in Northern Ireland. As a young man I was reasonably well off; I could afford to put petrol in a car and pay the household bills. But I was also aware that there was a whole community that was not so lucky, with a level of poverty that would be seen as totally unacceptable today. I was also becoming conscious of serious discrimination. As early as 1963 something happened that began to open my eyes. A friend of mine, Harry McGeown, lived with a family of twelve in a small dilapidated house in Keady Street, with neither water nor electricity, and had gone to the local unionist councillor to apply for a council house, because in those days councillors had the power to allocate houses. Councillor George Woods' reply to him was: 'No Catholic pig or his litter will get a house in Markethill while I am here.'

Harry came to me for help and I asked him to let me think about it. I was angry and felt I had to do something. I had not been involved in any kind of politics up to then: I was very comfortable as a primary school principal. So I went to see two prominent local Protestants: Jim Nelson, the local doctor, and Tommy Robinson, a local publican and member of the Royal Black Preceptory (and father of Bruce Robinson, a future head of the Northern Ireland Civil Service). I also went to see the Catholic curate, Charlie Devlin. Jim Nelson said, 'I don't want to live in a village that does things in that way.' The upshot was that we made an appointment and went up to see the local MP for this constituency, Sir Norman Stronge (later murdered by the IRA) in Stormont; he was also the Speaker of the Stormont parliament. Stronge did not seem at all interested: he hardly spoke to us, but I hoped he would do something behind the scenes. The local papers did a good spread on it. A short time later the Northern Ireland Housing Trust, a public agency, began building some new houses on Newry Street, and some of those eventually went to Catholics, including Harry McGeown. Out of that intervention came a small group we called the Mid-Armagh Anti-Discrimination Committee, which campaigned for fairness in housing and public employment.

Around that time Patricia McCluskey and her husband Dr Conn McCluskey were beginning to collect information about discrimination in housing and jobs from their home in Dungannon and to campaign against that discrimination under the banner of the Campaign for Social Justice in Northern Ireland. A few years later the civil rights movement started. It can't have been a coincidence that it was led by the eleven-plus generation of young people who were starting to come out of the universities: John Hume, Austin Currie, Bernadette McAliskey, Eamon McCann, Michael Farrell. Also television had become a household thing for the first time, and we were seeing those gripping pictures of Rosa Parks on the bus in Alabama, and hearing the speeches of Martin Luther King, with black and white people singing 'We Shall Overcome' together. That began to focus people's minds and to make them ask, 'What the hell have we got here in the North of Ireland?'

2. *Early Years in Local Politics*

I find it difficult to write about the civil rights movement because it was so disparate. There was Austin Currie squatting in a house in Caledon, on the other side of Armagh, to protest against a nineteen-year-old single Protestant woman (secretary to a local unionist politician) being housed by Dungannon Council while Catholics with large families were overlooked. He never received the credit he deserved for that courageous action. Derry was in many ways the spiritual centre of the movement, whose street protests were to lead to the RUC bludgeoning civil rights marchers in Duke Street in October 1968.

There was the Belfast group, which saw an ongoing struggle between a range of left-wing and not-so-left-wing groups: People's Democracy, the then Marxist-inclined IRA, what was to become the Provisional IRA, trade unionists, students and intellectuals. Remarkably, there was no stirring in the republican heartland of south Armagh until Harry Thornton from Ballsmill on the Armagh–Louth border was shot dead by the British army in Belfast in August 1971. Meanwhile at Westminster Gerry Fitt was doing an enormous amount of work to educate MPs – people like Paul Rose and Kevin McNamara – about the discrimination in Northern Ireland; he never got the credit for that either.

I was not on the Derry march in October 1968, although like everybody else I saw the TV pictures of Gerry Fitt being one of those batoned by the police, with blood flowing out of his head. I was one of the organizers of a civil rights march in Armagh in the following month. The Paisleyites were staked out around the town, all of them with cudgels of some kind; it was said that they had broken into a local hardware shop to help themselves to pickaxe handles and other implements. As we marched along Ogle Street, we saw the armed Paisleyites blocking the street ahead; at a certain point the police told us we would not be allowed to go any further. There were some angry speeches, which did not help when we were trying to get people away to safety. There were a few cracked heads before it ended. It was frightening: for the first time in my life, I saw close up the awful snarl of sectarian hatred on the faces of those people, people I knew and met every day of the week. That was followed by a march in Newry – Sean Hollywood, later of the SDLP, was the main organizer – and it was a good march up to the point when a few heroes pushed a couple of police vehicles into the canal.

The last protest march I attended was an anti-internment march from Castlewellan to Newcastle in March 1972. It was stopped at an army checkpoint on the edge of Newcastle; there was a brief altercation at the front of the march, and the army fired off CS gas canisters and charged the crowd. I fell over a small hedge into a garden, retching painfully as the gas filled my lungs. But I remember long before that becoming aware that you can only march up and down so often. Many of the pioneers of the civil rights movement – John Hume, Gerry Fitt, Ivan Cooper, Paddy Devlin, Paddy O'Hanlon – had come to the same conclusion and decided in 1970 that a new political party was needed to take the campaign further.

It took me another three years before I became fully involved in that new party, the Social Democratic and Labour Party, and then it was almost by accident. I had been impressed by seeing John Hume, clearly a sensible man with real gravitas, on television. Then in May 1973 a local election with new, more democratic structures was about to take place. The SDLP in this area had a good candidate, a well-known farmer from Tassagh. On nomination day I came home from school and my wife Gertrude said the farmer had phoned to say he was pulling out. The deadline for nominations was 5 pm in Armagh city. In a panic I rang three or four people, asking them to stand. I then realized that if I didn't do it myself we would miss the deadline. I called into the council offices to get the nomination form and found the requisite number of people in Armagh to sign it for me. I then discovered I needed a deposit of £25, no small sum in those days. I went into a shop where I knew the owner and said: 'Could you lend me £25? I'll not tell you now what it's for and I'll let you have it back tomorrow.' That was the beginning of a 32-year-old treadmill of politics for me. In those days I had absolutely no desire or inclination to be a politician. I was perfectly happy with what I was doing. But I felt I had no choice but to do what I did.

The new district councils at the time seemed to herald some change in the political life of Northern Ireland. These structures, brought in after the recommendations of the McCrory Report, scrapped the old, highly discriminatory system of local government. Election to the new councils was for the first time based strictly on 'one person, one vote' through proportional representation. Planning, housing and roads were taken out of the councils' remit to be dealt with by central government agencies. The Housing Executive – one of the North's very few success stories – was given almost total control of the provision and allocation of public housing. 'Bins, bogs and burials,' in the words of one wag, was what the local councils were left with.

Sitting on Armagh district council was an eye-opener. I saw for the first time the way in which the politics of division operated on a unionist-dominated council. I spent sixteen years on that council and I was never on a subcommittee, nor was I ever on a council visit to anywhere. But I had the issues I wanted to raise and I kept raising them, and I had very good colleagues in the SDLP: Oliver Toibin, Pat Brannigan and Jimmy McKernan. We kept hammering away.

It was Dickensian in many ways. Most of the unionists were chisel-faced remnants of the ancient regime, anachronistic old men determined to hang on to their privileged positions. The SDLP members, first-timers all, learned early that we would have to battle for everything, with the unionists always voting as a block. They regarded us as intruders into their rightful domain, and were unable or reluctant to understand that the world was changing and their days of supremacy were over.

There were some lighter moments. A debate about Irish place names raised the temperature considerably. Some declared that such names would never be allowed because Northern Ireland was British. Others vowed to 'stamp out these Fenian practices whatever the cost'. One DUP councillor, Dougie Hutchinson, thumped the table and declared: 'There will be no Irish place names about Drumnahunsion as long as I am here.'

Nobody on the unionist side saw anything wrong with the way things were done. We had our usual quota of religious fanatics, drunken officials and small-town affairs, sometimes all happening together. The Ulster Unionists, and then the DUP, did their stuff for the local newspapers, ranting and raving. We kept trying to exercise the very limited powers councils then possessed in a fair and proper way. It was very hard to do anything against unionist vested interests.

We took at least two cases of maladministration to court. One was against a well-qualified Catholic who had been working in Strabane Council running their sports facilities who was blatantly overlooked for the equivalent job in Armagh; we won that case.

I remember a motion coming before the council to deplore quarrying at Navan Fort (*Emain Macha*) outside Armagh city, one of the great sites of pre-Christian Gaelic Ireland and capital of the people of north-east Ireland (the *Ulaidh*). The company doing the quarrying was owned by a prominent unionist. When I told one DUP councillor, the same Dougie Hutchinson, the story of Cuchulainn tied to a stake on what is now the border and dying to defend the North from invaders from Connacht, he changed his mind and voted to save the ancient site. It was indicative of a thaw in relationships between the SDLP and some of the unionist councillors that I saw happening during my period on the council.

I used to dream that *Emain Macha* could become a future symbol for a new Ireland and a new North of Ireland, of a common Irish and Ulster identity. The old Gaelic capital, home of kings, identified as such by Ptolemy in the second century BC could become the beacon light for a new country whose people were at peace with each other. It could become the centre stone for a common heritage that, in Dougie Hutchinson's words, 'could greatly help to heal the wounds and divisions on each other by Planter and Gael, and God knows how much healing is needed at the present time'. It would be a new vision of a dynamic Ulster neither Catholic nor Protestant, Celtic nor Scottish, Gaelic nor Anglo-Saxon, but an Ulster of generous, garrulous, combative, hard-working and poetic people united for the first time in common love of their home place.

Armagh in the 1970s and 80s was a town that was being bombed into a state of shock by the Provisional IRA. Back in 1969, the first person outside Belfast and Derry to be killed in the Northern Ireland Troubles was John Gallagher, a young Armagh man shot by the B-Specials on the Cathedral Road as he walked home from the cinema. Then the IRA's bombs tore the heart out of Armagh. The SDLP used to hold its meetings in the Irish National Foresters' club in the town centre. One night there was a bomb scare and the next minute the main department store on the other side of Market Square, Lennox's, exploded; it was a horrible experience to stand there and watch it burn down. There were sectarian fights in the streets. Catholic lads could not go down Scotch Street because groups of young Protestants would come up the street to beat the hell out of them. Victoria Street, the essence of Armagh middle-class respectability, became almost a battle ground. Nobody knew what was going to happen next.

I left a council meeting early one evening in 1983 because the business was over and someone was coming to my house to see me. Before I got home I heard my fellow SDLP councillor Pat Brannigan on the radio describing how the Ulster Unionist council chairman, Charlie Armstrong, had been blown to bits. Charlie was a thoroughly decent man, and a member of the Ulster Defence Regiment, who had joined up only because he saw it as his duty to protect his neighbours. He had left the same council meeting I was at, went to the same car park I had just driven my car out of, and an IRA car bomb put an end to him. Before that, another councillor in the UDR from the Keady area was shot dead. You can imagine the atmosphere in the council at that time.

3. On the Brink of Civil War

The period from the early 1970s to the mid-1980s was a very harrowing one in County Armagh, and there were times I believed we were on the brink of actual civil war. Per head of population more people were killed in the Troubles in Armagh than any other county in the North.[1] When I decided to undertake this memoir I knew I would dread the section about sectarian violence and its effects on the area where I was born and bred, represented in the House of Commons, and still live. I have spent over forty years trying to distance myself from the sorrow and pain I felt at the slaughter of people I knew: decent, honest individuals who had no act nor part in the bitter near-war of attrition that enveloped us all.

It was a dreadful time. This lovely county was cloaked in a permanent black pall of fear and deep suspicion. Neighbour watched neighbour, wondering whether he or she was a secret IRA or loyalist terrorist, or maybe a clandestine police or army agent whose job it was to keep a close eye and report on the everyday movements of ordinary people. Many Protestants regarded each and every Catholic as, by definition, a supporter of the IRA who would, when needed, provide succour, information and protection to that enemy organization. In their jaundiced eyes Catholics were at best 'sneaking regarders', and at worst activists who were the IRA's eyes and ears in their small towns and farming communities.

1. D. McKittrick, S. Kelters, B. Feeney and C. Thornton, *Lost Lives: The stories of the men, women and children who died as a result of the Northern Ireland troubles* (Edinburgh 1999), 1481.

Similarly, many Catholics saw Protestants as agents of the police and army, active supporters of loyalist paramilitaries, and thus protectors of the sectarian murderers who were particularly active in my home area. This irrational equation of a person's religion with military or paramilitary affiliation was poisonous. People who had been good friends for decades began to doubt each other. The resulting febrile atmosphere allowed a vicious rumour mill to flourish, leading to the fingering of 'targets', completely innocent people then either outcast by their own community or targeted by the terrorist organizations operating out of the other community.

The toxic effects of violence and counter-violence seeped into every aspect of life. It was tragic to watch as the lives of so many good people, Protestant and Catholic, were blighted by violence and its consequences. Young people who should have been finishing their education and starting their careers were being murdered or spending the best years of their lives in jail. The chasm between unionists and nationalists deepened by the day, so that community cohesion in many places was simply non-existent. As a public representative I saw this at first hand, and it saddened me deeply that there was no right way to deal with it so long as the violence continued.

Neighbour killing neighbour has a putrid smell of evil that seeps into an entire community. Each murderous act begot its counterpart, until revenge almost became a duty to be fulfilled. It enveloped every crevice of life, spreading anger, suspicion, fear, hatred and ultimately despair. It left a dark cloud of deep suffering and loss that will endure for many decades.

I have often spoken of a man I knew who was killed during that time, whom I will call Jack Adams (not his real name because I know the family very well and don't want to cause them further suffering). Jack was a farmer by day and a good and decent neighbour. At night he would put on his part-time policeman's uniform. That meant that to some of the Irish republican persuasion he became dehumanized, a 'legitimate target', part of the British 'war machine', shot dead while ploughing his fields as part of the campaign to drive the 'Brits out'. But Jack's family has lived in County Armagh and farmed its lands for 400 years, as much a part of the landscape of this small part of the world as the soil they have tilled and the sweat they have spilled. This was their place, their home. The warped ideology of violent republicanism denied him that birthright: for these physical-force republicans he was an invader, planter, member of the British security forces. Their little Green Book said that he had to be murdered as he ploughed his ancestral land. Is his land Irish land?

Or British land? Or just the Adams land on which this family have lived and worked for four centuries?

There is another side to the story too. The very large number of murders committed by republican and loyalist paramilitaries often clouded the brutal fact that many innocent people were also killed by the security forces. Between 1969 and 1986 166 civilians who were not members of any violent organization or involved in any paramilitary activity were killed by the British army, the RUC and the UDR in Northern Ireland. During this time there were only two convictions obtained in connection with these killings: a 98.8 per cent non-conviction rate.

Examples of innocent lives being shattered and tragically ended were legion. John Pat Cunningham was a young man with special educational needs who could neither speak nor hear, but who loved the simple things in life like wandering into his family's fields near Benburb, on the Armagh–Tyrone border, to keep an eye on the cattle. When in June 1974 he saw soldiers with guns and blacked-out faces in those fields, he became terrified and began to run towards the safety of his home. The shot that killed him was fired by a highly trained soldier. A local doctor said John Pat had been born with an incomplete development of mind and required special care. The doctor said about a year earlier he had come across soldiers pushing the boy into a Saracen armoured car. The soldiers told him he had been hiding in the bushes and acting suspiciously. The doctor told John Pat's mother about the incident and advised her to keep a special watch on her son's movements, in view of his fear of soldiers and their uniforms. This innocent young man was doomed to become just the latest statistic in the official report about the Troubles that the British government regularly published.

John Pat would not have known twelve-year-old Majella O'Hare, who lived fifteen miles away at Ballymoyer, near the village of Whitecross. Majella's killing near her home was particularly shocking as there was absolutely no IRA activity there. On a bright crisp day in August 1976, the wee girl was on her way to confession with two friends. Perhaps she and her friends were singing as they walked along that country road: all her family were gifted with fine singing voices. It was the kind of summer's day that children's voices and birdsong would normally have made alive with happiness. The tranquillity was shattered when a soldier discharged a single shot and Majella fell to the ground, mortally injured. Her father, cutting grass in the nearby churchyard, heard the shot and ran towards the girls. He gathered Majella into his arms until an ambulance came. She was dead when she reached hospital.

After her killing there were the usual lies and excuses: there had been an IRA sniper unit in the area, the soldiers had been fired on, and the soldier who killed her thought it had come from people walking near her, so he opened fire. The paratrooper who had killed her was acquitted of her manslaughter. Thirty-five years later, in 2011, there was an unprecedented apology from the Ministry of Defence to her 88-year-old mother, after the Police Service of Northern Ireland's Historical Enquiries Team (HET) found there was no evidence to suggest there had been an IRA gunman in the area. It recalls *King Lear*: 'As flies to wanton boys are we to the gods. They kill us for their sport.' Majella's brother Michael was a close friend and I campaigned for many years for justice for Majella.

Then there was the Reavey family, who lived nearby and were good friends of the O'Hares. The father, Jimmy, also a friend of mine, had three sons, John Martin (twenty-five), Brian (twenty-two) and Anthony (seventeen), shot by a UVF gang who smashed into their home in Whitecross, just beyond Glennane, in January 1976 as they sat watching television. It was such a lovely, cosy farmhouse and living room with a big fire, and pictures on the wall of the father and mother and the boys in a football team; the whole family was involved in the local St Killian's GAA club. Another brother helped run a youth club at St Killian's, which kept local young people away from the paramilitaries, who were banned from the club. They weren't interested or involved in politics, except the oldest son Eugene used to help me occasionally at election time. According to the Historical Enquiries Team's report into the killings, and in the words of the family members: 'They were all workers, mainly on labourers' wages, at a time when work was not easy to come by, but were all "brought up in a happy family environment where the father grew the vegetables and the mother cooked their bread".'[2]

In that small space three young men were shot dead, the safety and sanctity of the home, something treasured by all rural dwellers, murderously violated. From then on, no Catholic family living in an isolated country place would be safe. The father Jimmy was a thoroughly decent man who worked at the hard trade of 'scutching' in the flax mill and then on the roads. He did not have a sectarian bone in his body. He immediately went on radio to appeal for no retaliation. The mother, Sadie, an outgoing and very talented lady, was a home baker and lace-maker, whose cakes won top prize in the Newry Show for many years; she was a particular inspiration to me. I went up there the morning after and it was very distressing: the 35 bullet holes on the inside walls told their own sad story. Her

2. HET Review Summary Report concerning the deaths of John Martin, Brian and Anthony Gerard Reavey, 7.

youngest son Anthony, who had been dragged out from under a bed and shot in the legs, died four weeks later from a blood clot on the brain.

Agony was piled on agony, horror on horror. The day after the attack on the Reaveys came the Kingsmill massacre less than a mile away, in which ten Protestant workmen were murdered by the IRA, who decided it was too monstrous to claim responsibility for it openly. This was apparently in reprisal for the Reaveys and the killing on the same night – in what appeared to be a coordinated operation – of three members of the O'Dowd family near Gilford, fifteen miles to the north.

A minibus carrying linen workers at the end of the day from their work at the linen mill at Glennane to their homes in Bessbrook was stopped at a bogus checkpoint by around twelve men, unmasked but with blackened faces. They were ordered off and told to line up with their hands on the side of the vehicle. One of the gunmen, apparently with an English accent, asked each of them for their religion. The men thought that the lone Catholic, Richard Hughes, was being singled out for assassination. The men on either side of him, the Chapman brothers, pressed each of his hands in an attempt to keep him safely and anonymously in the line. But one of the gang pulled him out and shouted to him to start running down the road and keep running. The others were then mowed down by automatic rifle fire. The only survivor, Alan Black, was hit eighteen times. Then there was silence and the IRA gang melted into a night made hellish by such a slaughter of innocents.

It was a tragic irony that the two Reavey brothers' coffins in hearses, accompanied by family and friends, were approaching the place of the massacre shortly after it happened. The procession was diverted away from this latest horror scene. Dead almost met dead on that dark, silent County Armagh back road: thirteen people cruelly sacrificed to satisfy the bloodlust of Provisional and loyalist warlords.

The way the Reavey family was treated when stopped by British army and RUC patrols on the roads in the weeks and months after the killing of their sons was outrageous (I write more about this in Chapter Eleven). The older Reavey brother, Eugene, who was in his own house two miles away when he heard about the shootings, remembers arriving a short time later to find a policeman searching the drawers in the sitting room where his brother John Martin lay dead. When asked what he was doing, the policeman said: 'I'm looking for ammunition. I believe there's ammunition stored in this house.' An incensed Eugene retorted that the only ammunition he was likely to find was ammunition he was trying to plant. He and a cousin who had also arrived took the policeman by the back of the neck and threw him out of the house.

The Historical Enquiries Team, set up by the Police Service of Northern Ireland to investigate unsolved killings during the Troubles (and wound up in 2014), spoke of evidence of 'the harassment the family endured from members of the security forces after these terrible murders. They were the subject of disinformation, rumour and innuendo, which has caused them great distress for many years.' The HET concluded: 'The murdered young men were entirely innocent victims.' The team failed to find any reason why the three Reavey brothers 'should have been attacked in this brutal and horrifying manner; the likelihood is that it was an instance of senseless sectarian violence'. They noted: 'Post-incident intelligence indicates that a loyalist paramilitary gang (which included members of the security forces) was responsible for the murders, and that the murders were linked to others in the area.' In another section on the possible passing of intelligence from RUC and UDR members to the UVF, the group responsible for the Reavey murders, the HET team commented: 'Given the crossover between some security force members and paramilitaries in the so-called Glennane Gang, the seeds of the eventual tragedy are perhaps clearly seen.'[3]

We were indeed close to civil war in the North after the Reavey and O'Dowd murders and the Kingsmill massacre. In her book *Lethal Allies*, Anne Cadwallader reports claims by policemen turned terrorists, John Weir and William McCaughey, that the local UVF planned to retaliate by attacking a Catholic girls' grammar school in Newry (Our Lady's Grammar School) or a primary school in the village of Belleeks, five miles from Kingsmill. Speaking to the BBC *Spotlight* programme in 2004, McCaughey said:

> The intention would have been to kill the occupants of the building, quite simply, and it would have been nuns and anyone else who happened to be there. It would have been a case of meeting republican terror with greater loyalist terror. That would have been the rationale behind it. Pretty sectarian, pretty extreme stuff, but the murders of ten innocent, working class Protestants was pretty sectarian, pretty horrific.[4]

In the end, according to John Weir, the UVF leadership in Belfast vetoed the plan precisely because they feared that civil war would be the outcome.

These were the among the most emotionally draining times of my public life, made more difficult by my being the SDLP's spokesman on justice: in that role I had to highlight the need for fundamental RUC reform, and in particular

---

3. HET Review Summary Report on the deaths of the Reavey brothers, 46–51.
4. BBC Northern Ireland, *Spotlight* progamme, 25 May 2004.

those instances when policemen were involved in terrorist activities in collusion with loyalist paramilitaries. And of course, being a Catholic and a nationalist, it was easy for Protestants and unionists to label me as an IRA supporter. I went to several of the funerals of those who died in the Kingsmill massacre. I was well received by most there, but I shall never forget walking up the street in Bessbrook on my own to the funeral of one of those victims. The constant drizzle and a dank grey mist added to the pall of grief that seemed to envelop the silent, heartbroken village. I felt desperately alone as a nationalist politician among those grieving unionists; I could hear my own footsteps.

Early on I made a promise to myself that I would show my abhorrence at political and sectarian violence by visiting the homes of the bereaved – all the bereaved, whatever their background – and if at all possible pay my respects by attending the funerals of everybody who was killed by such violence in my constituency. It was my statement to the IRA and to the loyalist paramilitaries, but it was often a difficult thing to do. In July 1990, when I was the MP for the area, a young policeman from my village, David Sterritt, was killed, along with two fellow RUC men and a nun, in an IRA landmine explosion outside Armagh. I went that evening to the wake. It was an eerie feeling; all the doors on his street were open as I drove up, the people watching to see what would happen. I parked my car at the Sterritt family's house and rang the bell. His uncle came to the door and I said I'd like to express my condolences. 'Get the hell out of here,' he shouted.

In October 1982 Thomas Cochrane, a lorry driver and part-time UDR sergeant from Loughgilly, was kidnapped by the IRA, who kept him for five days and then left his body beside the road on the other side of Camlough. His wife had been the district nurse, visiting the schools, a lovely woman whom I knew well from my years as a school principal. I went up to the house and she came to the door. She was crying and I sympathized with her, and she asked me to come in for a cup of tea. Then a male voice came from the corner of the big kitchen cum living room: 'Show Mr Mallon the door, please.' I said I'd go and wait outside. A neighbour who was also there at the time, Snowdon Corkey, who was in the police reserve, got up and said: 'Seamie, I'll walk down to the car with you – there are a few chancey boys around at the minute.'

Three weeks later I went down for a message in the pharmacy in Markethill. My daughter Orla, who was thirteen, came with me, because she loved going into the village to the shops. Because it was market day, it was very busy with lorries and vans parked everywhere. Orla went into the pharmacy and I sat waiting in the car. I was daydreaming when I heard loud metallic sounds. For a moment

I thought it might be timber being unloaded at the local hardware shop. But then I recognized it as the sound of gunfire, and I knew instinctively that the targets were Snowdon Corkey and his fellow RUC reservist, young Ronnie Irwin. They had just walked past my car on the way from the police barracks towards the barrier they were manning. They gave me the usual friendly wave and a few seconds later they were dying. I ran towards a cattle truck under which Snowdon had rolled and knelt beside him. The effluent from the cows was seeping down on top of him. So there I was on my knees and the young policeman dying beside me: 'Seamie,' he said, 'tell them all I love them.'

Ronnie Irwin was a particular favourite of Orla and her friends: they called him 'Chuckles' because he was so full of smiles and chat when they regularly walked through his checkpoint. When the local doctor, Jimmy Nelson, and local Unionist councillor Jim Speers arrived a few minutes later, both young men were dead. Orla was still sitting in the car, terrified I had been killed too. We both went home in tears. That really put calluses on my soul.

Then there was a young UDR man from Armagh. It was particularly heart-breaking. The father was a lecturer in Armagh Technical College. The son had driven up to the front of his parents' house and then the IRA opened up. They could hear the gunshots and one scream out of their son, but could do nothing about it. So I went in and spoke to the mother and father. They were very polite but it was as if there was a Chinese wall between us. The RUC had a unit of people whose job it was to comfort the bereaved. There was a young policewoman in the house and she said: 'I think, Seamus, that the best thing you can do is to go home.' That was the sheer awfulness of that time.

I had a good friend, Denis Mullen, who was active in the SDLP. Denis was the first Catholic to be employed as an ambulance man in the South Tyrone Hospital in Dungannon, and had just been appointed head of the ambulance service there. He was having a house built for himself outside the south Tyrone village of Moy and living temporarily in a small house at the end of a lane. I was driving through Armagh one evening and something happened to me that had never happened before or since: somehow my radio tuned into the police radio's wavelength and I heard there was a shooting in a particular townland in Moy. I said to myself, 'That's Dinny's place.' So I drove on out to the house and Denis was lying there dead and his wee three-year-old daughter was sitting beside him in her nightdress. That image of Denis lying dead beside his tiny daughter will stay with me for as long as I live on this earth. He was a victim of the same loyalist gunmen (some of them policemen) who had killed the Reaveys. And there was one final twist: I couldn't believe the ugly verbal abuse I took from a couple of the RUC men who were on duty outside that house on that night. At Denis' funeral, my SDLP colleague Denis Haughey described him as 'a kindly and gentle Christian, a man of peace. He served the community in innumerable ways.'

What effect did all this violence and hatred have on me personally? I was not particularly good at articulating my feelings and I admit I sometimes suffered from short periods of depression: 'black dog' I called it, echoing Winston Churchill's phrase. When I came back from a particularly bad incident I some-times went over to my sisters Maura and Peggy in Newry, and sat drinking tea, giving monosyllabic answers to the questions they would ask me. Gertrude and Orla used to say: 'Dad's in one of his moods again.'

What kept me in politics during that period? Sure I was in danger, but so were the people who lived in this village, so was every farmer, Catholic and Protestant, living in an isolated area of this constituency. How do you walk away from that? You hang in and you do your best. Many in the Protestant community would quietly say to me: 'Don't worry, Seamus, keep going – you're on the right lines.' Several times people warned me that they had heard about a threat to me here in my own house. So we had to put in bulletproof doors, and I had to warn Gertrude and Orla to stay away from the windows. And of course when I was going out in the car with either of them, I had to keep them back in the house while I checked under the car for explosive devices.

One night, at around one in the morning when we were all in bed inside, three or four men came to burn the house down and they got the fire started at the front door, but the fire went out; they were incompetent arsonists. On another evening, at around ten o'clock, a man appeared and marched around the house playing the flute. The police must have been following him because they imme-diately pounced. I told them: 'I'd like to chat to that fellow – coming up here by himself to play the flute takes a bit of courage. It was after all a flute he took out, not a gun.' I asked the police not to charge him, but they charged him anyway.

I was caught in the middle in those years. I knew the UDR had to be disbanded because of its abuses against nationalist people, but also that every time I voiced this in public I was adding further suffering to the relatives of those UDR men who had been killed by the IRA. I knew what those people were going through. I knew they saw me almost as a public spokesman for what the IRA was doing. It is not hard to understand how those violent events damaged the psyche of the unionist commu-nity and how long it will take for those memories to recede. I see in my unionist neighbours not just the pain and suffering caused by the loss of their loved ones, but also the pain of betrayal: their belief that the British used and then abandoned them.

4. *Sunningdale, Power-Sharing and the 'Dog Days'*

For the nationalist community, there was a short step in the early 1970s between the democratic political process chosen by the SDLP and the violent republicanism represented by the Provisional IRA. It was difficult for young people to choose between the two, especially after the Bloody Sunday killings in Derry in January 1972. It took nearly thirty years of killing and dying and suffering before people began to realize that the one thing in this whole miserable period that was an abject failure was violent republicanism. I remember talking to a young republican in Long Lartin prison near Birmingham. I asked him how he was doing. 'Next year there will be a big change, next year we'll get the Brits out,' he said. 'Oh no you won't,' I kept saying. That was the great lie that prevailed for most of that period.

Meanwhile we in the SDLP got massive abuse for taking the political road, being called things like the Stoop Down Low Party. The North of Ireland is full of people, good and decent people who would not hurt a fly, yet saw no contradiction in giving support to those who were killing their neighbours. That is something only time can change. I joined the SDLP because I wanted a political party that was viable, credible and contained the ideals of republicanism without the murderous nonsense of violent republicanism.

When you start to strip down my brand of republicanism, the definition that remains is a belief in the capacity of the people of this island – whatever the barriers of history – to learn to live together, to respect each other's traditions and to bring up their families and develop their culture in peace and mutual understanding. As Irish republicans, we need to help our unionist fellow Irish people to be part of this beautiful island we both call home. That may not have much of the blood and bugle stuff that all Sinn Féiners and Orangemen love so much, but it's what the vast majority of ordinary people want. I believe this is the true republican spirit: Wolfe Tone's uniting of Catholic, Protestant and Dissenter, not the vengeful 'Defenderist' culture that has often appeared to replace it.

In June 1973 I was elected as one of nineteen SDLP members to the new Northern Ireland Assembly; we were the second largest party after the Ulster Unionists. During the election I did my first television interview, a scary experience. The litany of political insights I had nurtured in my mind for days beforehand proved utterly superfluous; I never used one of them. I learned quickly not to clutter my mind with complex issues because one central point is all that you will have time to make. The wise advice of my first interviewer – 'no affectations, no fancy stuff, no being eloquent – just be yourself' has stayed with me to this day. I think I was also one of the first interviewees of Eamonn Mallie, then a cub reporter on work experience with the BBC, now a celebrated author and media personality.

My first day in the new Assembly the following month was a strange one. As a new young party, the feeling in the SDLP was one of hope. Yet as I drove around Edward Carson's statue in front of the Stormont parliament building, part of me was saying 'What am I doing here? How can we as a party create a new inclusive society under this symbol of supremacy and exclusion, of a unionism and Britishness that has always regarded the likes of me, as an Irish nationalist, as an alien being?'

Meeting my colleagues and hearing Gerry Fitt give a little welcoming speech changed my mood. But nothing could have prepared me for the naked aggression and sheer vulgarity that met us as we entered the parliament chamber from sections of the unionist and loyalist benches. The spectacle that greeted us was grotesque. At the start of proceedings a character called 'Professor' Kennedy Lindsay jumped onto the table in the centre of the chamber, grabbed the mace, the symbol of British royal authority, performed an outlandish dance, and led a shouting, conga-like procession out of the room. Did Queen Elizabeth realize that this clownish performance was meant to express loyalty to her office and person? I never saw nor heard of 'Professor' Kennedy Lindsay again.

If that was a farce, there was also an undercurrent of menace, which found its final form in the intimidating weeks of the Ulster Workers' Council strike in May 1974. On one occasion Ulster Unionist Party leader Brian Faulkner was getting up to leave the chamber, and three or four of the anti-power-sharing unionists were waiting at the door looking as though they were about to do him harm. I told Paddy O'Hanlon and Tom Daly, who was a big tall fellow, to get over there fast. And we went over and scattered them and got Faulkner out of the chamber safely. His colleague Herbie Kirk was not so lucky: he had just finished addressing the Assembly when a loyalist member caught him with a hefty uppercut to the chin.

On 1 January 1974 came the short-lived power-sharing Executive and the all-island Council of Ireland agreed in the Sunningdale Agreement. There was great hope and optimism and a bit of naivety at the beginning of that period. This was the first time since 1920 that nationalist representatives were up at Stormont as part of a ruling administration. Politics was a new thing to us. The basis for our optimism was the confidence of believing that never again would there be a society run by a one-party regime based on a gerrymandered electoral system; never again would there be an administration without representatives of the minority community; never again would there be a negotiation without Irish government input, and never again would the British government try to impose a solution that didn't have an all-Ireland dimension.

As a newly elected Assembly member, I had not been part of the negotiating team at Sunningdale, but we were all so elated when the Sunningdale Agreement was signed in December 1973. It was the most marvellous feeling. We were on Brian Faulkner's side and he was on our side – it was near to heaven. I'll never forget it: suddenly everything was possible. However, I put a bet on with the *Irish Times* journalist David McKittrick who said it would not last six months. I lost my bet.

I liked Brian Faulkner: he could be aggressive, but he had a decent core. The shock of the suspension of Stormont in 1972 had obviously affected him deeply. British Cabinet Secretary Robert Armstrong and his Irish opposite number Dermot Nally did a tremendous amount of work to persuade him to sign up to Sunningdale. He was ahead of his time; I was sorry to hear of his death in a horse-riding accident only three years later.

John Hume was Minister for Commerce so he was away most of the time trying to attract foreign business to come to the North. Paddy Devlin was Minister for Health: Armagh City Hospital was closed during his time; he wouldn't listen for a moment to all the representations we made to him to try to keep it open.

Gerry Fitt was Gerry. I always liked him immensely. He was not the party leader in intellectual terms. Even then John Hume was essentially the leader, but Gerry had done huge work at Westminster at the most difficult times over the previous decade. Austin Currie was Minister for Housing. I remember saying to him: 'Don't rush your fences.' He was getting ready to go in and clean up the whole discrimination in housing mess, but he soon realized it was not going to be easy.

I will never forget the day that the Executive fell on 28 May 1974, brought down by the Ulster Workers' Council (UWC) strike. John Hume, Tom Daly, Paddy O'Hanlon and Frank Feely had stayed with me the previous night because of the danger of violence at loyalist roadblocks that had sprung up almost everywhere (and because I could obtain petrol across the border), and we drove up to Stormont together that morning. As I knew the byroads of County Armagh well, we arrived unhindered at the edge of Portadown where the Mahon Road British army base was situated. I tried to gain entry to the base, but was refused by a disembodied English voice on the intercom. I stated who I was, that a senior SDLP member of the Executive, John Hume, was with me, and asked for an escorted passage to get us safely through the loyalist stronghold of Portadown and onto the M1 motorway to Belfast. After what seemed like an eternity, the voice returned and very curtly informed me that the army 'could not accede to my request'.

When I had run out of colourful expletives I went back to the car and using small back roads we managed to get onto the motorway. Tom Daly, who had tried his hand at navigation in road rallies, was eagle-eyed for the entire journey. Paddy O'Hanlon's gallows humour kept us amused. John Hume, who had swapped his ministerial car for my little Volkswagen Beetle, sat moodily silent except for asking every ten minutes: 'Where are we now?' O'Hanlon, becoming exasperated, replied at one point: 'For Christ's sake Hume, don't you know that we're on our way to our political funeral?'

We arrived at Lisburn in one piece and turned off the motorway onto the road to Shaw's Bridge, the quickest route to Stormont. We had gone about three miles when a police car screamed to a halt in front of us and another cut us off at the rear. 'Out, out, out' were the words that some years later had a different and more politically weighty resonance. When we emerged from the car, a fresh-faced young policeman pushed back his cap and, almost as an act of contrition, stuttered: 'Sorry lads, when we saw Mr Hume crammed in the back between two men in a very small car like this we thought he might be being kidnapped. Very sorry – we know you all have a busy day in front of you.' Before he could say anything else, O'Hanlon in a gravelly voice retorted: 'No, you are wrong again, constable. It won't be a busy day. We will just be signing on the dole.' He laughed, we all laughed, or at least we tried to. 'Sorry again lads, do you mind if we escort you up to the big house?' It was a new experience for all of us, speeding through paramilitary road checks with a police escort and all lights blazing. As we stopped at the gates of Stormont, and said our thanks and goodbyes, Hume broke his long silence and said: 'Those policemen knew who I was, isn't that right?' O'Hanlon's reply was pitch perfect, 'Yes, Minister.'

When we reached Room 17, our SDLP party room, most of our colleagues were already there. Brian Faulkner and his ministers had already resigned. Our ministers – Fitt, Hume, Devlin, Currie, Cooper and McGrady – had rightly refused to follow suit. They were then sacked by the Secretary of State, Merlyn Rees.

As we gathered up our papers and belongings word came through that Rees was coming down to our room to explain the British government's position. He was accompanied by Frank Cooper, the permanent secretary at the Northern Ireland Office. There was an embarrassing silence as both men sat down and Rees stuttered and stammered through the most abject litany of excuses I have ever heard from a grown man. One of these has stuck in my mind ever since. When pressed on why his government had totally failed to confront an illegal coup that had put an end to Northern Ireland's first ever cross-community government and shut down every facet of life in the region, he appeared to compare those cudgel-wielding, balaclava-wearing mobs with the Czechoslovakian people who had protested against the Russian invasion of their country six years earlier. 'Did you want me, a Labour minister, to bring army tanks on to the streets to break up a workers' strike' he asked, 'just like the Russian generals did in the city of Prague?' His pitiful performance in our party room was later followed by Prime Minister Harold Wilson's infamous speech when he upbraided the unionist people for being 'scroungers'. When wise and courageous political leadership was so urgently needed, a bad conscience provoked him instead to crude verbal abuse. The unionist community are a proud people; they wouldn't owe you a shilling.

The use of the British army in 1974 was sectarian. The British government had no problem putting the army into Derry, west Belfast or south Armagh. But they had big pangs of conscience about putting them into loyalist east Belfast, even if it meant that the legitimate, democratically elected government of the day would be brought down. They were forewarned about the UWC strikers taking over the power stations, and could have put a static military presence there. They could have done more and done it earlier to keep the roads open.

Rees had been a rear gunner under the command of his top civil servant, Frank Cooper, in the RAF during the Second World War. I remember on a later occasion after the fall of the Executive, we were sitting having coffee with Cooper and chatting about what would happen now. He said the British government had a way of making the SDLP move from its position of demanding nothing less than power-sharing with an Irish dimension: 'We'll starve you out.' They very nearly did, with the SDLP largely reduced to sitting without salaries on virtually powerless local councils for the next decade and longer.

At some point during the strike, the junior minister at the Northern Ireland Office, Stan Orme, came into the SDLP members' room to offer a deal. He promised an end to internment in return for our agreeing to suspend the Council of Ireland. We had a heated discussion after he left and eventually a motion to this effect was passed, with Paddy O'Hanlon, Hugh Logue, Paddy O'Donoghue, Frank Feely and myself voting against. I could not see the logic of it: we had fought hard for years to get a British government to recognize an 'Irish dimension', as it was then called. I strongly believed that if we had given way on such a point of principle once, we would have been asked to do so again.

More importantly, the Provos would have condemned us from a height and the nationalist community in general would have abandoned us; that could have been the end of the party. I felt at that late stage the Executive was doomed anyway. It is salutary that at the 1975 Constitutional Convention the United Ulster Unionist Council put down a motion (overwhelmingly supported by its elected representatives) rejecting power-sharing, sending the clear message that this was the issue to which unionists most objected to, not the Council of Ireland. Brian Faulkner himself was 'convinced all along that the outcry against the Council of Ireland was only a useful red herring – real opposition was to sharing of power'.[1]

It is extraordinary that much of the most far-sighted thinking about a Council of Ireland had been done by a group of senior Northern Ireland civil service departmental chiefs, led by the head of the Northern Ireland civil service Sir David Holden, in consultation with the then Secretary of State, William Whitelaw. In one of three 'secret' papers produced in late 1972 this 'future policy group' proposed that to acknowledge the 'special relationship' between Northern Ireland and the Republic of Ireland, a joint North–South Council for cooperation and consultation should be set up at once, but without – in the first instance – major executive functions.

1. E. Moloney, *A Secret History of the IRA* (London 2007: second edition), 324.

But the civil servants went much further. In his 2017 book on Sunningdale, the former head of the Irish Department of Foreign Affairs, Noel Dorr, quotes the most surprising of the papers they produced:

> … the redefinition of the constitutional status [of Northern Ireland] should proceed from this to set out an acceptable means for movement towards Irish unity in stages, *subject to consent at each stage.* This would again represent an acknowledgment of reality – that unity can never be achieved unless the people of Northern Ireland can be convinced that it is in their interests; that even in calmer times people will not take such a vital decision without knowing the 'terms of entry'; and that if unity is ever to come about at all, it must be in a staged, orderly way [emphasis in the original].[2]

The fall of the power-sharing Executive and Assembly and the Sunningdale Agreement did not completely destroy the new sense of hope that had pervaded our party, and indeed much of the general public. For the first time in its history, it was shown that unionist and nationalist, Catholic and Protestant, could work together in government, learn to trust each other, and to have mutual respect for the tradition from which each came. One could almost sense that there never would again be a single party government in Northern Ireland; that a marker had been set down. Whatever about the debris of the power-sharing experiment's last few weeks, something new had happened, which could, if allowed to grow, have changed the face of Northern Ireland for good.

Looking back at that period now, it could be said that the IRA and the loyalist paramilitaries were both responsible for bringing down the Sunningdale experiment. I would put more blame on the IRA, who understood politics better, and certainly people like Dáithí Ó Conaill would have known it was a very substantial advance. For the first time you had an Irish government involved in the solution of the Northern problem. For the first time you had an all-island Council of Ireland with executive functions. For the first time you had political representatives of the nationalist community involved in the Northern Executive. And for the first time you had a unionist leadership that showed great courage and vision both in their negotiations to set up and then their practice in implementing a power-sharing administration. Martin Luther King's 'precious stone of hope, hewn out of the mountain of despair' was brought down by an unholy alliance of the Provisional IRA, the Ulster Workers' Council and the loyalist paramilitaries.

2. N. Dorr, *Sunningdale: the Search for Peace in Northern Ireland* (Dublin 2017), 161–3.

The failure of this brave experiment was like a jumplead to many in the nationalist community who might have been somewhere in the no man's land between Sinn Féin and the SDLP. Ever since the latter was formed, there has been a dichotomy between its peaceful republicanism and republicanism as defined by the violence of the IRA. I know of many instances where members of our party had relatives in the IRA, relatives in jail, and relatives killed. So there was always an emotional tug towards that kind of republicanism, and that tug of war for the hearts and minds of northern nationalists between the two parties has continued ever since. The collapse of Sunningdale was one of the factors that tipped those people towards the IRA and Sinn Féin.

Power-sharing and Sunningdale, had they survived, could have saved several thousand lives in the remaining years of the Troubles up to 1998, particularly of young people. The IRA felt hugely threatened by the possible success of this dramatic new attempt at cooperation between ancient enemies and were determined to bring it down. This was despite, or perhaps because of, the fact that it represented a huge step forward for the nationalist community. If you believe members of the republican movement are patriots, this was a very twisted form of patriotism. In his history of the IRA, journalist Ed Moloney describes how that organization reacted:

> There was widespread agreement within the republican movement that the IRA had better move to kill off Sunningdale before Sunningdale killed it. As a key strategist of the time recalled: 'Our objective was to ensure that the Sunningdale Agreement would not succeed. [Dáithí] Ó Conaill was pushing us to blow up [the] Stormont [parliament] with a massive bomb and the Belfast leadership was trying to devise a method of getting a bomb onto a ship and blow it up in order to block the main channel in Belfast harbour. We wanted to make our presence felt as a force without which there could be no solution that was not to our liking.'[3]

There was not the slightest let-up in the IRA campaign during the five months of the power-sharing Assembly and Executive. They continued to operate on two levels. The big bombs were placed in Belfast and other urban areas, with pictures on television of people carried out in body bags and all the bloody mayhem that went with that.

Their other tactic was the continuing murders of Northern Irish people in the police and the UDR. It was not so high profile but it was that, more than

---

3. Moloney, 139.

anything else, which struck at the heart of the Protestant community. How many can remember horrific IRA atrocities like Bloody Friday in Belfast in 1972 or the firebombing of the La Mon Hotel in 1978 in which large numbers of people were killed? But even now people in the Protestant community in Markethill can tell you the day and the hour when a certain part-time RUC or UDR man, a farmer or a lorry driver, was killed by the IRA. That hit hard and deep because it hit families. Northern Ireland is a small place and each of those murders affected mothers and fathers and wives and brothers and sisters and sons and daughters and relatives and friends and work colleagues throughout the North of Ireland. That poison was wide and deep, and it is still there.

On the other side, the question was 'Who speaks for unionism?' I believe Brian Faulkner could have changed the face of politics in Northern Ireland. He had the intellect and he had the courage. He was the first of two leaders of the Ulster Unionist Party – the other one was David Trimble – I have seen politically assassinated by their own parties. Having had unfettered power from the 1920s onwards, the unionist people in 1973–4 saw that slipping away, and they were full of fear about the future. The slogan on the unionist side in the February 1974 Westminster election was: 'Dublin is only a Sunningdale away.'

Ironically one of the lessons of the collapse of the Sunningdale experiment (for everybody except the unionists and some British politicians) was that henceforth there could be no solution in Northern Ireland without the involvement of the Irish government. One of the secrets to having a stable Northern Ireland was close cooperation between the British and Irish governments to ensure its peaceful future. Anybody thinking his or her way through the situation would have seen that if we were ever going to get an end to violence and the beginning of peace, the role of the Irish government was going to be very important. One example was intelligence about IRA activities, which was far better in the Republic than in the North. A key factor there was an unarmed police force, the Garda Síochána, which enjoyed a high level of public confidence and therefore received considerable intelligence on the ground. In the North the section of the community where the intelligence lay that could point to the IRA was completely alienated from the RUC, particularly after internment, which deeply affected all nationalists.

After the collapse of the power-sharing Executive and Assembly came the 'dog days'. We did not see it then, but part of our role after that collapse was to keep the political process alive, because if it is not alive you add legitimacy to violence. Many nationalists saw the failure of power-sharing and Sunningdale as a failure of that democratic process to solve the deep problems of the North.

So, despite significant doubts, the SDLP made the decision to fight the October 1974 election to the Constitutional Convention, which was meant to try to find a new way forward. It was a very difficult election for us. Many in the Catholic community were torn; some followed the advice of two distinguished priests, Father Denis Faul and Father Raymond Murray, and boycotted it. I knew both of those men well enough not to question their motivation. They were good and sincere men, although wrong in that instance.

There was open intimidation in south Armagh, with *An Phoblacht* telling people not to vote and implying what would happen to them if they did. At one polling station in Mullaghbawn, I turned up with my election agent and standing at the door of the polling station was a man writing down names and another man with a gun. I went up to the former and asked him what was going on. 'You know what's going on,' he retorted, 'and it's none of your business.' 'It *is* my business that you're under the tutelage of the polling station and you've no right to be here and doing what you are doing,' I replied. I went inside and spoke to the election officials and not surprisingly they were very frightened people. In neighbouring Newry my SDLP colleague Frank Feely had shots fired over his head in one housing estate.

The intimidatory message from the IRA was absolutely clear. If they were brazen enough to show their guns to me and to shoot at Frank, both elected representatives, what were they doing to the brave people who went out to vote and lived next door to the gunmen and their followers? That was a major reason why a constitutional party like the SDLP had to keep going in those bad years. The Ulster Unionists and Alliance were doing it as well, but because so much of the paramilitary activity was within the nationalist community, it fell to us to keep the flame of peaceful, democratic politics alive in that community.

I smile grimly when I hear Sinn Féin talking about their democratic mandate and think of a man called Patsy Gillespie who became the IRA's first 'human bomb' when he was chained by the Derry IRA into a lorry load of explosives and blown to smithereens at a border checkpoint (along with five British soldiers). And when I look at Gerry Adams, I can't help thinking of Jean McConville, that poor mother of ten children, being driven away to her death by an IRA unit of which former members say Adams was the overall commander. When I go out into my home village of Markethill, I will meet the father, mother, brother or sister of somebody who was shot or bombed by the IRA, in the street, in the shops, in the pub. What is remarkable about the human spirit is the way in which so many of those people, somehow or another, are able to forgive. I'm not sure I would have the ability to do that.

Everybody in the SDLP was understandably depressed, even despairing, during that period. The low point was probably the 1976 annual conference, when there was an angry division between the party leadership and a group of which I was a leading member, who put forward a motion calling on the British government to declare its intention to withdraw from Northern Ireland. I attacked the Irish government for erecting 'a Berlin Wall of indifference between North and South', which was having a devastating effect on Northern national-ists. Gerry Fitt attacked us for having the same objectives as the IRA. John Hume said he also wanted the British to go, but the real problem in the North was one of conflict between the two sections of the community and Britain alone was not the problem. Our motion was defeated, but with most of those elected to the Constitutional Convention voting for withdrawal. Several leading party figures said all the good young people in their areas were joining the Provisionals since they saw in them the only way forward. A visiting Irish Department of Foreign Affairs official, Seán Donlon, wrote: 'Fitt and Hume now find them-selves leading a party of public representatives, a majority of whom are not prepared to accept official policy.' He said Hume had to be persuaded not to resign and Fitt's private assessment was that it was only a matter of time before the party disintegrated.

As the 1976 conference showed, there were plenty of divisions within the ranks of the SDLP in the late 1970s, which continued into the 1980s. There were those who had been in the Stormont parliament before it was prorogued in 1972: Fitt, Hume, Cooper, Devlin and Currie. There were the newcomers, including people like Eddie McGrady, Paddy Duffy and myself, who were sometimes viewed by the first group as something of a nuisance. Then you had tensions between the urban 'socialist' and the rural 'nationalist' wings. I have to say the former never convinced me of their socialism. Much more service was given to the community by those who were termed non-socialists than the so-called socialists. You had people like Paddy Duffy, Frank Feely, Paddy O'Hanlon and myself, who were regarded as kind of half-Provos. I remember one Belfast coun-cillor referring to us as 'the enemy within'. At that time John Hume was working in Europe as a member of Irish Commissioner Dick Burke's Cabinet, before he won a seat in the European Parliament in 1979. Gerry Fitt spent most of his time at Westminster. I devoted myself to keeping the party's branches open in County Armagh. I ran twice for Westminster for the old Armagh constituency in the 1970s, but it was not winnable. The Ulster Unionist Harold McCusker was always going to win with a built-in unionist majority.

Organization was a huge challenge. We had no resources, no money, no back-up. Very often my branch met in the living room of my house because nobody would rent us a room, worried that a bomb might be planted in it.

The 1980–1 hunger strike period was ghastly. Once again I believe we were in a situation which could have tipped over into civil war in some areas. The Catholic community was deeply affected by the deaths of the ten young men in Long Kesh prison. County Armagh was particularly volatile and community relations, or rather non-relations, plummeted to a new low. There was a real danger that the hunger strikes, and particularly Bobby Sands' election to the House of Commons, were beginning to create a powerful political movement towards Sinn Féin in the same way that Bloody Sunday in 1972 had effectively created the powerful paramilitary force that was the IRA. Voters were turning towards Sinn Féin in the way that recruits flooded towards the IRA back then. Successive Irish governments were in despair at the intransigent way in which Margaret Thatcher and her government handled the issue. In the South, the election of two abstentionist anti-H Block candidates to the Dáil contributed to the worst Fianna Fáil performance for twenty years and cost Charles Haughey the June 1981 election.

The IRA's murder campaign continued unabated: it is sometimes forgotten that sixty-nine other people were killed during the seven months of the 1981 hunger strike, thirty-seven of them by the IRA. Some killings were particularly shocking: for example, the shooting dead of Joanne Mathers, a young farmer's wife and part-time census-form collector in Derry. The British army was killing children like eleven-year-old Carol Ann Kelly and fourteen-year-old Julie Livingstone with plastic bullets. Loyalists were taking innocent Catholics off the Belfast streets and beating them to death. The rumour mill in the Catholic community went into overdrive after ugly events like the British army firing plastic bullets at mourners during hunger striker Joe McDonnell's funeral. Families of hunger strikers were verbally abused by policemen and soldiers while they were bringing the bodies of their sons to be buried.

In this area we had hunger striker Raymond McCreesh's death and funeral in Camlough. The IRA and Sinn Féin milked it to the hilt. There were people out kneeling in the street and saying the rosary; there were black flags everywhere, and uniformed men marching to slow drumbeats. I remember driving up from Dublin and there was no motorway then, so I had to drive through Dundalk. There was this big march of men and women through the town, all in black, all extremely tense and threatening.

In unionist areas, by contrast, the reaction was one of utter incomprehension, indifference, disgust and even triumphalism, with people saying things like 'slap it into them, we're winning now'. Most unionists agreed with the DUP's Peter Robinson who said, 'society properly deals with them [the hunger strikers] like the low and common criminals they are'. Then after the IRA assassinated the hard-line unionist MP Rev. Robert Bradford in November 1981, the first time they had targeted an MP, there was the appearance of Ian Paisley's Third Force, an attempt to raise a new loyalist militia, which imported guns from South Africa. Many of those guns were stored at and distributed from the property of a unionist farmer not far from my home. The North was polarized as never before.

We had to fight the local elections in May 1981 in the middle of the hunger strike. It was a pitched battle. Our canvassers were frequently assaulted. Character assassination was another weapon used by those who claimed to be freedom fighters. *An Phoblacht*, which was full of venom and lies about the SDLP, and about me personally, was sold at the chapel gates. One article stated I was living with the wife of a policeman. A later article said we were living in a villa in Italy that I had bought with my pension from Seanad Éireann – which I had attended for nine months!

In the following year we also had to fight an election for a new Northern assembly set up by then Secretary of State James Prior. There would be no power-sharing nor Irish dimension in this new body. After a robust meeting in Dungannon, the SDLP decided to contest the election to maintain its credibility as a democratic party, but not to take our seats. I remember John Hume eloquently making the case for us to take the high moral ground in this way. My good friend, the notably lean Frank Feely from Newry, who like me was a long-time unemployed politician, said this was fine, but added: 'I'm beginning to feel like Gandhi when it comes to taking the high moral ground, and very soon I'll look like him if I don't get a paid job from somewhere.' It was a very difficult to get up the energy to organize and canvass in such a meaningless election, barely a year after the hunger strike and Sinn Féin's successful entry into the electoral arena.

One of the worst things about this time was that I didn't want to turn on the radio because I knew I was going to hear more bad news; I even found myself thinking 'Thank God that shooting is in County Tyrone and not here.' Maybe there was an element of stubbornness too. My friend and SDLP colleague Joe Hendron used to say it was like the way I played football – stay on the field until the last man dropped. I just kept going, hopeful that the human spirit of ordinary good people would triumph.

During the ten years between the end of the Northern Ireland Constitutional Convention in 1976 and being elected to the House of Commons in 1986, our family largely lived from Gertrude's earnings. I got occasional fees for writing articles or doing lectures. We just cut back, we existed. A doctor told me at one point during that period that I had a bronchial illness and was not fit to work: I needed to stop running about and take three or four weeks off. I was called to a health tribunal in Armagh that adjudicated on my ability to work. One tribunal member said: 'I saw you on the television so you shouldn't be claiming.' For the next short period I received four pounds something in sickness benefit per week.

It was a humiliating time. We couldn't afford to go on holiday. I went back to work for a few years as an English teacher at St Catherine's College girls' secondary school in Armagh. I enjoyed being back teaching and in a strange and dark Northern Irish way it was even inspirational. I had one small class, and every one of those girls had somebody belonging to them killed. That made me put things into perspective: if I thought I was hard done by, I only had to look at those young women. I got them to talk about it and remarkably they hadn't much talked about it, in their families or anywhere else. It was heart-rending to hear them. Their stories made me even more determined to keep going in politics.

Politically in that period I was probably doing more constituency work than ever. There was a price to pay for being active in the SDLP in south Armagh in those days. One of my closest friends and strongest supporters in the area was John Fee, son of a local doctor (and nephew of Cardinal Tomás Ó Fiaich), a Crossmaglen SDLP councillor on Newry and Mourne Council. He came to work for me as my parliamentary assistant when I was elected to the House of Commons. This multitalented poet and traditional musician had a great way with words, writing quickly and accurately and producing speeches and statements that reminded me of the old poets of south Armagh.

John and his friend from the same area, Ann McGeeney, like him an outstanding worker for peace and reconciliation (and who was also to die young), epitomized the peaceful struggle of some people in that area against the awfulness of the Provisional IRA: not just physical violence but also intimidation, blackmail and character assassination. John lit up my office with the quality of his work and conversation and friendship, his integrity and courage. In 1994 he was badly beaten up by an IRA gang who broke into his house and attacked him with clubs and baseball bats after he had spoken out once again against that organization's violence. He never completely recovered from that terrible beating. They then spread foul rumours and lies about him to justify their attack. He got better but he was never the same again. He was to die in 2007 of a brain tumour at the tragically young age of forty-three.

We were cursed with a series of appalling secretaries of state in those years. After the craven Merlyn Rees came Roy Mason, who made no secret of his intention to pursue a security solution to Northern Ireland's problems, whatever the consequences for stability and consensus. He quickly ruled out a return to a power-sharing Executive, and even more forcefully, an Irish dimension. He announced that 'Ulster has had enough of initiatives, White Papers and legislation for the time being and now needs to be governed firmly and fairly.' Needless to say, any attempts he made to get political talks going were doomed to failure.

Mason was succeeded by the equally ineffective Humphrey Atkins. As a pipe smoker, I noticed that he carried with him at all times a small bolt-curved pipe, but I never saw him fill it or light it. Was it perhaps a stage prop to give him confidence? He quickly lost the confidence of the SDLP when he called on us to stop using Dublin and Washington to influence British government policy on the North. He also made it clear that an Irish dimension would be a non-runner.

Atkins was in charge during the 1980–1 republican hunger strikes, although the really deep, dark crisis was caused by Prime Minister Margaret Thatcher's intractable stance on the hunger strikers' demands. The harsh reality was that ten men died because of the clothes they wore in prison and who they were allowed to associate with, demands largely met shortly after their deaths. The hunger strike led to a huge sense of hurt and alienation, and even despair, within the nationalist community. Support for the IRA rose alarmingly. So too did the sense that this tragic course of events was manipulated by senior Sinn Féin figures to leverage maximum political support from the men's deaths. The Iron Lady's iron stance brought the Northern Catholic community face to face with a question it had been asking for sixty years, and Irish nationalists in general had been asking for several hundred: can Britain ever be the agent for justice and peace in Ireland?

Our job in the SDLP was to keep alive the hope that the day might come when the practice of democratic politics might bring that justice and peace to Northern Ireland. Our party's public profile had been badly affected by the resignations of two of its most important founding fathers, Paddy Devlin and Gerry Fitt (even though the latter's resignation in November 1979 led to John Hume's election as leader with me as his deputy leader). Although I didn't always see eye to eye with Paddy, his close connections with the international social democratic and trade union movements were invaluable for the development of our left-of-centre policy platform.

Gerry was a lovable man, a former merchant seaman hooked on Labour politics from an early age. He learned the rules of politics fast and how to break them even faster. His stories about Belfast elections could capture any audience. For example, he told of the Stormont election in his Dock ward in north Belfast in which three nuns came in to vote; they voted, left the polling station, but instead of returning to the convent, they went to a certain house, changed into civilian clothing and went back separately, one by one, to vote again. From his election as Republican Labour MP for West Belfast in 1966 Fitt was a voice in the wilderness at Westminster because of the strictly observed convention in the House of Commons that Northern Ireland's sordid affairs could not be debated there. Nevertheless Gerry used his contacts with politicians and journalists to great effect to highlight the discrimination and injustice the Catholic community had been suffering for decades, thankless work for which he did not receive the proper recognition. He worked closely with the group of Labour MPs – notably Kevin McNamara and Paul Rose – who had formed the Campaign for Democracy in Ulster to press for the reform of discriminatory election laws, to set up a Royal Commission to investigate the workings of the Stormont government, and to amend the Race Relations Act to outlaw religious discrimination.

After his house in the Antrim Road was burned down by a republican crowd in 1983, he moved his family to London, and in the same year was made a life peer. In the mid-1990s his beloved wife Ann, a warm and generous woman who fretted about Gerry as one would a wayward child, died. A short time later his son-in-law, Vincent Hanna, the prominent BBC journalist, on whom he had come to depend for advice and company, also died at the early age of fifty-seven. One could sense his increasing loneliness. He used to attend twelve o'clock Mass in Westminster Cathedral and then make his way to the Houses of Parliament, and inevitably into the Strangers Bar.

I remember him pushing back his spectacles, as he always did when under pressure, and calling to the barman: 'Two more G and Ts, Ted, and make them large ones, and one for yourself.' With that he threw back his drink, bade me farewell with a 'See you soon Seamus' and shuffled out of the door to the taxi rank, gone from the building he loved most in life and where he now found himself almost a total stranger.

In 1982 I was one of Taoiseach Charles Haughey's nominees to the Seanad. It came out of the blue: he sent his adviser Martin Mansergh to invite me and I accepted. John Robb, the Protestant surgeon from Ballymoney, was appointed at the same time, and John and I became good friends. We decided we would speak on everything; we were not going to be the token Northerners. I remember us discussing how we would approach a Litter Bill; that pushed us to the pin of our collars. I gave a dissertation on how the cross-border Annaghmakerrig Arts Centre should be developed. A motion on extradition was put down – at that time it was a huge issue – and as the debate went on it became obvious that neither John nor I were going to be called. I sent a note up to Tras Honan, the Cathaoirleach of the Seanad, asking to speak. When that had no effect, I said to her that we were going downstairs to hold a press conference to say that we were being stopped from speaking on this vital issue for the North. There was immediate panic. She ran up to Charlie Haughey, and we were suddenly allowed to speak. It was an indication of the attitude to Northerners: keep them in their box if at all possible.

My period in the Seanad only lasted nine months but it meant that I was disqualified from sitting in the Northern Ireland Assembly set up by Secretary of State Jim Prior in the following year (which in the end the SDLP decided to boycott because of its utter powerlessness). The local Ulster Unionist MP Harold McCusker cited a British electoral law requiring me to be prosecuted because I had been a member of a 'foreign parliament' when I was elected to the Prior Assembly. I did my speech from the dock in the Armagh courthouse: 'I have nothing but contempt for this legislation and nothing but contempt for the people who wrote it.' The judge stopped me a couple of times and told me that I was in contempt of court. Finally he said: 'Arrest this man.' A policeman had to come across the courtroom and put his hand on my shoulder. He was a guy I went fishing with. We went down to the cells and he threw his cap off and asked if I wanted tea or coffee. 'Coffee,' I said, 'and have you anything stronger to put in it?' 'We'll find something,' he replied. So we sat there talking until the word came down that my contempt had been purged. I have never understood why no senior member of the SDLP nor Irish government representative attended this court case, even though the legal issues being decided hinged upon North–South political relationships.

I was a constant critic of the Ulster Defence Regiment for its harassment of Catholics, but I also went to a lot of funerals of UDR men killed in County Armagh. There were two kinds of people in the UDR: those who were clearly in it because they liked kicking Catholics around, and others who joined because they saw it as their duty to serve their community. I respected that; they were mostly courteous. How they were not able to root out some of the bad guys around them, I don't know. The son of my near neighbours in Markethill was one of the 'UDR

Four', who killed young Adrian Carroll, brother of an INLA man shot dead by the RUC, as he walked home from his work as a painter for the council in Armagh, a killing claimed by the UVF. There were four UDR men in the Land Rover at the time. I'm quite sure that young fellow didn't shoot anybody. He may have been sitting in that Land Rover without a clue about what was going on. He went to jail and eventually got out on appeal. But it ruined his life; he's dead now.

My attitude to the RUC was ambivalent. Having lived all my life in a largely unionist village, I knew a lot of RUC men and some very good ones. Unfortunately there were also rogues, some of them at a high level. The good men talked to me. They were not breaking any rules; they would give me a flavour of things. An excellent relationship with a superintendent in Armagh ended when he left the force early, disillusioned by what he had seen, and went to Africa as a lay missionary.

Some men were joining the RUC in County Armagh as a rite of passage into the UVF and UDA, and it was obvious to me that they had cover for such paramilitary activities at very senior level. For example, the ex-RUC whistle-blower, former Sergeant John Weir (whose testimony must be treated with caution in that he himself was a convicted murderer), described how in the 1970s a named Assistant Chief Constable, while visiting his Special Patrol Group unit in Armagh, 'asked us for our views on how best to combat the rise in IRA activity in south Armagh'. He listened to SPG members expressing

> some extreme solutions to the [IRA] problem, such as that we use commercial lorries with armoured plating, which would enable us to remove illegal IRA roadblocks by shooting everyone dead, or that we should perform road stops wearing civilian clothes and carrying illegal weapons, pretending to be either UVF or IRA units, thereby learning the true allegiance of those we had stopped.

This very senior police officer 'expressed his support for these proposals and other extreme measures, with the result that some of us later implemented them'. Weir said one of his colleagues, who later murdered an innocent Catholic, tried to justify his action by saying that this Assistant Chief Constable, on one of his visits to Armagh SPG, 'had authorized an RUC shoot-to-kill policy'.[4]

I believe Brigadier Frank Kitson's strategy (when he was the British army's Belfast commander in the early 1970s) of setting up 'counter gangs' like the Military Reaction Force – effectively anti-IRA killing squads – was also adopted by the

---

4. John Weir sworn affidavit (1 March 1999) https://wikispooks.com/wiki/Document:John_Weir
   _Affidavit .

army and the RUC in Armagh. For example, the way in which the Glenanne gang was operating – apparently with specific intelligence from the Special Branch and British military intelligence – could not have happened without approval from on high. When people in the Catholic community knew that there were policemen involved in such killings, they would ask: how can we support a police force that is murdering people?

That's what made it so difficult. I know there was a policeman involved in the murder of the Reavey brothers. I know it was policemen who shot up the Rock Bar; and Donnelly's pub in Silverbridge. and the Step Inn in Keady. All those attacks happened in my area. And the same guns were used in the killing of my friend Denis Mullen in Moy in County Tyrone, so it was more widespread than just Armagh.

The case I really want to get to the bottom of was the murder of Sergeant Joe Campbell in the quiet seaside resort of Cushendall on the Antrim coast. He was a Catholic, originally based in Crossmaglen, and very well liked in both Crossmaglen and Cushendall: a good community policeman, the type of man you could trust. I believe it was a notorious loyalist murderer from south Down, Robin Jackson, who killed him. I also believe he must have been assisted in this by members of the RUC: somebody within the force was telling Jackson that Campbell was soft on the IRA. I still meet Joe Campbell's son and daughter because I have some lines of inquiry into his case.

Then in the early 1980s there was the series of RUC shoot-to-kill operations. I remember, in particular, the killing of Seamus Grew and Roddy Carroll, admittedly INLA terrorists but unarmed at the time, who were shot dead by the RUC in Armagh in December 1982. I had heard that there was a shooting incident, so I went into the police station and talked to the superintendent. He emphatically told me there was no incident, and there were no policemen on the Killylea Road where it was supposed to have happened. He rang me the next morning to apologize. He had not known that there was a police unit, the RUC's Headquarters Mobile Support Unit, in Armagh and that they had shot two men. He had not even been told about this operation; I know he was a very disillusioned man after that.

The chain of command in the shoot-to-kill strategy, I believe, went right to the top, which is why I called for Chief Constable Sir John Hermon's resignation after the Attorney General, Sir Patrick Mayhew, announced in 1988 that there would be no further RUC prosecutions, following the acquittal of four RUC men in connection with the shootings. It would be impossible to imagine that such an operation would have been carried out without the authority of the Chief Constable. Disciplinary proceedings were taken against twenty more junior RUC men, but the Police Authority decided by a majority of one that Hermon, his deputy, Michael McAtamney, and the head of the Special Branch, Trevor Forbes, should not face further investigation. Hermon later admitted that charges were considered against senior officers who had lied to protect intelligence sources during that period.

The late Deputy Chief Constable of Greater Manchester, John Stalker, was appointed to investigate those incidents because he was a very senior police officer of great experience and integrity. He was appointed because the police service he was investigating, the RUC, did not have integrity in relation to these events. The way he was hounded out of Northern Ireland and serious unproven allegations were made against him pointed to a high-level conspiracy to get rid of him because of what he might uncover. A few months after he was suspended from the inquiry in 1986 he told Noel Dorr, then Irish Ambassador in London, that that he had been trying to get a direct line to the Home Secretary, Douglas Hurd, to tell him about six murders, but he had been blocked by the RUC Chief Constable among others. He said he had completed five of six reports into the killings but 'very much feared now that what he had written will be rewritten by other hands'. He found that 'the RUC were all right except for some people very near the top who were very much to blame'.[5]

It seemed to us in the SDLP that the government was seeking to defeat terrorism while acting as terrorists. The prime examples were the Glenanne gang near Markethill and the shoot-to-kill policy. Ordinary people, entitled to the protection of the police, were seeing the police bending the law, breaking the law and even on occasions being involved in gangs murdering their neighbours. Was it right for the RUC to shoot to kill suspected terrorists because of what they had allegedly done in the past, even when they were unarmed at the time? It was indefensible morally, and in so doing they were breaking the law they were supposed to uphold.

---

5. 'Police chief John Stalker who probed RUC shootings was concerned about "six murders", files show', *Belfast Telegraph,* 30 December 2016.

5. A Loyalist Murder Gang near Markethill

Collusion between the security forces and murderous loyalist paramilitary groups – and the involvement by RUC and UDR men in attacks on ordinary Catholics – was one of the worst human rights abuses by the British government in the North of Ireland during the Troubles period. The Police Service of Northern Ireland's Historical Enquiries Team (HET) did immense work in highlighting these abuses in all their grim detail. There has been surprisingly little public outrage at these activities, which served to utterly undermine the rule of law in this society. If the HET's detailed revelations that members of the RUC and the UDR were routinely consorting with loyalist paramilitaries, and planning and executing terrorist shootings and bombings with them, had come out twenty or thirty years earlier, they would have dramatically confirmed the Catholic community in its fear that those forces were untrustworthy and compromised.

The most notorious of these loyalist groups was the Glenanne gang of paramilitaries, RUC and UDR men, based three miles down the road from my home in Markethill. For a time in the 1970s this band of sectarian murderers were allowed to kill and bomb seemingly at will throughout counties Armagh, Tyrone and across the border as far as Dublin. They were based on the farm of an RUC reservist called James Mitchell outside the village of Glenanne, and may have been responsible for up to 120 deaths, including those in the May 1974 Dublin and Monaghan bombings and the July 1975 Miami Showband attack. The detectives on the HET said that Mitchell's farm was the centre of allegations, which are 'the subject of continuing research … that loyalist paramilitaries used it as a base for planning and launching terrorist attacks, and that members of the security forces – both police and military – colluded with and actively engaged in these activities'.[1]

In November 2017 Mr Justice Treacy in the High Court in Belfast said he would make an order compelling the PSNI Chief Constable to complete an investigation into the Glenanne gang's killing spree. It is believed that a draft Historical Enquiries Team report into allegations of security force collusion with the gang was 80 per cent complete when the HET was wound up in 2014. The PSNI is appealing this ruling: counsel for the Chief Constable argued that it was an unnecessary step to force the police to finalize a report he claimed had yielded no new investigative opportunities.

The judge also said 'the very sad inescapable fact is that while these debates rage on at huge public expense, the victims' families languish with no end in sight and the ever increasing realization that nothing much may happen in their lifetime'. The case was taken by the brother of a thirteen-year-old boy who was killed in a 1976 bombing in Dungannon linked to the Glenanne gang.[2]

A 2003 report ordered by the then Taoiseach, Bertie Ahern, and carried out by a retired Supreme Court Judge, Henry Barron, concluded that James Mitchell's farm probably played a significant part in the preparation of the UVF bombings of Dublin and Monaghan in May 1974, in which thirty-three people and a full-term unborn child were killed. The ex-RUC whistle-blower, John Weir, said the bombs had been assembled at the farmhouse. Mr Justice Barron said it was neither 'fanciful nor absurd' to believe that members of the Northern Ireland security forces could have been involved, and it was likely that individual members of the RUC and the UDR had participated, or were at least aware of the attack at the planning stage. Judge Barron said that within a short time the RUC had good intelligence to suggest who was responsible and 'a number of those suspected were reliably said to have what his report called "relationships" with British intelligence and/or RUC Special Branch officers'.[3]

---

1. A. Cadwallader, *Lethal Allies: British Collusion in Ireland* (Cork 2013), 319.

2. https://www.belfasttelegraph.co.uk/news/northern-ireland/glenanne-gang-witnesses-and-victims
   -relatives-are-dying-without-closure-on-suspected-state-collusion-high-court-hears-36297954.html

3. Cadwallader, 226.

This was some kind of gruesome nadir in the activities of those security forces. It convinced many nationalists that the British government had abandoned all standards of justice and integrity in their running of the North. The HET said it was difficult to believe

> when judged in concert with other cases emerging around that time, that such widespread evidence of collusion was not a significant concern at the highest levels of the security forces or government. It may indeed be that there were fears that to confirm suspicions of collusion and involvement of RUC and security forces personnel in these terrorist crimes would have fatally undermined the credibility of the organization, and possibly compromised overall political stability ... it may have been viewed as seriously as that.[4]

Apart from terrorizing the whole Catholic community in this area, can you imagine the impact these kinds of murderous activities by the forces of law had on the good policemen and women who were risking their lives to uphold that law? At least some must have been conscious that such active collusion in sectarian murders and bombings was corrupting the RUC.

Because of the lenient sentences handed down on those few eventually made accountable for their actions, it was also apparent that the criminal justice system itself, which should have been offering every person in Northern Ireland the full protection of the law, was being compromised. The justice system was allowing itself to be part of the 'security offensive' against communities perceived, often wrongly, to be supporting the IRA, rather than the upholders of the highest standards of jurisprudence. Lord Denning's injunction, 'Be you ever so high, the law is above you', clearly ceased to be applied in many instances in Northern Ireland, and particularly in County Armagh, during this period.

A Protestant friend first told me what was going on in Glenanne. 'They're at it,' were his exact words. 'Who's at it?' I asked. 'The police and the UDR are working with James Mitchell,' he replied. I knew James Mitchell to see, nothing more. The HET's investigations revealed that the same guns were used by the same Glenanne-linked killers in scores of incidents, including the Reavey brothers' murders; the double bombing of pubs in Dundalk and south Armagh in which five people died; the Rock Bar attack; the killing of two young men coming home from a GAA match; the killing of a Protestant woman, Dorothy Trainor, in Portadown; the murder of my SDLP friend Denis Mullen, and a married

---

4. HET report on Michael McGrath, shot and badly wounded outside the Rock Bar, Granemore, 5 June 1976.

couple, Peter and Jenny McKearney in Moy; of dairy manager Fred McLoughlin in Charlemont and of three members of the Miami Showband near Banbridge.[5] It was extensive; it was not just a few bad eggs in the RUC and UDR who went out to kill Catholics and nationalists because that was their way of hitting back at the IRA. I believe it was an organized thing: an undercover operation in this area bringing together members of the army, the UDR and the RUC with loyalist terrorists that was sanctioned at a high level.

An early indication of this collusion in terrorism was the random murder of two young Catholics, Seán Farmer and Colm McCartney in August 1975 on the road between Newtownhamilton and Armagh. An RUC superintendent in Armagh rang me at around three in the morning to tell me about the incident and that there had been a UDR patrol from Glenanne in the vicinity. According to the HET, what had happened was that Farmer and McCartney, who were coming back from an All-Ireland football semi-final in Croke Park, were taken out of their car at a fake UDR checkpoint and brutally shot dead. A short time earlier an RUC patrol car with three policemen had come upon the same checkpoint, become suspicious, and informed both the army in Newtownhamilton and the Garda Síochána across the border about its presence. A group of GAA supporters returning from the same match in Dublin arrived a short time after the killings and raised the alarm.

Over thirty years later the HET was scathing about the RUC's investigation into this double killing of two men it concluded were innocent victims, singled out as Catholics and caught in a 'murderous ambush':

> Members of the Nationalist community and relatives of the victims in cases such as these are convinced that investigations were not rigorously conducted in a deliberate effort to conceal security forces' involvement and perpetuate a campaign of terror by loyalist paramilitaries against Catholic citizens. The HET is unable to rebut or allay these suspicions.
>
> The HET review has uncovered disturbing omissions and the lack of any structured investigative strategy. Junior officers seem to have been left unsupported and uninformed; indisputable evidence of security forces' involvement with loyalist paramilitaries in one case, followed by significant evidence of further cooperation just weeks later, should have rung alarm bells all the way to the top of government; nothing was done; the murderous cycle continued.[6]

---

5. Cadwallader, 301 (ballistics links table); HET Review Summary Report into deaths of Reavey brothers, 26–7.

6. HET report, Seán Farmer and Colm McCartney.

The following December five people were killed and many injured in a double Red Hand Commando gun and bomb attack on a pub in Dundalk and at Donnelly's Bar at Silverbridge in south Armagh. The HET found that the RUC's investigation into the Donnelly's Bar attack was full of flaws, with the man heading it, one of the relatively few Catholic detectives in the force, receiving little support from his colleagues. The main suspect, a well-known Portadown loyalist, was named on Special Branch databases as having been involved, but the lead detective was never told this and the suspect was never questioned.[7] Not until three years later, as part of the investigation of police involvement in the 1977 murder of a County Antrim shopkeeper, did an Armagh-based RUC constable admit that he had been there on the night of the attack, had driven the attackers to Donnelly's Bar and picked them up after the attack. In the end charges of withholding information were dropped against this officer because of insufficient corroborating evidence that those he had driven there had actually carried out the killings, or that he had known where it was to take place.

Robert McConnell, a UDR corporal from Tullyvallen, four miles from Markethill, later killed by the IRA, was one of the most active loyalist terrorists. He was one of the men driven by the RUC constable to Donnelly's Bar. He was named in a 1993 Yorkshire TV *First Tuesday* investigative programme – 'Hidden Hand: the Forgotten Massacre' – as having been involved in the UVF Dublin and Monaghan bombings. In a *Sunday Independent* article the programme's chief researcher wrote that McConnell had also been involved in the murder of the Reavey brothers. He was also believed to have acted as a go-between for British military intelligence and the UVF.[8]

After the double attack on Dundalk and Silverbridge, the new British army commander, Lt General Sir David House, ordered a call-up of the UDR in south Armagh. I was outraged. In a statement I said I regarded this as

> utter and dangerous madness in view of the cloud hanging over the force as a result of at least circumstantial evidence of their connection with loyalist para-military activists. Until it has been proved conclusively that this force has not been infiltrated by loyalist murder gangs, it should not even be contemplated using them in a full-time capacity in south Armagh or any other area. It is the

7. Cadwallader, 137.

8. D. McKittrick, S. Kelters, B. Feeney and C. Thornton, *Lost Lives: the stories of the men, women and children who died as a result of the Northern Ireland troubles* (Edinburgh 1999), 562.

surest way of swinging support back to the Provisional IRA … because local
people will look at the UDR presence as blatant harassment and intimidation
carried out to placate extreme loyalist politicians.

In June 1976 there was a bomb attack at the Rock Bar at Granemore, three
miles outside Keady, which was owned by a friend of mine, Joe McGleenan, an
SDLP councillor on Armagh District Council for a number of years. The loyalist
terror tactic in those days was to fire shots outside to keep people inside the pub
while the bomb was being placed. On this occasion the three masked attackers
shot and seriously wounded a man who had just left the bar and shot through
the windows, but only the bomb's detonator exploded. The HET concluded that
all three attackers were RUC men. John Weir claims they were members of the
RUC's Special Patrol Group in Armagh.[9]

In 1980 Laurence McClure, an RUC man who lived close to James Mitchell's
farm in Glenanne, received a suspended two-year sentence for his role in planting
the bomb at the Rock Bar; a charge of attempted murder was dropped. A second
Armagh-based RUC man who was present, William McCaughey, was later
convicted – along with John Weir – of the murder of a Catholic shopkeeper,
William Strathearn, in Ahoghill in County Antrim (although Weir says the actual
killing was carried out by UVF man Robin Jackson). This was called the 'Good
Samaritan' killing because Strathearn answered the door in the middle of the
night to a man who told him that a sick child needed aspirin.

McClure and McCaughey were among the four RUC men convicted for
offences at the Rock Bar by the Lord Chief Justice of Northern Ireland, Lord
Lowry, who imposed extremely lenient, two-year suspended sentences on all of
them. His judgement included the notorious lines:

> All of the accused have admitted their offences and all of them have acted either
> wrongly or emotionally under the same powerful motives: in one case the mortal
> danger to their service and in the other the feeling that more than ordinary
> police work was needed and was justified to rid the land of the pestilence which
> has been in existence … It can be said of each of the accused that he has done
> the State some service. Ordinary people can only imagine what is being done for
> them by the police in these days and at what cost to themselves.

I often thought how I would feel if the murderers of my father or son or brother
were described by an eminent judge as having done the state some service. Is

---

9. Cadwallader, 187.

it any wonder that nationalist confidence in the police and judiciary was all but destroyed?

Two months after the Rock Bar attack, the Step Inn Bar in Keady was bombed on a lovely summer evening in August 1976. The HET believes this large bomb was assembled at a garage near James Mitchell's farm.[10] The whistle-blower John Weir said the original target was in Clontibret across the border in Monaghan, but when they ran into unexpected garda activity, the bombers changed the target to the predominantly Catholic town of Keady. Betty McDonald, the young wife of the bar owner, was serving customers at the time. The car bomb blew a huge hole in the side of the Step Inn, and Betty's dead body lay mangled in the wreckage of her family's home with her four-year-old son crying 'Mammy' over it. Gerard McGleenan was killed by shards from the bomb as he left his house opposite to go for an evening pint.

Once again the HET found that the RUC investigation was full of holes. Four days after the bombing intelligence was received that four UVF men (their names and addresses were supplied) had stolen the car used in the attack on Belfast's Shankill Road. Nobody was arrested or questioned. The following day another piece of intelligence was received by Special Branch, naming the four men who had driven the bomb to Keady. One of these men was interviewed but released without charge. There is no police record that the other three were ever arrested or interviewed about the Step Inn bombing. Judge Barron's 2003 report said three of the suspects were 'reliably said to have had relationships with British intelligence and/or RUC Special Branch'.[11] I have been told that when the gang returned to James Mitchell's farm after the abortive run to Clontibret, they considered bombing my house before finally deciding on the Step Inn.

The Glenanne farmhouse was finally raided by the RUC in December 1978, where the police found homemade sub-machine guns, ammunition and Cordtex bomb fuse wire. Seven of the nine police officers subsequently arrested were convicted of various offences. Incredibly, James Mitchell, the former RUC reservist, was given a one-year suspended sentence, despite the size of the arms haul on his farm and the clear evidence, according to the HET, that the farm had been used to relay the bomb used in the Step Inn attack.

In her book about collusion, *Lethal Allies,* Anne Cadwallader claims that among the attacks known to have been planned and carried out from Mitchell's

---

10. Cadwallader, 198 and footnote.

11. *Ibid*, 203, footnote.

farm were the Dublin and Monaghan bombings (thirty-four dead), Donnelly's Bar in south Armagh (three dead), the Reavey family (three dead), the Step Inn (two dead), the Seán Farmer and Colm McCartney murders and the Miami Showband killings (three dead).[12] Judge Henry Barron concluded that the statements of the whistle-blower John Weir about widespread police collusion were corroborated in four attacks in which eleven people had died: Donnelly's Bar, the Reavey and O'Dowd families and Seán Farmer and Colm McCartney.[13]

Northern Ireland's most homicidal UVF killer, Robin Jackson, the former UDR man from south Down believed to have been personally responsible for more than fifty murders, and who was the leader of the attack on the Miami Showband in 1975, was one of the top men in the Glenanne operation. Jackson seems to have been untouchable, perhaps because he was protected by the RUC Special Branch. Anne Cadwallader says that Jackson was arrested, questioned and caught with guns in his possession eight times over a twenty-year period, but was either never charged or had charges against him dropped.

How did I counsel and support the people in my constituency living in isolated farmhouses and bungalows, terrified that there was a gang of loyalist paramilitaries, RUC and UDR men on a farm in the vicinity plotting to kill them? I did this by just being there, prepared to speak out on their behalf and against the rogue security force members who were terrorizing them. I was out and about a lot, attending funerals almost as the people's representative, because they might not want to go themselves out of fear – and particularly to a funeral of somebody from the unionist community who had been murdered by somebody from the nationalist community.

The Reverend William McCrea of the DUP once declared that I was the OC of the south Armagh Provisional IRA. On another occasion he called me 'the man who has contributed more to the murder of innocent members of the security forces than practically any other person in the SDLP community ... by his words [he] is stained with the blood of innocent people'.[14] In one sense, of course, this was music hall stuff, dismissed by most sensible unionists. It was also dangerous in that other more extreme elements could, and did, see it as a justification for attacks on me and my home.

In particular, the constant threat from paramilitaries based in the loyalist stronghold of Portadown, only fifteen minutes' drive from Markethill, prompted

12. *Ibid*, 338–9.

13. *Ibid*, 316–17.

14. Northern Ireland Assembly, vol. 14, p.113–14, 4 March 1985. Similar views were expressed by Rev. Ian Paisley on a number of occasions.

people from the Protestant community to advise me to go away for a while. They would say: 'You have a wife and child – for their sakes you should go.' On two occasions tip-offs from Protestant neighbours may have saved my life. I stayed at home for a couple of days after those warnings: it was a safer place than being out on the roads.

After McCrea's first verbal assault on me, a mural appeared on a wall beside a children's playground in Markethill showing a poor fellow hanging from a gallows with the slogan 'Hang Mallon and Fuck the Pope.' I could never figure out why Pope John Paul had to answer for my sins, the most significant of which, perhaps, was my very existence as a nationalist public representative in a 90 per cent unionist village. Thankfully many good Protestant people let it be known that the street artist did not speak for them, and that they were disgusted and offended. I knew that disgust to be the authentic voice of Protestantism in my home village.

Most distressingly, my seven-year-old daughter Orla was playing with a friend in that playground and saw the mural. She came home in floods of tears, and I had to reassure her with the less-than-comforting words: 'Listen love, I'm in very good company.'

I believe the Protestant community were just as aware of the abuses within the RUC and UDR as we were. Could they have done anything about them? To use the old phrase: not in time of war. But they were as mortified as we were. People have often asked me why members of the Protestant community did not speak up about what they knew about the activities of loyalist paramilitaries and police and UDR working with them. The answer is twofold: firstly was the fear of repercussions in their own community; secondly, their revulsion at the constant killing of policemen and UDR men by the IRA. I remember going to the funeral of a policeman in Markethill and listening to a local Presbyterian minister, William Bingham, grandson of the Bingham family who were my next-door neighbours as a child, speak in a voice full of anguish that laid bare the sheer heartbreak of ordinary unionists about the killing of their loved ones in the security forces.

The Catholic community was equally fearful of loyalist killers in the area and appalled at the killing by the IRA of local Protestants, people they knew well. They were just as fearful about speaking up and informing the police about what they knew. That is what happens in civil wars: people's sense of right and wrong becomes dulled by terror and atrocities.

At this difficult time the threats came on a regular basis. I could get away from it for a brief period. After I was elected to the House of Commons in 1986 I could go to Westminster; I was safe there even if I was not safe coming or going. Gertrude and Orla stayed in Markethill, and so they were not safe. Orla remembers having a recurrent nightmare that the whole family were shot dead out on the main Armagh road. Gertrude was by nature a worrier, but never suggested leaving, perhaps because she knew my stubborn nature. I wasn't going to abandon people who needed me, people who were themselves in a dangerous situation. I had been the principal of the local school; I had known these people growing up, I knew the elderly people. I was not going to leave them with bullets flying around them.

I remember one attack in 1986, shortly after I had been elected to Westminster. I was on my way to a meeting of the Young SDLP at a hotel on the outskirts of Newry with Orla, then seventeen, and three schoolfriends in the car. As we approached the hotel there was a loyalist protest led by a DUP councillor from Kilkeel with around forty people, mainly young men, at the gate. They surrounded the car, shouting ugly and appalling things at us, and then, without warning, a concrete block smashed the back windscreen, followed by bricks, and the crowd tried to tip the car over. It was extremely frightening, particularly for the girls; I don't know how we escaped without serious injury. Like a fool I first tried to remonstrate. Then I wound the window back up and just drove through them.

Across Northern Ireland, and in particular in the picturesque border counties, small back roads, grass verges outside villages, panoramic viewing spots, river banks and sand dunes have all been violated by becoming places of torture and murder and the dumping of bodies; sometimes naked, sometimes in bags, but always maimed and desecrated. Those beautiful lonely places where foul things have happened are forever disturbed by a spirit of darkness that is always present, which never entirely vanishes.

Seamus Heaney was haunted by the murder of his cousin Colum McCartney at a fake road block on a south Armagh road. This is a road out of the lonely Fews Forest, between Armagh and Newtownhamilton, which I often take. In his poem 'The Strand at Lough Beg', Heaney imagines that he can accord his cousin's corpse the reverence denied him on that bleak roadside in the dead of night. He recalls in particular his cousin's gentleness, for he was a man for whom violence was abhorrent. He addresses Colum's ghost behind him on the strand at Lough Beg:

> I turn because the sweeping of your feet
> Has stopped behind me, to find you on your knees
> With blood and roadside muck in your hair and eyes,
> Then kneel in front of you in brimming grass

And gather up cold handfuls of the dew
To wash you, cousin. I dab you clean with moss
Fine as the drizzle out of a low cloud.
I lift you under the arms and lay you flat.
With rushes that shoot green again, I plait
Green scapulars to wear over your shroud.

Heaney suggests that nature can cleanse and restore the innocence of the body desecrated in a roadside killing. The strand at Lough Beg on the Antrim–Derry border is contrasted with the spot in south Armagh violated by murder.

As I walk or drive on my weekly rounds I am haunted by the places that have been violated; too many places violated in my parish, my county, my country, violated by murder and massacre, places I used to know and love as I passed by them on my boyhood bicycle.

6. *The New Ireland Forum and the Anglo-Irish Agreement*

Charles Haughey was a very able politician. As a minister, he did good work on many things and I liked him as a person. I thought that when it came to dealing with the British he would be a stronger and more incisive negotiator than Garret FitzGerald. I mainly knew him on a 'hello – how are you?' basis. We occasionally sat down and talked about things we had in common such as his ancestors from Swatragh in south Derry where I had an uncle who had been the local parish priest.

I thought his insistence on a unitary state as the central recommendation of the 1984 New Ireland Forum Report was an absolutely legitimate position to take. For somebody like him, the leader of Fianna Fáil, it would have been very odd if the Forum report had not made reference to a unitary Irish state.

I simply did not agree with Haughey's opposition to the Anglo-Irish Agreement and said so. He may have thought it copper-fastened partition, but you could have said that about Sunningdale, the Good Friday Agreement, any agreement short of unity. Apparently he was very taken aback by my strong support for the 1985 Agreement. In a message to London the British ambassador in Dublin, Alan Goodison, said my support had dealt 'a severe blow to the credibility of Fianna Fáil's opposition' and the *Irish Press* said that I had done 'the best sales job' for the Agreement of any constitutional nationalist politician. When he came back into power in 1987, Haughey was pragmatic and rowed back from his initial opposition to that Agreement, but he did not forgive me for my earlier support for it: after that there was no more contact between us.

Garret FitzGerald and I did not always see eye to eye on some of the fundamental issues and that became obvious during the New Ireland Forum, and particularly in its conclusions. I accept that he had come into power in 1982, along with Dick Spring and Peter Barry, with an absolute determination to do something about the disastrous situation in the North, which they believed was threatening the security of the Irish state itself. They set up the Forum with three aims: to redefine the meaning of Irish nationalism, hoping that this would make it more palatable to unionists; to address the discrimination and alienation felt by Northern nationalists; and to improve the British–Irish relationship, which had fallen to new lows after the republican hunger strike and the Haughey government's seeking an end to hostilities and EU sanctions against Argentina during the Falklands War.

One issue I could not agree on with FitzGerald was how that forum of nationalist parties could come to conclusions that did not include Irish unity. I thought that the nationalist people of Ireland would be sceptical if we did not have a united Ireland as one of our objectives. It would also have left one group of people both speaking and killing for Irish unity, the Provisional IRA. That would have been intolerable for the constitutional nationalist parties. As I told the 1985 SDLP conference: 'We can't, we won't, we must not put our united Ireland aspiration on the back burner. We cannot make liars of ourselves. We cannot leave it in suspended animation for any length of time, or, like in County Armagh, the men in balaclavas will come along and say "We are the only people pursuing this course."'

There were times when some people in the SDLP seemed to be in danger of losing our core belief in unity. That was a sore point for me. There was a form of 'Humespeak' that hinted at things without actually saying them. In contrast I was completely clear in my belief that Irish unity was the only long-term solution to the Northern conflict. The accusation against me at the time was that by sticking by this core principle of my own party I was acting as a straw man for Fianna Fáil; that was the view of some commentators and other political anoraks. For me, though, it was something different: I was concerned that at a time when Northern nationalists were taking a battering, the confidence of people on the ground in the SDLP would slip away unless we took a strong line on unity. It is not only in Ireland that when downtrodden people are taking a beating, there is a tendency to move towards the hardest line – and the hardest line for nationalists in the North of Ireland was the Provisional IRA.

It transpired that FitzGerald saw the Forum as a stepping stone into the negotiations with the British government that eventually led to the November 1985 Anglo-Irish Agreement, and that he saw the Forum Report as a kind of *aide memoire* from nationalist Ireland that he could use in those negotiations. The central demand of the Irish government in those talks was for it to be involved in the government of the North. I had no problem with that. I did have a problem with saying that as the collective nationalist parties in Ireland – Fianna Fáil, Fine Gael, the Irish Labour Party and the SDLP – we were going to negotiate with the British but we were going to leave out Irish unity as an option.

Nationalist 'alienation' was the buzzword at the time, meaning a total lack of confidence by the Northern nationalist community in the rule of law and justice and security, in the state forces who were debasing that justice and security, and in the ability of democratic politics to obtain that justice and security. The senior Irish government official Michael Lillis, one of the main architects of the 1985 Anglo-Irish Agreement, described the situation accurately: 'Trust on the part of the nationalist community in the British security forces, including the RUC and the UDR as well as the local judicial system, had completely broken down … a profound and imaginative transformation was urgently needed to address the spreading pathology of alienation.'

Nationalists in Armagh believed that the British government of that time – which at the very least was turning a blind eye to, and probably actively colluding with murders carried out by RUC and UDR men – was behaving like a terrorist organization. There was a kind of nihilism that creeps in when people despair of the political process. Looking back on that period now, it was very close sometimes to a Bosnian-style civil war in this area, and I know Dublin officials were concerned that it could spread across the border. The campaigning local priest Father Raymond Murray said in 1983 that the policing of an alienated Catholic population by the nearly 100 per cent Protestant RUC and UDR had given Armagh 'a terrible and emotional civil war tinge'.

The other problem between FitzGerald and myself arose from the bugging of the home of my good friend Micheal (whom I called 'Mackie' from our footballing days) and Marjorie Moyna in Kilbarrack in north Dublin during the New Ireland Forum's proceedings. I used to stay with them when I was a member of the Seanad and was there during my visits to the Forum. Both were cornerstones of our SDLP organization in Dublin.

Mackie rang me one evening at home in Armagh to tell me that he had discovered a bugging device in his house. The first thing I said was, 'don't touch anything' but he had already pulled it out. I got in the car and drove straight to Dublin.

Who was the target of it? Was it them or me? Was it a nephew reported to be in the IRA? I discounted that because Mackie disliked what he was doing so much there was no rapport between them and he was rarely in the house. We had to do something so we went to the media. I was particularly angry because it pointed the finger at Mackie, Marjorie and myself in a most unfair and defamatory way. An innocent, law-abiding family had their home violated, and I said as much. I contacted the government, and Garret FitzGerald in particular, but all I got back was stuff like 'Well, you know the nephew is involved.' I responded: 'But Mackie and Marjorie absolutely are not.'

FitzGerald, speaking in the Dáil, lumped together the Moyna bugging with representations I had made, as one does as a public representative, about another Moyna nephew who failed to get a job in the Irish public service after he'd been convicted of taking part in a riot outside the British Embassy in Dublin during the hunger strikes: guilt by association. I thought that beneath him: it was not the action of 'Garret the Good'. I told him so in the Forum the next day in no uncertain terms. After that I was excluded from any discussions preceding the Anglo-Irish Agreement until a late stage. John Hume told me nothing and the little I knew came from Peter Barry because we had been working on policing and UDR issues together. I always got on well with Barry. He was the Southern politician who first used the phrase 'the nightmare of the Northern nationalists'. If people said we were both old-fashioned Irish nationalists, I would take that as a compliment.

One senior Irish official told me later that the Moyna affair had nearly brought down the Irish government. Another said FitzGerald felt he had behaved badly towards me and was close to resigning over it. The government feared it might undermine my support – and that of the 'green' wing of the SDLP they believed I headed – for the upcoming New Ireland Forum Report, and for the negotiations that were to lead to the Anglo-Irish Agreement, going on in parallel with the Forum. Apparently they even worried that I might boycott the Forum in protest. I believed there could be only two sources of the bug on Mackie Moyna's house: the Garda Síochána or the British. Whoever it was destroyed my trust in the FitzGerald government at that highly charged time: it made me wonder why the hell the Irish government needed to eavesdrop on my conversations. In the end Garret FitzGerald and I buried the hatchet when he came to the party to celebrate my election to the House of Commons.

During those Anglo-Irish Agreement discussions, I was unhappy about the sectarian killings, particularly in the Armagh area, which were rife at that time. I was not confident I could get sufficient protection for the nationalist people living there. When you are excluded you think the worst. I knew any agreement would be recognizing the North of Ireland as *de facto* part of the United Kingdom. I knew the Irish government involvement would be less than at Sunningdale. As it turned out, the redeeming feature of the Anglo-Irish Agreement was the establishing of the Joint Secretariat at Maryfield outside Belfast through which the type of representations I had been making informally to Dublin on behalf of my constituents could be made in a more effective and sustained manner.

Friends in the Department of Foreign Affairs later told me that the Irish government was nervous almost up to the last moment that I would not support the Anglo-Irish Agreement. They knew I could not support any agreement that did not seriously deal with injustices against the nationalist community, and particularly the abuses by the UDR and RUC. When finally shown the draft agreement in the early autumn of 1985 I was won over by the new right of the Irish government to 'consultation and more than consultation' – in the phrase later used by the two governments in press briefings – in areas like policing and justice. Apparently there was a big sigh of relief when I indicated my approval with the rather Delphic phrase: 'A camel is a horse made by a committee. This is not a camel.'

The Anglo-Irish Agreement proved to be a real milestone and the beginning of new hope for nationalists. For the first time the British government was not overruled by the unionist veto. Mechanisms for dealing with the deep alienation of the nationalist community from the institutions of law and the state in Northern Ireland were to become more effective over the next decade and a half: there was a growing recognition of the need for a radical revamp of policing and the courts; for tougher fair employment legislation; and for North–South cooperation across a range of areas in recognition of the Irish dimension.

When nationalists saw what could and was being done through new Irish government involvement in the North, there was an easing of some of the tensions and a turning back to the SDLP. Symbolism was important here. In the words of a 1990 Department of Foreign Affairs memo:

> The sense among nationalists is that the Agreement and the [Maryfield] secretariat are the symbols of their reunion with the wider nationalist family on the island and of the recognition – for the first time – of their identity within Northern Ireland. As such, they have brought a very significant boost to morale and confidence within the nationalist community.

From the right to make representations through the Maryfield secretariat on policing abuses came the seed that eventually led to the Patten Report on the RUC and the total overhaul of policing in Northern Ireland. Also the extent of the sectarian murders in Northern Ireland, and particularly the collusion in those murders by members of the RUC and UDR, began to register in Dublin and London. Being the SDLP's spokesman on policing was a poisoned chalice in many ways, but I knew that any society that does not have a police service acceptable to the community is doomed. I worked hard to get people's complaints to the secretariat. And for the first time during the Troubles I saw actions being taken on the British side that I put down to the new role of the Irish government at their spartan base on the outskirts of east Belfast.

Maryfield was slow to get going and for the first few months I doubted whether it would deliver anything significant. The Northern Ireland Office under Sir Robert Andrew was bitterly opposed to it, and it was almost as if the NIO had gone out of their way to give the Irish officials posted to Maryfield as unpleasant a place as possible to live and work in; they had to do both in a bare, forbidding 1960s office block with no curtains in the windows and massive security all around it. As one Irish official said: 'We negotiated the Anglo-Irish Agreement with the most brilliant officials at the top of the British system, Cabinet Secretary Robert Armstrong and his deputy David Goodall. But its implementation was in the hands of the utterly obstructive Northern Ireland Office.'

In the early months of 1986 Maryfield was under constant siege from angry loyalists, with a crowd of 18,000 people protesting outside on one day of heavy rain in January. The two understandably anxious senior Irish officials inside were told by the RUC officer in charge: 'See that rain? It's worth a battalion of soldiers.' Those two officials were Michael Lillis and Dáithí Ó Ceallaigh, and I must pay tribute to their courage, determination and thoroughness in making sure that Maryfield worked and worked so well in exceptionally difficult circumstances. I also worked hard to submit detailed complaints from my constituents to the Irish side of the secretariat. In January 1986 I gained the added credibility of doing so as an elected member of the House of Commons. On the 23rd of that month I took the Newry and Armagh seat from the Ulster Unionists in the by-elections caused by the resignation of all the unionist MPs in protest at the Anglo-Irish Agreement.

At first the Northern Ireland Office was unresponsive to issues raised by the Irish side. Then the Irish officials proposed a joint log to record topics or incidents and to track responses on a regular basis. It was only when confronted by this log and its threatening implication that, unless the NIO responded, they were risking being in breach of an international treaty, that they began to move. It helped that the Irish side, thanks to the Department of Foreign Affairs (DFA) 'travellers', officials who regularly visited key political, legal and religious figures throughout the North, were frequently better informed than the British side. There were only two DFA 'travellers' in the early 1980s; this was increased to five or six after the Anglo-Irish Agreement. It was also valuable that security chiefs such as RUC Chief Constable Sir John Hermon and the British army commander in Northern Ireland were visitors to Maryfield, where they sometimes stayed late into the night sampling the fine whiskey and good conversation supplied by the diplomats from Dublin.

After this, I started to notice a change in the way my complaints about Catholics and nationalists being mistreated and harassed by the security forces began to be dealt with. The Northern Ireland Office officials at the Maryfield secretariat started reporting back that a soldier had been spoken to or carpeted or fined. Then after around eighteen months came the first example of a soldier being dismissed. The Irish officials used to say to their British counterparts: 'We have reports from Mallon country and what the British army is saying about this incident is simply not true.' Here is another example of how the system worked: in the spring of 1986 my SDLP colleague Bríd Rodgers was trapped in a Catholic estate in Portadown under attack from loyalists. She phoned the Department of Foreign Affairs in Dublin; the DFA phoned the Irish secretariat at Maryfield; they phoned the RUC and the police moved in to remove the attackers.

The Irish side of Maryfield was very active. Dáithí Ó Ceallaigh says around forty issues were formally raised with the British side in the first seven weeks of Maryfield's existence, including several cases of UDR harassment. Michael Lillis listed sixteen areas where there was progress during the first fifteen months of the joint secretariat: repeal of the Flags and Emblems Act; strengthening of the law on incitement to hatred; improved rules for fair employment; vastly improved representation of Catholics on public bodies; the demolition and replacement of three notorious 'ghetto' flat complexes, Divis and Unity in Belfast and Rossville in Derry; better rules for the routing of controversial, mainly Orange, parades; the establishment of a Police Complaints Commission; fuller reporting and investigation of sensitive incidents involving the security forces; improvement in *habeas corpus* rules and procedures; a new code of conduct for the RUC; substantial improvements in prisons policy and on issues such as prisoners' compassionate parole; shifting of the onus of proof to the prosecution in bail applications; tighter rules on admissibility of evidence; measures to reduce delays in bringing trials to court; and some (although not nearly enough) improvement in the rate of RUC accompaniment of the UDR, a measure that I always saw as a poor substitute for the disbandment of that force.[1]

The continued harassment of Catholics by the UDR was an issue I reported regularly to Maryfield. There was an SDLP colleague on Armagh Council, Martin Cunningham, who had a brother involved with the INLA. He was murdered in 1987 by a fellow member of that organization, who buried his body under a disused cowshed. I was with his funeral cortège on the road between Armagh and Keady when it was stopped by the UDR. Their assumption seemed to be that everyone in that cortège was a republican terrorist. I told them what I thought of them. They kept us for nearly an hour and eventually phoned for the RUC. The police arrived and I heard one policeman telling the UDR platoon commander: 'Catch yourselves on.' This was the kind of incident that left a very bad taste.

The UDR had to be disbanded. Its members were seen by the nationalist community simply as an armed and anti-Catholic loyalist militia (one of its commanders once said it was better to have loyalist terrorists inside rather than outside the UDR!). I regularly raised the high level of criminality in its ranks in speeches in the House of Commons. A Department of Foreign Affairs memo in 1989 called it 'a well-trained and well-equipped unionist army, more threatening to nationalists than at any time in its history'. Three years later it was wound up, merged into a new regular unit of the British army called the Royal Irish Regiment.

UDR excesses was one area where it took some years for Irish warnings to sink in. Eddie McGrady's enormous and largely unrecognized work in pushing a greatly improved Fair Employment Act through the House of Commons was a post Anglo-Irish Agreement success story. But pressure from me and the Irish government to replace the one-judge Diplock courts with three-judge courts as they had for Troubles-related trials in the South did not work. On the security side, it was more a question of mitigating the worst excesses of the security forces – whose harassment of people, and particularly the young, did not greatly improve – than in gaining significant reforms. The level of IRA violence was also rising again in the late 1980s. After the Remembrance Day bombing in Enniskillen in November 1987, I raised the issue of the threat posed to the Irish state by the IRA following the seizure of 150 tons of Libyan weaponry from a ship, the *Eksund,* off the French coast and the revelation that five shipments of Libyan arms had been successfully landed in the South.

---

1. 'Emerging from Despair in Anglo-Irish Relations' in *Franco-Irish Connections: Essays, Memoirs and Poems in honour of Pierre Joannon* (Dublin 2009).

One thorny local issue whose resolution gave me particular pleasure was the end of quarrying at the important archaeological site of Navan Fort (*Emain Macha*) outside Armagh. I had been lobbying about this for many years. Cardinal Tomás Ó Fiaich requested action through Maryfield to stop severe damage to the site. Earlier the Northern Ireland Civil Service and Armagh Council had ignored complaints from the public. Four or five months of difficult negotiations were required before the North's Environment Minister, Richard Needham (furnished by Irish officials with poet Thomas Kinsella's translation of the great Homerian epic *Táin Bó Cúailnge*, that centres on *Emain Macha*), personally overruled the civil servants and stopped the quarrying.

It was more though than just being able to make representations. Under the Anglo-Irish Agreement the British government was required to 'make determined efforts to resolve differences' in response to those representations from Dublin. The way in which the Irish government now had a defined role in Northern Ireland was groundbreaking. We had come out of twelve years of nothing: no forum for democratic politics, widespread murder by paramilitary groups on both sides, the system of law tearing itself apart. Now we were able to move away from sectarian confrontation. Before the alienation of Northern Catholics had been almost total. Neither the political nor legal process operated as it should have to protect them. As the political vacuum in the North deepened, our focus on the need for a role for the Irish government got stronger.

As long ago as 1969 the Irish government had been sending up officials – the so-called 'travellers' – to talk to people in order to assess the situation in the North. However, this did not become systematic until after the Anglo-Irish Agreement. Many passed through my door, and some, like Dáithí Ó Ceallaigh and Tim O'Connor, became good friends. They were particularly interested in nationalists' complaints of security force harassment. After Maryfield was set up, a system was developed whereby reports of such incidents were circulated to selected Cabinet members and senior officials in Dublin.

I believe these served to change Irish government policy significantly. More people in the North, like the campaigning priests Denis Faul and Raymond Murray, and nationalist lawyers like Paddy McCrory, who previously had doubts about the Irish government's sincerity, began to believe that Dublin was serious about trying to address their problems. Increasingly, Northern nationalists began to trust the Irish government.

The Agreement also led to law-abiding nationalists starting to look with a new eye at the judiciary. Up to then they could not understand how Chief Justice

Lord Lowry could deliver a judgment as when passing extremely lenient sentences on those police officers involved in the bomb attack on the Rock Bar and praising them for having 'done the State some service'. They could not understand how Lord Justice Gibson (later murdered by the IRA) could have acquitted police officers involved in the shoot-to-kill operation involving unarmed IRA men at Craigavon with praise for their 'courage and determination for bringing the three dead men to justice, in this case to the final court of justice'.

As the RUC's 'supergrass' system of evidence-giving informers was discredited in the courts, Catholics began to believe that the judges were starting to realize such abuses damaged the whole process of law. I was surprised I was able to get an Early Day Motion on supergrass trials in the House of Commons, which was allocated fifteen minutes speaking time for me and fifteen minutes for the relevant minister to respond. The Anglo-Irish Agreement may not have been the sole reason for the change, but it was a harbinger of a changing judicial climate. Peter Barry's active personal interest in such issues meant the Department of Foreign Affairs also took an interest and that was helpful to me as the SDLP spokesman on policing and justice.

However, the Anglo-Irish Agreement's success in beginning to tackle injustices against nationalists was not properly publicized. The Agreement was an extremely carefully worded document and the ordinary nationalist seeing it reported on TV might not have appreciated its importance. The volcanic unionist opposition to it frightened the Irish government into largely keeping quiet about its many successes. It should have supported constitutional nationalism by sending out its best people to shout the Agreement's achievements from the rooftops.

7. *An Irish Nationalist in the House of Commons*

The January 1986 by-election that saw my election to the House of Commons as the second SDLP MP after John Hume was a great day for the party. It had been a superb campaign. My tireless election manager, Mary McKeown, had organized a huge canvass in sometimes foul weather of every area of the Newry and Armagh constituency, with as many as fifty to sixty people calling at doors at any one time. Senior party colleagues like Mark Durkan, Bríd Rodgers and Joe Hendron were prominently involved. There was huge jubilation when we won, with a victory motorcade of nearly a hundred cars touring the area and a great hooley with people hanging out of the rafters in The Welcome Inn in Forkhill, owned by Art O'Neill and his wife Maura, formerly of New York.

I came into the House of Commons at a good time for an Irish nationalist from the Parnellite parliamentary tradition. Two months earlier the Commons had voted on the Anglo-Irish Agreement by 473 in favour to a mere 47 against, the largest majority of Margaret Thatcher's premiership. This surely must have demonstrated to the Ulster Unionists that, after sixty-five years as the Northern Ireland wing of the Conservative Party, they now had virtually no parliamentary allies, including among their erstwhile friends on the Tory benches.

On the other hand I seemed to have supporters everywhere. The Speakers of the House were very good to me. In my early years Bernard 'Jack' Weatherill, a Conservative who represented the London suburb of Croydon, saw it as part of his role to protect the minority parties. If John Hume or I asked a question, he would ensure that the relevant minister answered it. Another Speaker, Betty Boothroyd of Labour, became a good friend.

Others were Kevin McNamara, Labour's spokesman on Northern Ireland, Clive Soley, and my two proposers, Clare Short, whose father was from Crossmaglen, and Alf Dubs. Alf, who when he arrived in the UK as a *kindertransport* child taken out of Nazi-occupied Czechoslovakia had spent some time with a family in Cookstown, is a gentle and idealistic man. Michael Foot was always helpful as was Enoch Powell, even though our politics were radically opposed. I had never met Powell before. In my maiden speech I quoted lines from Wilfred Owen's First World War poem *Dulce et Decorum Est*. I could hear Powell muttering and banging the bench behind me. So when I finished and sat down, I turned to him and asked 'What's wrong with you?' 'If you must quote from Owen's poetry, quote it properly,' he grumbled. I expressed my confidence that I had quoted it correctly, and suggested we go to the Commons' superb library to check. When we had confirmed that I had quoted Owen right, he started to talk about his friends who had lost their lives in the Second World War, questioning why they had died. I asked him: 'Was the war you and your friends fought in an acceptable war?' He growled: 'There's no such thing as an acceptable war.' After that he was occasionally helpful with advice at the committee stage of emergency security legislation in Northern Ireland.

I remember the day he lost his seat in the 1987 general election to my SDLP colleague Eddie McGrady in South Down. My count in Banbridge was finished and I had won. The news was that Eddie was doing well up the road in Dromore. They wouldn't let the SDLP people with me into the count centre there so I stayed outside with them. A raucous cheer went up inside and we knew Eddie had won. Then the door opened and out came Powell with his wife and stood on the steps, blinking in the evening sun and putting on his homburg hat. And there was not a unionist in sight. I went over to him and wished him well and walked him down to his car. Our group of nationalists from south Armagh applauded him as he passed. I recalled his famous comment that 'all political lives end in failure'. He was a brilliant man out of his time; a man who could have been prime minister had it not been for his infamous 'river of blood' speech against immigration.

I had a good relationship with Ken Maginnis. We would occasionally go out in London together for something to eat. We were both first-time MPs from rural, border areas of Northern Ireland. I enjoyed his bluster; I always thought he was at his best when he got angry in a one-to-one argument. My relationship with Ken went back years before we both got into politics. Back in the 1950s a cousin of mine had bought a bar in Warrenpoint and wanted to get it open in time for the big holiday on 15 August. He asked me if I would go down to work for him for a while as a barman. His other part-time barman turned out to be Ken. On that opening day the place was packed; I was behind the bar and he was on the floor. There were three fellows, members of the same family, who were misbehaving, knocking over drinks and barging into people. Ken put them out and then went for his lunch. I was standing at the door when the three men came back looking for Ken. When they couldn't find him, they turned on me. I fought back as well as I could, but I was no match for those guys and they gave me a kicking. So when Ken came back, I said: 'You owe me one.' He frequently referred to that in later years.

Although in my maiden Commons speech I paid a warm tribute to my Ulster Unionist predecessor, Jim Nicholson, as MP for Newry and Armagh, I did not have any kind of relationship with him. I wonder if he ever regretted saying once that in his opinion, 'There is not a coat of paint between Seamus Mallon and the Provisional IRA.'

I called on the unionists to 'come and build with us', emphasizing that my aim was to create Irish unity by peaceful and democratic means, and in such a way that it would not cost one drop of blood. I quoted the philosopher Spinoza describing peace as 'not an absence of war, but a virtue, a state of mind, a disposition of benevolence, confidence and justice'. Only through benevolence would unionists and nationalists in the North of Ireland begin to understand the other person's point of view and end the utter obscenity of violence, paramilitary, military or institutional.

In that speech I was appealing to the unionists to help build the conditions for peace. You cannot impose peace and unity, the best you can do is create the conditions in which they will grow. What does unity mean? Is it a 32-county unitary republic? Is it a federal or confederal arrangement? Does it mean complete British withdrawal? Should other options be on the table? I do not see the options being confined to a 32-county context. I don't think in my lifetime or for a considerable number of years after is there is going to be a 32-county unitary state.

Seamus Heaney touched on the importance of courageous benevolence in everyday life in his Nobel prize acceptance speech when telling the story of the one Catholic workman among the ten Protestants about to be shot down at Kingsmill, who felt the Protestant worker beside him take his hand and squeeze it in a signal that said no, don't move, we'll not betray you, nobody need know what faith or party you belong to. As Heaney said: 'The birth of the future we desire is surely in the contraction which that terrified Catholic felt on the roadside when another hand gripped his hand, not in the gunfire that followed, so absolute and desolate.'

If we live on a diet of division, it is hard to be benevolent. If you live in a society that is divided and unjust, you have to get as much as you can – you're not giving, you're taking. How can we create the circumstances where a new generation of young people don't once again divide a whole society into friends and enemies? What creates the circumstances in which people can cherish their own culture without feeling antagonistic towards or threatened by a neighbour's culture?

There is a cultural imbalance in Northern Ireland. Going back into history, the Protestant and unionist community, as the people who were settled here, never identified with the culture and folklore of the region, but kept themselves separate because they had been given a different role and had a different culture.

What is that Ulster–British culture? I find when I go for a drink in the local pub in Markethill, I will often get into an argument with unionist neighbours, and I will find that by and large they are not aware of their own culture; they don't want to talk about it; they want to get away from it; they want to change the subject. They don't even want to talk about why the Presbyterians had to go to America in the time of Charles the First because of religious persecution by the English state and the Anglican Church. They are almost in denial about it, and about the role they played in kicking the British out in the American War of Independence. That is something they should be proud of: an extraordinarily large proportion of US presidents – eighteen by one calculation – have come from the Scots–Irish tradition.

I remember being in Richmond, Virginia, many years ago and a lovely young woman was showing me around the local museum of the American Civil War. I asked her why there were no artefacts from the Union side, only from the Confederates. 'Sir,' she said, 'this is not a museum, it is a shrine.' It was she who gave me directions to a Civil War cemetery about fifteen miles outside Richmond, where every single grave had a headstone with the name of someone from townlands in this part of County Armagh. They were all people of Protestant stock. That intrigued me. I have often wondered what took them to that American battlefield.

The unionists are a martial people; back to the early 1600s when they first arrived here as colonists, they have made their political decisions by force or threat of force. More recently, events from the mobilization of the original Ulster

Volunteer Force in 1912–14, through the outbreak of the Troubles in 1968–9 to the murderous activities of the modern UVF and Ulster Defence Association (UDA) show that if threatened with Irish unity by coercion they will resist by force. That tradition is still there, and is exemplified by their passion for marching. They have shown their willingness to push this society to the edge of civil war – as they did at Drumcree in the 1990s – by demanding their right to march along what they declare as their traditional routes, even if they are now through areas which have become overwhelmingly Catholic.

That defensive culture has always been there. Now, with the DUP in charge, they often appear more defensive than ever. Everywhere they see the rise and rise of Irish culture: the Irish language; Irish poetry and drama and literature; Irish traditional music; Irish people being successful and lauded everywhere; Ireland at the centre of new technology; Ireland as a country loved and admired internationally, and strongly supported by its EU partners. What do they have to offer in return: the Orange Order, marching bands, loyalty to the English monarch, evangelical Protestantism? It's not a very attractive offer in this cosmopolitan, multicultural, globalized world.

Another problem is that self-examination does not come easily to unionists. As the *Irish Times* columnist Una Mullally put it recently: 'Self-examination is not a pastime of those who navigate society easily. It's obvious to see why. If everything bends to your will, then why would you ever need to question the structures that allow you to "be" so smoothly?' If one is black, or gay, or a woman, or a Traveller, or working class, or a Catholic in Northern Ireland, in order to navigate a world where the cards are stacked against you, 'a degree of unpacking one's identity or place in society is required. If one views one's identity as default, self-examination and reflection don't necessarily occur.' She put her argument in the context of a large group of British voters – reflected in the 2016 vote for Brexit – who continue to believe in British identity as superior and exceptional, and in the idea of colonial dominance long after the empire has fallen. Unfortunately there are many of these people in the ranks of Northern Ireland unionism.[2]

In that first Commons speech I also said the unionist community suffered from a lack of confidence and appealed for a unionist leader who would not threaten, and would not continuously say 'no', but would try to lead that community to peace and reconciliation with their nationalist neighbours. David Trimble

---

2. 'Brexit chaos rooted in British lack of self-examination', *The Irish Times*, 19 November 2018.

had a tremendous opportunity to do that. I believe he would have succeeded if he had gone out and sold the Good Friday Agreement by saying 'Here is where I want to go and here is where we can go together to make Northern Ireland, as part of the United Kingdom, a more fair and equal place.' I believe he would have got a positive reaction in most parts of the North.

In Britain, and that includes at Westminster, we are all, nationalist and unionist, seen as Paddies. As they walk into 10 Downing Street to have a private audience with Theresa May, the DUP currently see themselves as important people because, in this passing moment of Brexit crisis, they hold the balance of power in the House of Commons. The reality is that Northern Ireland will always remain a very low priority in British politics. The DUP clutch at any straw, which might prevent them having to reassess their relationship with a Britain that has little interest in or sympathy for them.

For example, politicians like Arlene Foster and Nigel Dodds are adamant that there must be no post-Brexit arrangement that allows the slightest differentiation between Britain and Northern Ireland, even though the Good Friday and St Andrews agreements have already differentiated the North in significant ways from the rest of the UK. Rather than adopting this hard-line version, it would have been far more sensible for the DUP to have attempted to soften the impact of Brexit in recognition of the fact that most people in Northern Ireland and Scotland voted against it; it has real potential to break up the United Kingdom to which they are so attached, and would leave the weak Northern economy, with its low productivity and poor export performance, extremely exposed. It must be humiliating for people who avow their loyalty to Britain and its crown at every opportunity to see the way they are dismissed by all but the hardest of Brexit hardliners.

Some might believe that my twin belief in the absolute need to move towards unity and at the same time to reach out to unionists is a contradiction. But it is not for two reasons. Firstly, if I have the right to hold my view that eventual unity is the best solution, then I also have the duty to work towards it. The only way I can in conscience do that is by genuine consent, and the only way I can get that consent is through an engagement with the unionist people. Secondly, as a humanitarian, I would want to enter that engagement in a spirit of generosity and compassion towards those people who are my friends and neighbours.

I have always tried to ignore the insulting and sometimes dangerous remarks about me by some unionist politicians, although they can be very hurtful. I suppose I grew another layer of skin when I became a politician. Where it did hurt very deeply was being insulted within my own community. On several occasions I called at the houses of Protestants who had been murdered and was told unceremoniously to leave. That burned into me for days afterwards. And because of the rules I had laid down for myself, I had to go to their funerals the next day. I felt very lonely at those funerals; the worst part was standing on my own waiting to go into the church, trying to avoid the looks of pure hatred from some of my fellow mourners. It does not happen very often now that I greet somebody in a shop or a pub or on the street in Markethill and that person looks straight through me, as some did in the past. I would like to think that does not happen so much these days because they have got to know me better and even to trust me more.

At funerals there were nearly always people who would come up and stand with me and talk to me and let it be seen they were doing that; at Protestant and security force funerals as well. On the other hand I remember going to the funeral of Fergal Caraher, from a well-known IRA family in Cullyhanna, who was shot by Royal Marines in an incident the local community regarded as an example of 'shoot to kill', in that he could have been arrested before the soldiers opened fire. The graveside oration, a republican tradition, was given by the Sinn Féin politician James McAllister, who launched into a verbal attack on me across the open grave, calling me a UDA lover and a Brit lover, among many other terms of vilification. It was a lonely station, to say the least, being harangued in a cemetery, in the middle of a crowd of IRA supporters, where I had come to say my prayers for the dead. I could have walked away but did not. I stood my ground – cold, shocked and alone, but I was sure I was doing the right thing.

For all my long standing demands for the UDR to be abolished and the RUC to be radically reformed, I have never had any local Protestant saying to me: 'You were wrong about that.' I've occasionally had an ex-RUC man thanking me for what I did, although he had probably got out on a huge pension! I have lived in largely Protestant Markethill for many years now and I don't have any feeling of not being part of the community there, the whole community – I do feel very much part of it, in all its divided and binary nature.

During the Troubles I received death threats from both sides. On at least three occasions during the late 1980s I was faced with banners and signs on the roads (and in one case a wall painting) in south Armagh featuring a picture of a man kneeling with a bag over his head and a masked man levelling a weapon at his head, with the slogan 'Seamus Mallon is an informer.' The first time was after the IRA shot dead three policemen sitting in their car in Newry in 1986, when I said I hoped that the 'evil, squalid and vicious men whose perverted ideology inspires them to kill Irishmen in the name of Irish unity' would be brought to justice. The second was during the 1987 general election. My SDLP canvassers managed to take a few of the signs down, but it wasn't an easy and pleasant thing to canvass such areas. The irony was that I when I went into an RUC station it was often to make representations on behalf of republicans who had been arrested or ill-treated.

I remember a canvass in Jonesboro at the end of which a Newry supporter, Sean Gallogly, and I were heading back to our car. Two young men – yobs is what I would call them – followed us, hurling abuse. Sean asked them 'Is something bothering you?' One of them then went to hit him, but Sean felled him with one punch. The other fellow took to his heels. The most difficult thing about that kind of canvassing was the stones and other missiles that were thrown by people hiding behind walls and fences. Eggs were a particular favourite: it's remarkable how painful a hard-boiled egg can be if its pointed end hits you in an exposed place, and how much damage an unboiled egg can do to a suit.

We had enough strong men in our canvassing team who, if our attackers came out of the shadows, would have taken care of them. Somebody like John Fee, who became my parliamentary assistant, typified this determination and courage by my SDLP supporters. Being able to look after yourself in a fight was something of a pre-condition of canvassing for Seamus Mallon. Then, of course, Newry and Armagh was also unique among parliamentary constituencies in that there was a British army fortress for every 1100 inhabitants. It was all a very long way from Finchley!

It is fair to say that any time we went in to canvass a housing estate in Newry or south Armagh that was known for its republicanism, we were in danger of being attacked in this way. In addition the tyres of our supporters' cars were regularly slashed and their sides scraped and dented. They did not attack women, but there were other ways of intimidating them. One of my most faithful canvassers, Mary McNulty, remembers sitting alone in a caravan in Camlough, making a tally of voters as they went into the polling station, and being watched with fixed and menacing stares by twenty men standing beside the Sinn Féin caravan on the other side of the road. At other times women canvassers were closely monitored by men who drove slowly past them as they went from door to door. These were not things that my fellow members of the House of Commons had to suffer at election time. Sylvia Hermon and Ken Maginnis were a rare couple of unionists who came over to me and sympathized because of the difficult things I was experiencing.

I received voluminous hate mail. My long-suffering secretary Nuala Feehan has a collection of these ugly letters from both sides. One extreme unionist took 'great exception to Papist Republican Bastards like yourself being paid out of British taxpayers money when at heart all you are working for is a united Ireland. I should watch your step very carefully because a quick death isn't far away!' An extreme republican from New York found it 'difficult to understand the thinking or mentality of those like you, and that pig John Hume, who will sell out all that is right and just; who will join, in fact become a very part of that which is so evil and oppressive to the Irish. I suppose you should be pitied since you will spend a very long time in hell for what you are doing.' Another extreme unionist got straight to the point: 'I say replace [the UDR] with a lot that don't talk much but get on with the work, which is KILL, KILL. Their name is the Black and Tans, and I hope you are their first target.' Occasionally letters were laced with unconscious humour, such as the man from Downpatrick who wanted to talk to me about bringing about a united Ireland by hypnosis, or the 'constituent' who was of the opinion that a recent attack on my house was caused by my attitude to 'Early Renaissance Art'.

It was touch and go a few times with the loyalists. When Bernadette McAliskey was shot in 1981 by the Ulster Freedom Fighters (a cover name for the UDA), the RUC had intelligence that the same crowd were out to get me. So the police were camped out on the road outside my house for several weeks. The house was the target of arson attacks twice in 1989 when I and the family were away. There were constant threats. For example, typed notes used to come in the post warning me not to canvass in a particular unionist town or village or 'we'll get you'. We usually went and canvassed it anyway and found that people on the doorsteps were more than friendly. There was insidious pressure on people, particularly at election time and around the twelfth of July. One neighbour, a good Protestant man with whom I was friendly all my life, recently asked another friend, a Catholic, to help him put up a union flag on his house. 'If I don't put up the flag, the windows will be burst,' he said.

I liked the House of Commons very much. My first day there, on the steps of the St Stephen's entrance, a lady from the BBC asked, 'Coming from the hills of south Armagh, Mr Mallon, how do you feel to be in the Mother of Parliaments?' I smiled and replied: 'As good as any man here and better than most.' She laughed and the policemen standing there joined in.

That was the way I regarded the place. I was going to treat all of their conventions with respect; there would be no nastiness. I have to say it was a great place to work: marvellous library facilities to prepare for debates; the acoustics in the chamber were magnificent; the confrontational element in its procedures often made for a better debate. The Commons chamber was so much like a stage, built for fine oratory, and I liked the proximity of the journalists and broadcasting studios; I gave a lot of media interviews in those days and some people were kind enough to say that I was often at my best when in front of a microphone. When I went there first the Northern Ireland votes were at 10.30 at night, so in the middle of the day I was able to explore central London on foot.

I spoke on other issues apart from Northern Ireland. In a debate in 1993 I warned about the rise of an English nationalism that was 'introverted, inward-looking and blinkered' in its attitude towards the European Union. I warned many times against the reintroduction of the death penalty; in 1988 I said:

> Nothing is more potent in Irish political life than the martyr's gravestone. Nothing is so tuned to the bugle in the blood, whether it be Protestant blood or Catholic blood, than that feeling of martyrdom for the cause. That is the tremendous driving force which keeps this series of Troubles going four times longer than the last World War. And if someone tells me the death penalty is going to be a deterrent in the face of that motivation – it is not, and it never will be.

I then quoted Winston Churchill: 'The grass will grow green again on the battle-field, but never on the gallows.' I co-sponsored the Liberal MP David Alton's unsuccessful private member's Bill to stop late abortions. I was a member of the Select Committee on Agriculture.

Too often I met condescension in Westminster, which went something like this: 'Terrible situation over there. Can we not do something about it? These impossible people: two tribes beating each other up.' This was in the Mother of Parliaments that had been responsible for Ireland, and then Northern Ireland, for many centuries; who had sent Protestant settlers there to be the rulers and jailers of the Catholic Irish natives, and to seize their land; which in 1920 had put a boundary across Ireland to ensure that the North was permanently unionist. That was all done in Westminster. I used to rail against the lack of knowledge and the hypocrisy of such thinking. They have never accepted that they have a responsibility to this place, having ruled it for so long. For them it has always been just one more deeply troublesome colony, like India or Malaya or Kenya.

There were a few exceptions. Peter Brooke was clearly a Secretary of State who was prepared to think afresh about Northern Ireland and I used to talk to him regularly in Westminster. His statement in 1990 that Britain had 'no selfish strategic or economic interest' in Northern Ireland was a game-changer. Before that speech he had consulted closely with John Hume. I had a long discussion with him in my living room, and I had some idea of what was coming. It was crucially important because it represented a significant change in a fundamental British policy position going back hundreds of years. It started to open a door into what would a few years later become the peace process.

I had more dealings with Sir Patrick Mayhew because of the Brooke–Mayhew inter-party talks in the early 1990s, on which a lot of work was done, but in the end did not get anywhere. He confided in me once that he could not get Hume to talk to him; John treated him with derision, using 'uncouth language'. I thought that a man who was such a good judge of malt whiskey could not be all bad.

My main memory of Mayhew is an amusing one. We were in the latest round of talks in London's Lancaster House in July 1992. I had a friend in England who was a racing trainer, Terry Casey, and he was running a horse at a meeting in southern England on this particular day, a fast finisher whom he fancied. I sent a note to Mayhew about this and all of us – SDLP, unionists, British and Irish officials – put money on him. My colleague Frank Feely was given the collected bets and sent to the nearest bookies. 'Marvellous, Seamus, it won at 8–1,' a delighted Mayhew reported back to me. On that occasion it was the only thing we could all agree on.

8. *The Peace Process and the Good Friday Agreement*

The peace process of the 1990s was a well-deserved triumph for John Hume in particular. As his deputy leader for twenty years I recognized that the Good Friday Agreement was the culmination of more than three decades of work based on his dual principle for a just solution to Northern Ireland's problems, which had earlier been tried and trashed in the brief 1974 power-sharing and Sunningdale experiment. As the senior Irish diplomat Seán Donlon put it: 'The subsequent agreements, whether the Anglo-Irish Agreement of 1985 [or] the Good Friday Agreement of 1998, are all based on the Sunningdale principles, or the John Hume principles: unite the two communities in Northern Ireland; create North–South structures for cooperation.'[1] There is a greatness about John's political life, what he did and what he helped to change. I would rank him among the great leaders of Irish constitutional nationalism, men like Daniel O'Connell and Charles Stewart Parnell.

John and I pursued our agreed political objectives in different spheres. Sometime after the Stormont parliament was prorogued in 1972, John became convinced that the British government would not move towards any real solution of the Northern Ireland problem without pressure from American political and

---

1. M. Fitzpatrick, *John Hume in America: from Derry to DC* (Dublin 2017), 47.

public opinion. He therefore started to visit the US regularly and to make contact with leading politicians like House of Representatives Speaker Tip O'Neill, senators Ted Kennedy and Daniel Moynihan and New York Governor Hugh Carey. His single-minded crusade there would eventually lead to successive presidents, Jimmy Carter, Ronald Reagan and Bill Clinton, playing a critical role in the development of the Northern Ireland peace process.

My main political activity was in a different place, on the battleground that was policing and security. I never saw myself as being in John's shadow. He had chosen a role for himself that he carried out extremely well. I ploughed my furrow and did all I could to change the culture of violence and injustice endemic in our society. I was aware that for a long time I was a politician who did not have a job or an income or any kind of democratic forum. In many ways I did not have a future. At times John and I would have disagreed about some things, often about the tone of things, but we agreed on most of the fundamentals: Irish unity by consent, opposition to violence and commitment to the democratic process.

Much has been said and written about the relationship between John and myself. Some of this is real, some fanciful. What problems there were between us were largely caused by a lack of communication. John was a remarkable genius, extraordinarily talented, egocentric and very resistant to criticism. He much preferred working on his own. For such a gregarious man, John was very much a loner in his political life, reluctant to keep the party informed about matters important in the development of its strategy and policies; notably the early moves in the peace process. Sometimes I felt he disliked the routine business of party politics, and felt encumbered by the need to report his plans and actions to the rest of us in the SDLP leadership and party. This was nothing new, of course. There are politicians everywhere who are by nature independents, but it makes it particularly difficult when they are party leaders.

I decided that for my peace of mind I had to do and say what I thought right, and damn the consequences. Generally John and I got on well; we had great respect for each other. In a lighthearted moment my SDLP colleague Paddy Duffy once declared that Hume had 'become like Jesus Christ – he will be walking on water soon'. Seeing me enjoying the quip, he continued, 'And you Mallon – you've become like John the Baptist, wandering about in the desert and living on locusts and wild honey.' That wasn't a bad description of what I was living on for a long time!

Possibly my tone came across as harsher than John's. Living on the west bank of the Foyle, and as the man who was almost the uncrowned king of nationalist

Derry, it was perhaps difficult for him to understand the battleground I faced in south Armagh, between the IRA and Sinn Féin violently opposed to me on one side and unionists and loyalists violently opposed to me on the other. It was a harsh environment for a democratic politician to work in. A harsh tone was needed to describe the murder of innocent people, whether by the IRA, the UDA or the UVF, or by policemen, soldiers or undercover intelligence services. Repeating the same visionary message over and over – in the way John sometimes did with so-called 'Humespeak' – would not have got me into any position where I could do something about things like anti-Catholic harassment and collusion by the RUC and UDR. I saw myself as someone with firm views, but I hope I always showed in negotiations and in other forums that I was open to other people's views.

It is hard to talk about violence in a soft way. My voice had to be hard when describing the killing of my neighbours. If I had started to whisper that ugly truth, it would not have been heard. I was not looking for any thanks for my strong words. After forty years of having listened to me, I think people got the message that I was a fair-minded man in condemning violence from all sides. I remember at an SDLP valedictory function in Armagh for me a few years ago there were a surprising number of unionists present; that made my night.

My main criticism of the republican movement was their use of murderous violence. I believe the violent republicanism of the Provisional IRA has inflicted more lethal damage on the concept of Irish unity than many decades of unionism ever could. The IRA killed nearly five times more people than the British army, the RUC and the UDR combined. Of the 1771 people they killed, 636 were uninvolved civilians.[2] Throughout the years I consistently challenged the Provisionals' claim to be the champions of the rights of the nationalist people of the North. I said they were denying the right of self-determination to the Irish people, North and South, by their relentless campaign of violence to force unity. I saw this very much as a battle for the soul of the Northern nationalist community. The IRA were destroying the opportunities for even seeking Irish unity because with every bullet they fired and every person they killed they diminished and eventually almost destroyed the prospect of seeking to achieve that unity by agreement and consent.

A large proportion of those who died at the IRA's hands came from their own nationalist community. There were so many murders in my Newry and Armagh

2. D. McKittrick, S. Kelters, B. Feeney and C. Thornton, *Lost Lives: The stories of the men, women and children who died as a result of the Northern Ireland troubles* (Edinburgh 1999), 1473–84.

constituency that I sometimes became weary of issuing my incessant condemnations. A typical statement from me followed the murder in September 1986 of a Catholic from Lurgan, David McVeigh, whose hooded body was left in a ditch near the scenic Flagstaff viewpoint a hundred yards from the border south of Newry. The IRA had accused him of being a former member turned police informer. I said the murder showed

> the hypocrisy of the IRA who had attacked the injustice of the Diplock courts and the supergrass system and yet had terminated this man's life before a kangaroo court on the evidence of gossip. The people of the Newry area will no longer tolerate this kind of brutality, having seen so often the type of Ireland the IRA are trying to create at the end of a gun, built on suspicion and centred on fear.

So I did worry about the Hume–Adams talks only a few years later. I knew the Provos were still pushing their old line of the British setting a date for withdrawal and becoming 'persuaders' for Irish unity, with now an alliance with the Irish government and the SDLP to advance this strategy. I was concerned that democracy in the North – at that time riddled with mistrust and self-doubt after so many failures – was being bypassed, and I was worried what this would do to the SDLP, the Ulster Unionists and the other constitutional parties. I was not the only senior SDLP politician who was worried: Eddie McGrady, for example, was openly opposed to the talks. I believe, looking back, that our concerns were well founded.

I have heard that Gerry Adams is now saying he unsuccessfully approached me before he approached Hume about opening talks. I did have a conversation with Cardinal Tomás Ó Fiaich sometime in the late 1980s in which he asked me if I would talk to Adams and I replied I would think about it. Then two Belfast priests, Father Alec Reid and Father Des Wilson, came to see me at my home about the same subject. I told them this would have to be a matter for Hume as the party leader. Some time after that Gerry Adams wrote seeking a meeting, but I did not see what use it would serve so did not respond.

During the Hume–Adams talks in the early 1990s I seemed to become a particular bugbear for the Provisionals, with people like Martin McGuinness and Gerry Kelly accusing me of trying to undermine those talks. Why did they single me out? Because I was always very concerned that John would be used by them. I remember a testy SDLP meeting around a month before the August 1994 IRA ceasefire at which I expressed serious qualms about the likely trajectory of events. My strong view was that as a political party the SDLP would come out of this arrangement badly. I had made it clear to John that I fully supported him in his efforts to get an end to violence, but that as a political party we had to protect ourselves. The Hume–Adams channel was creating difficulties for the party. There was substantial opinion in the North and in Ireland generally that was uneasy about it. The unease was about the way the whole process was being led by Adams towards their form of peace: along the lines of 'We've tried violence and that didn't work, so now we'll try politics, and we'll use every possible tactic and one of those tactics is to take advantage of Hume's standing in Ireland and internationally.'

In retrospect that is what they did very successfully. In the first instance the person who suffered most was John, who was the target of horrendous media coverage, particularly in the *Sunday Independent,* for talking to Adams. What I was trying to get John to do was to engage with Sinn Féin as the leader of the SDLP, with its membership having a clear knowledge of what was going on, and so protect the party in this new and difficult phase of Northern Ireland's politics.

We had to protect the party because it had been formed in the worst of conditions back in the 1970s as the democratic voice of Northern nationalism, and remained that legitimate voice in the following period of violence. Now it seemed that John's relationship with Adams was being used by the Provisionals as a propaganda weapon that would do the SDLP no good. I believe they were happy to give the impression at times that John was closer to them than to his own party, and that instead of being the key instigator of the peace process, he was letting Adams make the running. As early as January 1995 the Catholic primate Cardinal Cathal Daly privately expressed concern to the Irish government that Gerry Adams appeared to be emerging as the leader of Northern nationalism.

I watched this happening when the two of them were in the United States, with Adams having a throng of media people following him everywhere while John sat in the corner almost unnoticed. I was at two conferences in the US and watched the lionizing of Adams and company, with leading Irish-American politicians like Senator Edward Kennedy meeting Sinn Féin delegations with respect and warmth. The image was created that these were the people who would get things done in the North, who had real influence in high places at home and abroad, who were getting to the people at the top: taoisigh, prime ministers, presidents. They got things done, but it was all for themselves.

I was critical of the Hume–Adams talks in the sense that peace was being bought in such a way that it was bypassing democratic procedures. I believe that before the parties came together to endorse the Good Friday Agreement, Sinn Féin had already obtained 'understandings' on the issues that were important to them: the release of prisoners; an agreement, leading to a letter of comfort, for IRA members who were 'on the run'; a deal to give them all the expenses and perks of membership of the House of Commons while refusing to take their seats there.

I said in several speeches in the early 1990s that I would not concede Irish republicanism to the IRA or Sinn Féin. When we entered into discussions with Sinn Féin, we handed the baton onto them in many ways. Maybe it was the price we had to pay for peace, but unfortunately we also legitimized them. The SDLP, who had struggled for so long to keep the flame of decency and democracy alive, paid a high price for conceding that republican ground to the Provos.

What is now creeping into the narrative is the claim that John Hume knew when he was in discussions with Gerry Adams that the IRA's campaign of violence giving way to Sinn Féin's involvement in democratic politics and government would damage the SDLP. That was not the case. Indeed he thought the opposite: he emphatically believed it would benefit our party. When I expressed a contrary opinion, I recall his exact words. 'I don't give two balls of roasted snow for what you think.'

Above all there was decommissioning. There was something unnervingly wrong about two sovereign governments, instead of dealing with the issue of paramilitary groups' illegal weapons themselves, making those arms part of the bargaining element within an ultra-sensitive political process between parties trying to reach a political settlement that had evaded them for a quarter of a century. This would be regularly derailed by that poisonous issue for many years.

I believe John should have told the Provos: 'I'm trying to help you towards a peaceful way to achieve a united Ireland. But you're holding on to your guns and Semtex – you've absolutely got to get rid of those.' In the end it took the IRA eleven years after their first ceasefire to put their arms completely beyond use, and that led to huge mistrust and misunderstanding, which has beggared the practice of politics ever since. During this period the more extreme DUP took over from the Ulster Unionists as the main unionist party, and the more extreme Sinn Féin replaced the SDLP as the main nationalist party. So the IRA keeping their arms for so long enabled Sinn Féin to move to a central and decisive position in the politics of Northern Ireland. In the end, with the extremists in charge, it led to the collapse of the North's political institutions in January 2017.

By the late 1990s the republican movement was too far down the road to peaceful politics to go back to violence and the two governments should have called their bluff and demanded they give up their arms by a certain date on pain of not being allowed into the new Northern Ireland Executive. The paragraph in the Good Friday Agreement (drawn up between the two governments and Sinn Féin) may have fudged this issue, with its obfuscatory language about Sinn Féin and the loyalist parties using 'any influence they may have to achieve the decommissioning of all paramilitary arms within two years' of the May 1998 referendum. But everybody around that negotiating table understood that there was an obligation on the IRA to decommission its arms as an essential part of the peace process. Except, as it turned out, the IRA themselves, who continuously insisted that decommissioning was not part of that Agreement and dragged it out for many more years.

They may have engaged with General John de Chastelain's Commission on Decommissioning. However, General de Chastelain told us that for a long time all the IRA representatives did when they came in for meetings with him was 'drink tea and eat biscuits'. In the end it was the Americans, amazed at the indulgent attitudes of the British and Irish governments to IRA criminality, who forced Sinn Féin into pressuring the IRA both to begin decommissioning in 2001 and to complete it in 2005. In September 2001 a furious US government special envoy, Richard Haas, accused the IRA of supplying the FARC terrorist group in Colombia with bomb technology and asked whose side they were on after the 9/11 attacks on New York and Washington. Four years later Senator Kennedy memorably said: 'Sinn Féin cannot be a fully functioning democratic party with the albatross of the IRA around its neck. I believe Mr Adams wants to see the IRA disbanded, but there is a time to hold 'em and a time to fold 'em and we are long overdue.'

In 2008 Richard Haas's successor as US special envoy to Northern Ireland, Mitchell Reiss, wrote:

> The peace process devolved into an exercise in serial concessions and indulgences, first to Sinn Féin and later the DUP. Moderate political voices from both traditions were shouted down and marginalised by more polarising figures. The British government never seemed to ask why any of the Northern Ireland political parties would ever agree on closure when they could always expect to extract more concessions at the next meeting or after the next crisis.[3]

I saw the way in which the decommissioning issue – and the cynical way in which the Provisionals dragged it out – destroyed middle unionism, and did enormous damage to the SDLP. My party colleague Sean Farren put it well when he criticized the Irish government for its position that 'the silence of the guns was

---

3. R. Wilson, *The Northern Ireland Experience of Conflict and Agreement: A Model for Export?* (Manchester 2010), 159.

sufficient'. He quoted from the Catholic catechism: 'A sacrament is an outward sign of inward grace.' So decommissioning would have been an outward sign of an inward disposition towards peace on the part of Sinn Féin and the IRA. In my speeches I often emphasized that holding illegal weapons was not just a matter of what unionism required or what the British government required. It was a matter of what the Irish people required; it was a challenge to the sovereignty of the Irish people.

Could it have been done differently? I believe so. Could those three powerful men, President Clinton, Prime Minister Blair and Taoiseach Ahern, not have come together to say to the IRA and Sinn Féin: 'We want you in this process, we'll facilitate you getting in, but only when you've got rid of your arms'? If that did not happen after the Executive was set up in December 1999, it should have happened after the Good Friday Agreement's proposed decommissioning deadline of May 2000. I remember arguing with Tony Blair and Bertie Ahern in February 2000 that in the absence of sanctions against them Sinn Féin were leading everyone 'a merry dance'. The more difficulties there were, the more they were pampered. Blair said both Sinn Féin and the Ulster Unionists were 'completely and bloody unreasonable', but declined to threaten them with sanctions or alternative approaches.

I also have a vivid memory of saying to Tony Blair at a dinner in Hillsborough that the SDLP was the largest nationalist party in Northern Ireland and yet he was doing a lot of talking behind our backs to the smaller nationalist party, Sinn Féin. His answer was breathtaking: 'The trouble with you fellows, Seamus, is that you have no guns.' That was a seminal moment for us. It also sent the message to unionists that if you have guns and the brutal willingness to use them, you can get concessions out of governments.

I know there was some sympathy for my views in government circles in Dublin. But Bertie Ahern, backed by key senior officials like the Secretaries of the Department of Foreign Affairs and Justice, Dermot Gallagher and Tim Dalton, believed that by far the most important thing was to keep the IRA and Sinn Féin on board, and thus constant attention had to be paid to their needs and demands. The sympathetic officials I knew now admit this meant the Irish government took the Ulster Unionists and the SDLP too much for granted, and this contributed to our electoral decline as the governments gave more and more credence to the hard-line parties. But they still feel this was the price they had to pay to keep the fragile peace process going. In the words of one official:

It didn't bother John Hume too much if the SDLP paid an electoral price for the greater goal of a lasting peace in the North. Seamus Mallon, who was closer to the party's day to day needs and interests and had always fought so hard to defend them, was the man who had to make all the compromises, both in negotiation and then in government with the Ulster Unionists. He had to put up with an awful lot of shit, which John never had to. So emotionally I might be with Seamus to a significant extent, but rationally I felt we had to do what we had to do.

There wouldn't have been lasting peace and stability in the North without an inclusive agreement, and if the unionists kept demanding immediate or quick decommissioning there wouldn't have been an inclusive agreement, because the republicans wouldn't have signed up to it. We kept pointing out the error of their ways to the republicans and in the end they did come around to seeing it.

That may be the argument of *realpolitik.* But looking back, it is extraordinary that the two governments did not tell Sinn Féin after they went into the Executive in December 1999 that now they were in government, alongside other democratically elected parties, they could not have an illegal, secret army with all its weapons intact at their back.

The IRA declared their first ceasefire in August 1994 and it lasted just over seventeen months, until February 1996 (when they bombed Canary Wharf in London), with Sinn Féin accusing the British government of bad faith in not allowing them into all-party talks. Sir Patrick Mayhew had announced in Washington the previous March that partial decommissioning by the IRA of its weapons was required before Sinn Féin could be admitted to the talks. Prior decommissioning was not part of the deal as far as they were concerned, and at that point I agreed with them. One problem was a hung parliament at Westminster. John Major's government was being kept in power by the Ulster Unionists (a foretaste of the balance of power held by the DUP during the Brexit crisis). The Unionists were panic-stricken at the prospect of all-party talks that would include Sinn Féin, and with the government's support, were using the prior decommissioning demand to block them. Even Senator George Mitchell's six principles for exclusively peaceful means and total paramilitary disarmament, and his proposal that some decommissioning should happen *during* all-party negotiations, failed to move them.

In October 1994 John Hume asked me to lead the SDLP's delegation at the Forum for Peace and Reconciliation in Dublin, which was an Irish government-established platform for discussion on ways forward for the North, in which Sinn Féin could be included. I found the experience of that forum energizing.

Despite the absence of the two Unionist parties, Alliance, victims' groups and the Protestant Churches put the unionist point of view. It also engaged in some important exercises in new thinking, notably a report called *Paths to a Political Settlement: Realities, Principles and Requirements,* which was in my view an important precursor to what eventually became the Good Friday Agreement.

Eventually, after long months of prevarication and delay, the crucial all-party talks began in Stormont's dreary Castle Buildings on 10 June 1996 with the two prime ministers, John Major and John Bruton, in attendance. Sinn Féin were not: the previous week the IRA had killed detective garda Jerry McCabe in the course of a botched robbery in County Limerick and the following weekend they bombed the centre of Manchester, injuring several hundred people. Senator George Mitchell arrived to chair the talks two days later at the invitation of the two governments. They were conducted on the basis of the three sets of relationships outlined by John Hume many years before as essential to a solution: Strand One dealt with new arrangements for the internal governance of Northern Ireland; Strand Two with the North–South relationship; and Strand Three with relations between both parts of Ireland and Britain.

At that stage I laid more blame at the British government's and Ulster Unionists' doors for the lack of movement towards substantive negotiations than at Sinn Féin's. I said in September 1996 that the government's 'Washington Three' prior decommissioning precondition was a 'paramilitary quartermaster's dream' in that it 'handed those quartermasters a veto over the political engagement of their associates'. I asked: 'Why should unionists destroy the process by insisting on unreal conditions before or at the table, when they could have the support and solidarity of all to make decommissioning a precondition for rising from the table, and thus embark on the best prospect of actually achieving this goal?'

The SDLP's bottom line in those negotiations was always a North–South structure with strong powers to encompass the whole range of socio-economic relationships on the island; a limp and anaemic Strand Two would be totally unacceptable. I said unionist fears that this new body – which eventually emerged as the North South Ministerial Council (NSMC) – could be used to achieve Irish unity by subterfuge were entirely unjustified. The small price the Ulster Unionists would pay for a return to devolution in Northern Ireland and unity only by consent would be an NSMC on which unionists would sit; which would operate by agreement only; which would be accountable to a Northern Ireland Assembly and which would be a key element in bringing the prospect of permanent peace to the North for the first time since 1920. I said that inside the North, progress on practical issues of equality in policing, employment and recognition of the Irish language were also vital.

The talks dragged on with little progress until Labour under Tony Blair swept into power in May 1997 with a huge majority. I was one of Tony Blair's greatest admirers. I was there when he came into the House of Commons. I saw him when he was shadow Home Secretary at the despatch box and he was very, very able. He was completely focused on how he was going to get into power, and did it by concentrating on the middle ground in the British electorate. I then saw him surprise everybody by bringing that extraordinary focus of his to the apparently intractable problems of Northern Ireland. I later lost my respect for him over the Iraq war.

Those talks were a strange business. The loyalist groupings were sitting next to us. One of their representatives was John White, the UDA man who had stabbed my friend SDLP Senator Paddy Wilson and his girlfriend to death in a particularly gruesome manner back in 1973. I felt if this was what I had to put up with to get an inclusive political settlement, so be it. As usual Rev. William McCrea was talking bigoted nonsense. The maverick unionist lawyer Robert McCartney was posturing. I said I was sick of listening to the village idiot and the school bully. In the words of *Irish Times* journalist Dick Grogan, the parties had 'dug themselves into a pit of depression and confrontation which matches the mood of the Northern Ireland community at large'. Nothing was progressing; there was a sense of *déjà vu*, same old faces, same old politics, but it was your job to keep at it. There were a few glimmers of light: we were having sessions with the Ulster Unionists and we sensed that, like us, they wanted something to move.

Then in September Sinn Féin joined the talks – the IRA having declared its second ceasefire two months earlier – and signed up to the Mitchell principles of commitment to 'exclusively peaceful means' and 'the total disarmament of all paramilitary organizations'. At this point the DUP walked out, which was probably the most helpful thing they could have done. During this second round of talks John Hume was not well. So I was leading for the SDLP. The negotiations were once again extremely difficult. We were certainly the centre of international attention. There was a feeling sometimes that the whole world was coming to Northern Ireland: Senator George Mitchell with the glamorous and razor-sharp Martha Pope, Tony Blair with Secretary of State Mo Mowlam, Bertie Ahern, President Bill Clinton, General John de Chastelain from Canada and former Finnish Prime Minister Harri Holkeri (both were working with George Mitchell).

For the first few weeks people were on their best behaviour. There seemed to be senior British and Irish civil servants everywhere, keeping an apparently never-ending flow of discussion papers going through the party offices.

After that it was back to the grindstone. The Ulster Unionists appeared still to want total integration with Britain, and were deeply alarmed at the prospect of a three-stranded settlement with a strong North–South dimension. An added difficulty lay in the UUP negotiating separately with the British government and Sinn Féin with the Irish government outside the talks. No written reports were ever received from these meetings. It was very hard to get a handle on these different and separate negotiations: it was like having to play high-stakes poker at several tables at the same time. By December it was looking hopeless again. We and the UUP had reached some agreement on an agenda, but then Sinn Féin and the Irish government baulked at some of its provisions, and we were forced to back off. The debate turned nasty and I remember saying in all my years in Northern Ireland politics I had never seen such resentment, suspicion and pain as I'd seen in the previous few weeks.

We did a lot of work through bilateral meetings with the Ulster Unionists on Strand One – the power-sharing and other institutional arrangements within Northern Ireland – until they were sick looking at us and we were sick looking at them. There were something like twenty-eight different drafts of a Strand One agreement between ourselves and the UUP: twenty-eight different ways of saying the same thing. But we were inching into each other's negotiating minds, so that when it came to the final days and hours at least we had a clear idea of where we each wanted to go.

Outside the talks, the violence was continuing. A month before the Good Friday Agreement there was a particularly poignant double murder by the Loyalist Volunteer Force of two young friends, one Protestant, one Catholic, in the hitherto unscathed village of Poyntzpass, a rare oasis of community harmony on the Armagh–Down border seven miles from Markethill. The double killing violated that quiet place, which was free of the flags, graffiti and slogans that deface so many towns and villages in the North. I knew the village well; away back I even played for their football team.

Philip Allen and Damien Trainor had been close friends for years; Philip had just asked Damien to be best man at his wedding. They were having a pint in the pub after work when the two masked gunmen came in and started shooting. Damien's uncle said: 'All Damien lived for was cars and a few drinks along with his mate who was murdered alongside him. They've grown up together as pals the way both their fathers did. The families have a long, long history; there was never any animosity among them, just the best of pals, the best of friends.'

I went down to the Railway Bar where the killing had taken place as soon as I heard about it that evening and talked to the owner, Bernadette Canavan, an SDLP supporter and good friend. She was totally shattered. A young policeman then told me the two men had died in hospital in Newry. I went back the next morning and David Trimble arrived at the same time, not by arrangement. We went to young Allen's house first and paid our respects. Then David offered to take his car up to Trainor's. I said, 'No, we'll walk up.' That was the best thing we could have done, it gave people some hope. There was a feeling that we were doing something good in those dreadful circumstances, one of those black moments when somehow inside it was a chink of light. People stopped us on the street every twenty yards to thank us for coming and to say it was good to see both of us visiting the bereaved families together and offering our condolences together and walking through the village and meeting people at the doors together. And then, of course, we went to both funerals together. It was heartening in a heart-rending situation. I think that experience stayed with Trimble; it certainly stayed with me. And it helped as we moved towards the crunch stage in the final weeks of the negotiations. There was hope in the air then that I had not experienced since the days of Sunningdale. It was a terrible but seminal moment.

There were two major differences in those talks compared to previous ones I had been involved in: firstly, Senator George Mitchell brought the aura of a US president with him, having been sent by President Clinton, and was a superb chairman, an extraordinarily patient listener, a brilliant presenter of compromise papers and exceptionally good at one-to-one discussions. Secondly, there was the heavy involvement of British and Irish government ministers, who were very much part of the negotiations.

Then, in that extraordinary final week – Holy Week, April 1998 – we had Tony Blair flying in with the hand of history on his shoulder, and a sleepless Bertie Ahern dashing between Dublin and Belfast to keep vigil over his mother's body and then attend her funeral. According to a confidential note three days later by Sir John Holmes, Blair's principal private secretary, it was in serious doubt whether an agreement would be reached right up to the last minute: late on the afternoon of Good Friday, 10 April. When Blair had arrived at Stormont on the previous Tuesday afternoon, 'the situation looked bleak'.[4] General de Chastelain put the chances of success at 20 per cent; George Mitchell even lower.

---

4. Quotes from confidential letter from Sir John Holmes, 13 April 1998.

The main issue at the beginning of that week was the long list of North–South bodies and areas for cooperation contained in George Mitchell's first document for discussion (i.e. the first draft of the Agreement). This had actually been drawn up by the two governments (with a strong input from Dublin) and it featured a wide range of all-Ireland functions and annexes listed in forty-nine areas for cross-border cooperation (including health, education, trade and the arts). UUP deputy leader John Taylor famously said he 'wouldn't touch this paper with a forty-foot barge pole'. The Ulster Unionists fought a successful rearguard action to have this reduced to twelve bodies and areas for cooperation. David Trimble's biographer Dean Godson calls this 'Trimble's greatest triumph during the talks.'[5] I was not at all happy with the kind of often minimalist bodies that eventually emerged – in areas like food safety and loughs and lighthouses – and at the fact that there were no bodies in key areas like agriculture, health or energy.

However, Holmes said that the long list of annexes of issues for North–South cooperation included in that draft agreement had 'pushed the Unionists over the edge'. The Irish government, Sinn Féin and we in the SDLP feared at one point that there would never be any North–South bodies at all because they would be sabotaged by the Ulster Unionists.

Things reached a low point late on the Wednesday evening when the Ulster Unionists and the Irish government met for a long and tense discussion. Holmes quoted Bertie Ahern as saying that 'it had finished just in time, before blows were exchanged'. On Thursday morning it became clear that the Ulster Unionists and Dublin 'were not capable of solving their problems bilaterally – the mutual distrust and hostility was too great. From now until virtually the end of the talks, we [i.e. the British government] negotiated with both by proxy, and kept them apart.' At midday on Thursday Trimble accepted a minimum of six North–South bodies and a longer list of sample areas for cooperation. But he also said that decommissioning would be a 'showstopper' unless the British government 'got right the link between this and Sinn Féin's ability to sit in the new Northern Ireland government'.

Bertie Ahern had made it clear to the British that a deal would be almost impossible for the Irish government if Sinn Féin did not sign up to it. Late on Thursday Sinn Féin's public line had turned very negative and it looked as if they were preparing to dissociate themselves from any agreement. They were demanding improvements on the Irish language, policing and security, and prisoners (whom they insisted all had to be out in a year).

5. D. Godson, *Himself Alone: David Trimble and the Ordeal of Unionism* (London 2004), 333.

A series of meetings during the night of Thursday 9 – Friday 10 April appeared to turn the tide. These included two very long meetings between Blair and Ahern on one side, and Gerry Adams and Martin McGuinness on the other; and a 3 am phone call from Bill Clinton to Adams. In Holmes' words:

> No concessions were made on Sinn Féin demands, but their concerns were listened to. Dr Mowlam wrote a letter of comfort on some of the issues. The Prime Minister promised to meet Adams after Easter to discuss them further. It eventually became clear early on the morning of 10 April that, while they would not sign up to the deal on the spot, not least because of their annual conference a week later, they were ready to make positive noises about it and argue for it. It was made clear in return that, while we would stick for now to the planned two-year release deadline for prisoners, we would be ready to advance this if Sinn Féin did sign up and circumstances allowed.

Meanwhile the deal on Strand Two had unblocked the Strand One negotiations:

> The SDLP's patience was rewarded and the UUP accepted early on Friday morning the essence of what they had rejected for so long: a Northern Ireland Executive, with a First and Deputy First Minister, and a reasonable form of sufficient cross-community consensus for voting on key issues. Other pieces of the jigsaw had also fallen into place, with new words on decommissioning and policing agreed, and the UUP having finally accepted the Irish amendments to Articles 2 and 3.

Good Friday saw two more last-ditch crises. There was one more row between the Irish government and the Ulster Unionists about the number of North–South bodies. This was resolved by David Trimble, 'at his most boorish', being persuaded to propose 'a pretty meaningless health body'. It was sold to an unhappy Bertie Ahern on the basis of an additional reference to other bodies to be considered by the new North South Ministerial Council.

Holmes describes the final impasse as:

> It quickly became clear that Trimble's troops were in general revolt, particularly his young staffers, but also major figures like Donaldson. Faced with the prospect of selling to their community a deal involving Sinn Féin at the Assembly and Government table with no guarantee of decommissioning, with all prisoners out in two years, at least severe doubts about the future of the RUC, a new relationship with Dublin, and a nationalist hold on major Assembly decisions, they were losing their nerve.

Trimble seemed to be losing the argument. 'It began to look hopeless, and despair took hold.'

Eventually, on Friday afternoon, Trimble, Taylor, Reg Empey, Ken Maginnis and Jeffrey Donaldson met Blair and told him the deal was 'unacceptable and unsaleable' to unionists, with the single biggest issue being the prospect of sitting round the Cabinet table with Sinn Féin when there had been no decommissioning. 'The Prime Minister let his despair show, but said he was ready to help if he could, but not by reopening the text itself.' 'When they had left, we concocted a letter to Trimble making clear that, if after six months of the new Assembly, the present rules to promote non-violent methods had proved ineffective, we would support changing the rules to give them teeth,' said Holmes.

They sent this to Trimble 'without much hope' and Blair asked Clinton to give Trimble a call. Suddenly, at around 4.30, the picture changed again and the news came through that Trimble had called a vote of his UUP delegation and narrowly won it.[6] 'This seemed too good to be true, but Trimble quickly rang to confirm it was now clear for the plenary to be held, and Mitchell arranged it for 17.00.' After the plenary's endorsement of the agreement by all the parties, followed by congratulatory speeches by the two prime ministers and the party leaders, the British government delegation left for London, 'scarcely able to believe what had happened'.

Throughout those final months and weeks I was always conscious of the elephant that was not in the room: the British and Irish governments (and even the US government) negotiating with Sinn Féin *outside* the room, outside the negotiations that the rest of us were involved in, on issues that were important to them, such as the release of prisoners. It was very difficult in a negotiating situation to know that one of the players had privileged access to the key decision-makers, the two governments.

Once the pressure came on in that final few days as we approached George Mitchell's Good Friday deadline, the SDLP focused on Strand One. I was very much of the opinion that you cannot keep negotiating every bit of an agreement right up to the final moment. But that is exactly what we did. When David Trimble came in with his team late on that final Holy Thursday evening, he showboated for quite a while, snapping at people and condemning everything we put on the table as 'nonsense'. That was mainly for Jeffrey Donaldson's benefit,

---

6. In his biography of David Trimble, *Himself Alone,* Dean Godson quotes delegation member Antony Alcock saying there was no actual vote on the agreement, but he saw it as 6–3 for a deal (350).

since Trimble knew he was having serious doubts about going along with what was agreed.

So we abandoned that meeting for a while and had a middle-of-the-night meeting with Tony Blair, who could not understand the need for one of our main proposals, 'Parallel Consent'. We explained this was to require that in any vote on legislation in the new Assembly, there would have to be a majority of both unionists and nationalists before it was passed. We needed this safeguard to ensure that no combination of unionist parties could come together to block key reforms. And we got that. Then we had a meeting with the Irish government delegation, although they seemed more interested in what Sinn Féin were negotiating with the British than in us: Sinn Féin had secured a substantial increase in that last few hours in the number of prisoners who were going to be released. Blair did that deal on his own; Mo Mowlam was excluded. She joked with black humour that she was 'Her Majesty's tea lady'.

Somewhere around 2 am on Good Friday morning we had a final meeting with the Ulster Unionists. Jeffrey Donaldson was absent and Trimble was very subdued by comparison with the earlier meeting. We had an amicable discussion, reached agreement on Strand One (apart from a few technical details) and shook hands on it. One of the last things they agreed was to our demand that the First and Deputy First Minister in any Executive should have joint and equal powers, which was always a problem for the unionists, who had been used to having the top government post for nearly eighty years.

Then, as we left the meeting with the Ulster Unionists, Pat Doherty of Sinn Féin came up to me and said Gerry Adams and Martin McGuinness would like a meeting about Strand One. Angry words in unparliamentary language were spoken by me, as I reminded him that they had had the best part of two years to come and discuss Strand One with us, and had not done so, so after all that time we were not going to change anything to suit them at the last minute.

Then John Hume and I went down to tell the Irish government about the agreement with the unionists and I think they were taken by surprise. We were understandably overjoyed and excited. While we explained the agreement to Bertie Ahern and his officials, the door opened and what appeared to be a sleep-walking Mo Mowlam, shoeless as usual, came in, looking like Lady Macbeth. She sat down beside me, put her head on my shoulder and went to sleep. I let her rest there and carried on speaking. A few minutes later she lifted her head and in pure schoolgirl English exclaimed 'Fucking brill, Seamus' and went back to sleep again. I think I may have been in tears at that point.

By six o'clock that morning, there wasn't a chair left in Castle Buildings. It seemed to me that every single member of the six negotiating parties had arrived to witness the climax: you couldn't sit down, you couldn't lie down on that freezing morning in that horrible office block. I woke up under a table beside a senior Irish government official, David Donoghue, and announced, perhaps slightly prematurely, that this was the happiest day of my life.

But we still had another eleven hours to wait. Trimble got his fateful side letter from Tony Blair promising that 'the process of decommissioning should begin straight away', a promise Blair was either unwilling or unable to keep. It was not until five o'clock that afternoon that George Mitchell was able to convene the final plenary session for the parties to endorse the agreement. As Mitchell said in a short closing speech:

> This agreement proves that democracy works, and in its wake we can say to the men of violence, to those who disdain democracy, whose tools are bombs and bullets: your way is not the right way. You will never solve the problems of Northern Ireland by violence. You will only make them worse. It doesn't take courage to shoot a policeman in the back of the head, or to murder an unarmed taxi driver. What takes courage is to compete in the arena of democracy, where the tools are persuasion, fairness and common decency.

Seamus Heaney welcomed the Agreement with the following words:

> If revolution is the kicking down of a rotten door, evolution is more like pushing the stone from the mouth of the tomb. There is an Easter energy about it, a sense of arrival rather than wreckage, and what is nonpareil about the new conditions is the promise they offer of a new covenant between people living in the country. For once, and at long last, the language of the Bible can be appropriated by those with a vision of the future rather than those who sing the battle hymns of the past.

In the House of Commons ten days later I welcomed the Good Friday Agreement as

> a massive victory. It is a victory for the political process over violence; of pragmatism over outdated ideologies. Above all, it is a victory of the human spirit, inspired by hope and confidence, over the twin imposters of hatred and bigotry. I believe that it should not be seen as a victory for either unionism or nationalism. It is a comprehensive and common sense set of arrangements that will allow people to be at peace with themselves, at peace with others, and united in the common purpose of resolving our differences only by agreement, only by

consent and only through working together to lay to rest the ghosts that have divided us for so long.

What did I bring to the talks that led to the Good Friday Agreement? I like to think I brought a questioning of things, and a refusal to nod things through without in-depth discussion. I suppose I would be called stubborn. For example, John Hume would often have decided on a policy position, and would have run it past Mark Durkan and Sean Farren. My role then was to say: 'Hold on a minute, we're not going anywhere until we discuss this seriously.' I think that perhaps I also brought a more conciliatory approach to add to my traditional tenacity, which may have come from my experience of interacting with unionists in the House of Commons.

I must also pay tribute to David Trimble. He genuinely wanted to make the new institutions work. If John Hume or Gerry Adams had faced the degree of division in their parties that Trimble had, they would not even have been at the negotiating table. Almost all his MPs were against him; as were half his Assembly members and a large proportion of his local councillors. George Mitchell was to write in his memoirs:

> Each day of the nearly two years of negotiations was for him a struggle to avoid being thrown off balance. Attacked daily by some unionists for selling out the Union, criticised often by some nationalists for recalcitrance, he threaded his way through a minefield of problems, guided by his intelligence, his sure grasp of the political situation and his determination to reach agreement.[7]

The day of the referendum, 22 May 1998, which saw 71.1 per cent of voters in the North and 94.4 per cent of voters in the South support the Good Friday Agreement, was the second most important day of my political life. It was the first time in my lifetime that the people of Ireland, North and South, had voted on the same issue on the same day, and the issue was the life and death one of peace and an end to conflict on our island. It was symbolically enormously significant. It gave the political process in the North a legitimacy it never had before. It was an all-Ireland vote, the first since 1918, for a solution that included a strong all-Ireland dimension. In that sense it wiped out eighty years of unionist dominance. If that overwhelming vote of the Irish people for peace had not happened, there would have been no second chance. It would have been the last chance of peace for a generation, maybe longer.

---

7. G. Mitchell, *Making Peace: the inside story of the making of the Good Friday Agreement* (London 1999), 180.

It was the final end of the unionist veto on progress involving an Irish dimension, which was first signalled in the 1985 Anglo-Irish Agreement. The unionist community voting by a small majority for the Agreement was itself a historic break with the past. If my thesis that unionists can be persuaded slowly to support some form of Irish unity is correct, then their vote for the Agreement, which had unity by consent as a central element, was very significant. Through the reform of the police and the courts that followed, it also represented the beginning of the end of the domination and corruption of those institutions by the unionist elite over the previous eighty years.

9. *In Government with David Trimble*

In April and May 1998 we might have signed, and the Irish electorate might have overwhelmingly endorsed, one of the most extraordinary and unexpected peace agreements of the modern era, but it was not long before we were again in the midst of a typical Ulster maelstrom. In early July, two days after David Trimble and I had been sworn in as First and Deputy First Minister, a huge security operation swung into operation in Portadown, nine miles from my home, to deal with the 'traditional' Orange march back from Drumcree Church through the Catholic Garvaghy Road area of the town, whose residents were bitterly opposed to its passage.

This had been a violent flashpoint for the previous four years and more. Probably the worst year had been 1996 when the RUC first banned the march and then, on the twelfth of July, after loyalists blocked hundreds of roads and attacked the police throughout the North, backed down, clearing the Garvaghy Road of its protesting residents and forcing the marchers through. In that year there were roadblocks everywhere: I was trapped between one loyalist barricade made out of a large fallen tree just below my home and one in the lane above it. I had to go to an important meeting in Newry about Daisy Hill Hospital with the then 'direct rule' health minister Malcolm Moss, but I simply couldn't get out of my house. When I heard that Moss was coming by helicopter I asked, tongue in cheek, if he could call in for me. The next thing I knew was that his helicopter was landing in the field behind the house. He didn't give me a lift back, so my SDLP colleague Frank Feely had to drive me back through the loyalist roadblocks. There was tremendous tension, with the kind of tactics last seen in the Ulster Workers' Council strike: masked men with cudgels at roadblocks, widespread intimidation of Catholics, appeals to sectarian Protestant solidarity.

A senior RUC officer told the prominent Belfast journalist David McKittrick: 'We were on the brink of all-out civil war. Letting the march through was bad, but the alternative was a thousand times worse. We kid ourselves that we live in a democracy. We have the potential in this community to have a Bosnian-style situation.' I recognized that possibility only too well. At least three times – in 1976 after the Kingsmill massacre, in 1981 during the republican prison hunger strike and in 1996–8 during successive Drumcree marches – I believe we were indeed close to a Bosnian-style civil war in parts of the North. And that citadel of loyalism Portadown, just down the road from my home, was often the epicentre of the conflict.

In July 1997 the RUC forced the Orange march down the Garvaghy Road again. In July 1998 it seemed to matter little that there was now a power-sharing government in Northern Ireland, which should have heralded some kind of new beginning. With the establishment of the Parades Commission, there had also been a change of policy on provocative marches: 2000 police and soldiers blocked the Orangemen at Drumcree Church and prevented them from marching through the Catholic estate. Once again there was murder, intimidation and mayhem all over the North, with more than 600 attacks on the police, most of them by loyalists, and seventy-six police officers injured. Once again we were very close to the brink.

That we didn't tip over was, I believe, largely because of the horrified public reaction to the burning to death of the three little Quinn boys, from a mixed Catholic–Protestant family, after a petrol bomb was thrown into their house by loyalists in the County Antrim town of Ballymoney. I attended the funeral of those boys, Richard, aged eleven, Mark aged ten and Jason aged nine, and watched those three small white coffins being carried into the local church. Even by the standards of the Troubles it was a pitiful and heart-rending occasion.

Northern Ireland is a very small place. Rev. William Bingham, the Orange chaplain who was one of the leaders of the Drumcree protest, was the son of Davy Bingham who was my best friend when we were growing up as neighbours in

Markethill. I had several meetings with him and urged him to end the stand-off before it came to a bad end. After the Ballymoney killings he told me he was going to call on the Portadown Orangemen to do just that, and this advance notice helped me to steady a very wobbly David Trimble, who was both an Orangeman and the MP for the Upper Bann area.

At the height of the 1998 crisis I went to meet the Catholic community in Churchill Park off the Garvaghy Road. My driver Paul Rice, a tough guy who was an Antrim county hurler, warned me not to go, and maybe he was right; I was on a hiding to nothing. Inside the hall the residents angrily denounced my suggestion that there might be ways of defusing the stand-off, such as David Trimble and I walking symbolically down the Garvaghy Road together (another suggestion at the time was that because of the massive security cost of Drumcree – estimated at £14 million annually by the police – it would be cheaper to build a whole new road for the Orangemen to march down!). Their leader, Breandán Mac Cionnaith, a convicted IRA bomber, was not amenable to any compromise.

Outside a mob was baying for my blood and I don't think I would have got to my car unhurt if it had not been for Paul. We literally had to fight our way out. We then drove the short distance to Markethill. I had told the RUC when I took the Deputy First Minister's job that I did not want a police escort because I didn't want any policeman killed looking after me. When we were nearing Markethill, there was a loyalist roadblock on the main road below my house and I saw they had guns, so we had to turn around in a hurry and once again you could hear the baying of the men on the barricade: different politics, same baying. We sought refuge in the nearby house of friends, Sean and Ann Conlon, and called the police, who said they would remove the roadblock. I must admit we were both a bit shaken. I sat there worrying that Gertrude was in our house just down the road on the other side of the loyalist barricade, perhaps in danger, and I could not get to her. Later that evening, with the roadblock still not moved, I got home by taking back lanes. That summer Northern Ireland came very close to a conflagration.

These horrible events were happening all the time. If it wasn't a loyalist sectarian murder or an IRA murder, it was a loyalist uprising like Drumcree or a massacre like the Omagh bombing. At times you would say to yourself: how do we get out of this? The only answer was to do what you do when you are riding a bicycle up a hill: keep your head down until you reach the top. At least we now had the hope that a new power-sharing dispensation and an Irish dimension might be given the chance to work in Northern Ireland.

Five weeks after Drumcree, I had just come off the golf course at Rosapenna in Donegal when I heard about the Omagh bombing. I jumped into my car and drove straight to Omagh. A young civil servant from my office who was from the town met me and we went in together. I had seen explosions and multiple deaths before, but this was on a different scale. The eeriness and stillness and smell of death in the streets was something new even to me. I went to the hospital and the police station and they were both in a state of shock and turmoil. The savagery of it was brought home to me by the sight of a strong young policeman bent over with his head in his hands, sobbing. There was a suggestion that the police had got their information wrong and had mistakenly directed the crowd in the wrong direction, *towards* where the bomb would explode. The young civil servant took me to meet his father. He was a nice working man, very much a unionist. He sat me down and poured me a glass of whiskey. Then both of us sat there without a word for at least ten minutes, dumbfounded by the sheer horror of it all.

Despite our different and often clashing personalities, David Trimble and I shared the same burning deck during those first few dangerous months. I believe that given the time and space he and I could have built a lasting partnership. Certainly that's what people who talked to me in the street in Poyntzpass, Omagh and at the Quinn boys' funeral in Ballymoney wanted: they felt that David Trimble and I working together meant a new and hopeful beginning to deal with all the historic enmity and deep distrust. The main problem for Trimble was that he saw himself on a tightrope within his own party, largely caused by the absence of decommissioning, and that prevented him from doing things he could have done such as openly selling the gains of the Good Friday Agreement for unionists. Unfortunately he couldn't allow himself to be seen standing and advocating openly and unashamedly alongside me while that toxic issue remained unresolved.

I had great sympathy for Trimble, just as I had every sympathy for Brian Faulkner before him. They were courageous men who tried hard to lead Northern Ireland to a better place in the face of a lot of very nasty stuff from their own people. Trimble could not even canvass in parts of his own constituency. I saw the most ugly abuse against him, both verbal and physical, at first hand. During the 2001 general election, when my count was over in Banbridge, I decided I would go and see how he was getting on. I saw him being physically attacked: people kicking and hitting him as he came out of the count centre, with the police doing their best to protect him.

There was immense pressure on Trimble inside the Ulster Unionist Party. With Jeffrey Donaldson, Arlene Foster and Peter Weir deserting him, he was losing the best young talent in the party. He knew the two governments were negotiating behind his back to keep Sinn Féin on board. In a way we were Siamese twins locked into the same problem: decommissioning was almost as much an issue for me as for him because it was the huge blockage preventing us getting down to the real business of governing Northern Ireland together.

I genuinely wanted to help Trimble with the problems decommissioning were causing him. Seven months after the Good Friday Agreement I told the party conference in Newry that the SDLP would support the exclusion of Sinn Féin ministers from government in the North if the republicans failed to meet their decommissioning obligations. I acknowledged unionist fears that Sinn Féin would 'pocket' concessions, such as the release of prisoners, but would fail to honour the Agreement's terms to work to achieve decommissioning by May 2000. 'I believe this will not occur, and that it is not intended. But no one should have any doubt that if it did happen the SDLP would rigorously enforce the terms of the Agreement and remove from office those who had so blatantly dishonoured their obligations.'[1]

I knew quite quickly after the speech that it was approved neither by John Hume nor the Irish government. Both of them thought that as long as the IRA's guns were silent, there was no major issue. In the end I was proved wrong about Sinn Féin and the IRA's good intentions. Its failure to decommission stretched from two years to more than seven: it was not until September 2005 that General de Chastelain, head of the decommissioning body, announced that the IRA had put all its weapons beyond use in a final act witnessed by Catholic priest Father Alec Reid and Methodist minister Rev. Harold Good.

Despite the overwhelming 1998 popular vote, I am convinced that peace for the IRA and Sinn Féin did not mean the right of the people of Northern Ireland to live content in safety and free from fear, but was a bargaining counter to be used for as long as it was useful and effective in getting what they wanted from the two governments. I had a real sense from nationalist people shortly after the IRA's 1994 ceasefire that now they had tasted peace they never wanted to let it go again. However, in an April 1997 radio interview I said I believed the republican strategy of the Armalite and the ballot box had never really been abandoned. I went on: 'You cannot play with peace, as Sinn Féin and the IRA have been cynically doing. Peace is a fundamental human right of each individual in the North of Ireland; it cannot be doled out to them by Sinn Féin, as you would dole out dolly mixtures to a child.'

---

1. D. de Bréadún, *The Far Side of Revenge: Making Peace in Northern Ireland* (Cork 2008, revised edition), 195; *The Irish Times,* 14 November 1998.

I also felt that by concentrating so totally on the decommissioning issue, David Trimble was fighting on the wrong hill, like the Confederate General Robert E. Lee at the US Civil War battle of Gettysburg. The more the unionists and the British obsessed about decommissioning, the more Sinn Féin knew they could use that issue as a bargaining counter; the more it made them the centre of political attention. They seemed to be never off the television in those years; it is little wonder that younger people in particular believed they were now the main party of Irish nationalism. They seemed to be able to get anything they wanted at every point of the negotiating process. They said: 'We'll not do peace unless Joe Cahill gets a US visa; we'll not do peace unless Gerry Adams gets a US visa; we'll not do peace unless the prisoners get out; we'll not do peace unless the "on the runs" get a deal,' and so on.

David Trimble's biographer Dean Godson believes that Sinn Féin had little interest in Trimble or in bolstering his position during this period. 'They believed that if he fell, another unionist leader could always come along, who would still have to do business with them.' If Trimble fell as a result of the IRA's failure to decommission, 'they would continue to benefit from aspects of the [British] Government's reform programme – changes to the RUC, prisoner releases and the equality and human rights agendas – whilst those aspects which were of less interest to them such as the Assembly (with its unionist majority) would disappear'.[2]

The story about how I became Deputy First Minister to Trimble's First Minister is an odd one. At the end of June 1998 I was away playing golf in Kildare when somebody came out onto the course to tell me that Bertie Ahern wanted to talk to me urgently. So I was taken in the Taoiseach's car into Government Buildings in Dublin with great secrecy and speed. We had a brief chat, but to this day I don't know why he wanted to see me. I then went over to the Merrion Hotel for a cup of coffee, and in came John Hume. He sat down and we were joined by a couple of senior people from the Department of Foreign Affairs, but nobody said anything about serious politics, let alone high office in the new Stormont administration. I was no wiser when I went to bed that night.

Two days later I was summoned to go to a party meeting in Belfast and headed for Stormont. I was there some time when John Taylor put his head around the door and said: 'I think you're in the wrong place. You should be in the Wellington Park Hotel. That's where your party is meeting.' I thanked him and drove across town. There was a meeting going on, and when I came into the room,

---

2. D. Godson, *Himself Alone: David Trimble and the Ordeal of Unionism* (London 2004), 410–11.

*Seamus Mallon's father, Frank, mother, Jane (née O'Flaherty),
and sister Jean in London's Trafalgar Square, 1962.*

*The St Joseph's College Belfast Gaelic football team in the mid-1950s,
with Seamus* (top left).

A teenage Seamus with sisters Kate and Jean out-side their home in Markethill, County Armagh.

Seamus with three of his sisters, Kate, Jean and Maura, and mother, Jane (back right).

On the day of Maura's wedding, April 1962. From the left: Seamus' sisters Peggy and Kate, his mother Jane and sister Jean.

Wedding party of Seamus and Gertrude (née Cush), July 1964.

Seamus on holiday in Ballinahinch, Connemara, with wife, Gertrude, and daughter Orla, 1986.

Graffiti on a children's playground wall in Markethill, late 1970s.

Mallon being taken to the cells in Armagh after being found in contempt of court, 1982.

Belfast cartoonist Rowel Friers' cartoon of Mallon and John Hume, early 1980s.

Mallon in combative form at an SDLP annual conference, early 1980s.

Mallon with Senator Ted Kennedy, 1985.

*Mallon with Cardinal Tomás Ó Fiaich
and Joe Kennedy outside St Patrick's R.C.
Cathedral, Armagh, mid-1980s.*

Mallon canvassing a Newry housing estate in the January 1986 by-election in which he won the Newry and Armagh House of Commons seat.

SDLP election workers in the Newry and Armagh constituency, January 1986.

Mallon walking past the British army post in Crossmaglen.

Mallon with three 'bodyguards' on an election canvass in the Barcroft Park estate in Newry.

Mallon in Pittsburgh, mid-1980s.

Mallon above the main Belfast–Dublin road at the border at Cloughoge, near Newry.

The SDLP's four MPs: Eddie McGrady, Joe Hendron, John Hume and Seamus Mallon.

SDLP campaign poster.

Mallon with Charles Haughey, early 1980s.

A difficult moment during pre-Good Friday Agreement negotiations, 1997.

Mallon with Senator George Mitchell, 1998.

Seamus Mallon with John Hume outside the Belfast count centre following the referendum vote in favour of the Good Friday Agreement, May 1998.

David Trimble and Seamus Mallon after they had been sworn in as First Minister and Deputy First Minister at Stormont on 1 July 1998 with Northern Ireland Assembly Speaker John Alderdice.

David Trimble, Bill Clinton, Seamus Mallon and Tony Blair, Stormont, September 1998.

*Frank Feely, Newry SDLP politician, Seamus Mallon and John Fee,
Crossmaglen councillor and Mallon's personal assistant.*

Mallon with President Clinton at the White House, St Patrick's Day 1999.

The party leaders and politicians who negotiated the Good Friday Agreement with President Bill Clinton, Senator George Mitchell and Taoiseach Bertie Ahern, the White House, St Patrick's Day 1999.

The Northern Ireland Executive with Taoiseach Bertie Ahern at the inaugural meeting of the North South Ministerial Council, Armagh, December 1999.

Trimble and Mallon with the President of the EU Commission, Romano Prodi, June 2000.

David Trimble, EU Commissioner for Regional Policy, Michel Barnier, Seamus Mallon and Finance Minister Mark Durkan (standing), *Stormont, March 2001.*

Minister for Foreign Affairs Dermot Ahern, US businessman Dan Rooney, US Ambassador to Ireland Jean Kennedy Smith, Seamus Mallon and Dundalk businessman Frank Toal (date unknown).

Trimble and Mallon with George W. Bush, Washington DC, March 2001.

Seamus outside his birthplace, Markethill.

Seamus with grandchild Lara and Jessie the dog.

John Hume caught me by the cuff and said: 'This Deputy First Minister thing – you're going to have to do it because the doctors have told me I shouldn't.' Apart from his health, I think John probably realized that when it came to the detail of day-to-day political engagement and horse-trading, especially with unionists, I was a better operator than him. He was the vision man; I was the negotiator.

On 1 July 1998, just under three months after the Good Friday Agreement, David Trimble and I were elected as First Minister and Deputy First Minister by the new Assembly. There was little time to feel any satisfaction in being the first nationalist Deputy First Minister of Northern Ireland holding equal powers with the unionist First Minister. Loyalist arson attacks took place against ten Catholic churches during the night after our inauguration, and we were four days away from the annual confrontation at Drumcree.

Trimble and I went over to Castle Buildings, where the government offices were, and announced ourselves with our new titles. 'The first I've heard of it,' said the woman on the reception desk. Eventually we were taken upstairs to a small, bare office with a couple of chairs and one phone. Later John Semple, head of the Northern Ireland Civil Service, turned up to make sure we were comfortable.

After my appointment, I was asked if I would like to have a chief of staff as David Trimble did. 'No,' I said, 'I think the North has had too many chiefs of staff.' Instead I appointed two advisers: Hugh Logue, a former SDLP colleague in the 1973–4 Assembly who had been working with the European Commission in Brussels, and Colm Larkin, head of the Commission's office in Dublin. Later I chose a Protestant civil servant, Billy Gamble, as my private secretary, while Trimble chose a Catholic, Maura Quinn.

Although they were totally unprepared for the arrival of a devolved power-sharing government, after a time I came to know and respect many of the senior civil servants. After their initial shock, they worked hard to make this unprecedented new system work. Because we had so many dealings with Dublin, we could all see the advantages their Southern counterparts had over the North's officials by being part of a national government with extensive exposure to the wider international stage, notably in the European Union and at the United Nations.

When Bill Clinton and Tony Blair joined David Trimble and me for a packed public meeting in Belfast's Waterfront Hall that September, I quoted the words of the black American poet Maya Angelou at Clinton's presidential inauguration five years earlier: 'Lift up your faces, you have a piercing need for this bright morning dawning for you. History, despite its wrenching pain, cannot be unlived, but when faced with courage need not be lived again.'

Deaglán de Breadún of *The Irish Times* was kind enough to write that I was the unexpected star of that event. I was full of hope for the marvellous tapestry of peacebuilding institutions that would emerge from the Good Friday Agreement. I said:

> The road to the future is always under construction. The democratic institution of the Assembly will take root to become a living symbol of hope and confidence for all the people of Northern Ireland. We will establish a North South Ministerial Council, which will serve as a model for inter-regional relationships. We will create a British-Irish Council to promote the totality of relationships among the people of these islands in a sense of harmony that benefits our membership of the developing European Union. We will build a new future based on the skills, creativity and character of our people. Our young people are a source of hope for our future. Consequently, we will give priority to education, sharing Prime Minister Blair's view that 'unless we get our education system right our children will not be prosperous and our country will not be just'.

I had Colm Larkin and Hugh Logue to thank for most of that speech, as well as Hugh's wife Anne for the quote from Maya Angelou.

Working with David Trimble was a roller-coaster ride. He was both a highly volatile and a highly intelligent man who was under tremendous political pressure. He had developed storming out of meetings into a new art form. Mo Mowlam used to say that she hardly ever finished a meeting without Trimble walking out. When we met in my office I used to lock the door to prevent this.

Trimble and I fought long and hard in sometimes tense and difficult meetings. I was determined that I was not going to be perceived or treated as his deputy, but as the equal leader I was legally entitled to be under the Good Friday Agreement. But when business had to be done he could knuckle down and show himself to be gracious under pressure. When we reached a compromise decision, we shook hands on it. I know from Reg Empey that he asked the people in his party not to publicly attack me. He was a man of great potential, badly treated by his own party, badly treated by the unionist community, and ill-used by Tony Blair, who gave him side promises on decommissioning that he was unable or unwilling to keep. I was very keen to work effectively in partnership with him.

We agreed on two key things: that Sinn Féin and the DUP were out to get us and the two governments were not reliable friends. I remember one occasion when Trimble and I were discussing Executive business in a room at Stormont and the television was on in the background. There was Gerry Adams and Martin

McGuinness smiling as they left 10 Downing Street. And the following week they would be in Government Buildings in Dublin. And perhaps in the White House the week after that. Trimble said to me: 'You know, Seamus, they're shafting us. We'll soon be redundant.' 'I'm afraid so,' I replied. We would be struggling with difficult issues like Drumcree or policing or trying to put a Cabinet together or working with civil servants who had been running the show for the previous twenty-five years, and there were Adams and McGuinness strutting their stuff in three capitals. It was hard to watch sometimes.

Neither Trimble nor I had ever run a government department, let alone a whole government, before. So we had to learn fast on the job. I was surprised at how hostile the unionist ministers were to the civil servants. The head of the Northern Ireland Civil Service (as opposed to the London-based Northern Ireland Office), John Semple, was a nice and self-effacing man, but he did not feel comfortable working in such unusual devolved institutions.

Like many senior civil servants who had been used to running the place for so many years during 'direct rule' from London, I think Semple felt intimidated by the arrival of local politicians to whom he was now answerable. When a group of department heads asked the new Executive's legal adviser, Dennis McCartney, what they should do if a Sinn Féin minister told them to do something they did not like, he replied: 'You have two choices. You can either do it, or you can say "no" – but if you say "no", you'll have to resign.'

In October 1998 David Trimble and I went on an intensive tour of eleven cities in America, seeking jobs and investment. Mo Mowlam, who joined us for part of the trip, said the only time during the whole peace process she cried was when hearing me speak emotionally at one of those meetings with business leaders about why peace was so utterly crucial for the North.[3]

That trip was good as on several occasions Trimble and I were able to have a meal alone together; to talk things out, to get to know each other better and become more at ease with each other. We shared a mutual liking for a few glasses of a good red wine; indeed Trimble, like most people, would be far more relaxed after a glass of wine. I have two stand-out memories of that US tour. Mowlam had arranged through the Irish government for the Irish and international paper and packaging entrepreneur Michael Smurfit to invite us up to the lap of luxury in his New York penthouse. Trimble was on a high that day. He tore into Smurfit for not investing in Northern Ireland. Smurfit looked at me and raised his eyebrows.

---

3. M. Mowlam, *Momentum: The Struggle for Peace, Politics and the People* (London 2002), 261.

He turned to Trimble: 'Do you not know, David, that I have a factory employing a large number of people in your constituency?'

Then in our hotel in Denver, Colorado, I had gone to bed when I was woken by a phone call telling me that Trimble was going to be awarded the Nobel Peace Prize. So I got up and went down to his room, dressed only in my pyjamas. 'Too late, too late,' he shouted when I knocked on his door. 'Open up – I've got a piece of news for you that you'd probably like to hear.' So I think I was the one who first told him. I congratulated him, adding that it was a great honour for everybody in the Executive. He went red in the face and spluttered, 'Thank you, thank you, leave it with me,' and went back to bed.

The low point in my relationship with Trimble was probably in July 1999 – a year after our appointment – when his behaviour forced me to announce that I was resigning. I was feeling the frustration of still waiting, fifteen months after the Good Friday Agreement, for the full power-sharing Executive to be set up. Trimble had used his weakness in his own party over decommissioning to force concession after concession from the British government, but even the latest package on offer – an agreed sequencing plan with clear fail-safe mechanisms and the Canadian General de Chastelain (whom the unionists trusted) in charge – was not enough to prevent him and his party from boycotting Stormont on the day the full Executive was meant to be nominated. There was a farcical nomination procedure in which SDLP and Sinn Féin members were named and immediately unnamed because there was no cross-community consensus. I then felt I had no option but to resign as Deputy First Minister Designate in protest, accusing the unionists of attempting to bleed the whole peace process dry with their endless demands. When my colleague Mark Durkan was asked afterwards, 'In the shadow Executive, what were you minister for?' he replied, 'Two minutes.'

I was very reluctant to do it, but I felt the deadlocked process needed a kick and resignation was the only way I had of kicking it. Mo Mowlam tried her best to get me to change my mind. That summer I received a mailbag of 3500 letters, the great majority of them supportive. An extraordinary half of them were from unionists, practically all supportive, and many pleading with me to come back. I think they trusted me, because I had never talked to them in any other than a straight way; I never told them any lies or garnished the truth in any way.

Perhaps I am the kind of straight-talking Ulsterman whom unionists tend to trust. They would have heard me in the House of Commons appealing to them to 'stand on their own feet and show that we can be sturdy, independent Ulstermen rather than whinge to ministers for a little more when we are getting a little less'. There is a difference between the two traditions, the two tribes. Unionists are a very literal people: they have to be able to quantify everything, to add and subtract it, to weigh and measure it; they want to see the lines of any agreement clearly and not be told to read between those lines. On the other hand nationalists never had much to add or subtract. So they had to deal in concepts, and that meant they had a skill at reading between the lines. Hence the ambiguity that they would sometimes use in their arguments.

There's a cultural difference here. A wise, now deceased friend used to say that a south Armagh man had to be able to tell the same story in five different ways, and at the same time keep an eye open to see who in the room was worth talking to and who should be avoided. I don't want to overstate it but that difference is still here. When I go up to the Carrickdale Hotel on the border between Armagh and Louth, they have a different way of talking, almost a different language. There's a softness there, almost a lyricism in their speech and sometimes a certain exaggeration and embroidery of the truth. But I'm a product of this Protestant village of Markethill, for good or ill, and I tend to try to tell things as they are. And if a Protestant told me that made me unusual as an Armagh Catholic, I would take that as a compliment!

It was one reason John Hume had such a problem with unionists: they never knew what to make of him. His 'Humespeak' frightened them; they couldn't translate it into their own more black-and-white language. They felt its cleverness and ambiguity represented a threat to them.

It took five more months for the full Executive, including Sinn Féin and DUP ministers, to be finally set up, with nominations on 29 November and its first meeting on 2 December 1999. A mechanism was found to enable me to withdraw my resignation. When unionists, nationalists and republicans sat around that Cabinet table for the first time in Stormont, I pointed out that the table had originally come from Gosford Castle in Markethill and that my mother had occasionally helped at the unionist gentry's dinner parties there. It was, in a small way, a symbol of how far we had come.

David Trimble's decision to go into power-sharing government without the IRA even beginning to decommission its weapons was a very brave step. Earlier in November there had been a breakthrough when Trimble said he would support the setting up of an Executive once the IRA's decision to appoint an interlocutor to the De Chastelain Commission on Decommissioning was announced, and Adams said his party accepted that IRA decommissioning was 'an essential part of the peace process'. I was happy to hear Adams say that. On the other hand, I had heard words like it so often, and I knew it was part of the ongoing power game being played by Sinn Féin.

Decommissioning was the real bugbear of the first two stop-start years of that new Executive, and the painfully slow progress on this issue constantly undermined Trimble within his own party. Even when we finally set up the Executive, in order to get the UUP's backing he was forced to give his party president a post-dated letter of resignation as First Minister to come into effect in just over two months in the event of inadequate movement on IRA arms. I have no regrets about having taken a firm line over that crucial issue within my own party and with the Irish government. In my opinion the republican movement were using it, and using it both cynically and effectively, for their political advantage, knowing that while they had those arms they were central to the whole process.

I believe, and I know senior Irish officials who share my belief, that Sinn Féin acted in bad faith in those first few months of the Executive. Trimble could not have made it clearer when he signed up to go into government with them in November 1999 that he could not sustain this for more than a couple of months without some kind of start to decommissioning. As one official said: 'They knew it was curtains for Trimble unless they gave him something. They played on that.' Irish officials would have remembered that as long ago as 25 June 1998 Martin McGuinness had told Bertie Ahern that the 'principle' that IRA decommissioning would happen by May 2000 was 'a Sinn Féin commitment'.

Insistence upon decommissioning as a condition for entering the Executive would have been the best way forward. It was not just a question of helping Trimble; more important was to protect the integrity of the all-party agreement. I told the 1999 SDLP conference: 'This impasse is not of the SDLP's making. For we hold no guns. We keep no bombs. We impose no preconditions. We exclude nobody. And we are fiercely proud of that.' However, that autumn, when George Mitchell came back to carry out a review of the Agreement and find ways of overcoming the decommissioning impasse, he was essentially talking to the Ulster Unionists and Sinn Féin. I remember sitting outside his door in Stormont for most of a day, telling him I would remain there until he brought our party back into the deliberations. That did not happen. Nevertheless at the end of his review, Mitchell told me clearly that out of his discussions with those two parties, his understanding was that the Executive would be set up at the end of November and decommissioning would begin at the end of January 2000.

Yet there was no start to decommissioning for another twenty-one months, and it was not completed until 2005. So here were the representatives of an organization that had caused untold misery to people with their weapons now using the continual holding of those weapons to block the democratic wishes of the whole Irish nation. It was a kind of republican veto to replace the unionist veto they had complained about so bitterly for so long. There was something obscene about using the weapons of war to establish a political base and move towards taking political power. This was after the Irish people, North and South, had by huge majorities voted for peace in the May 1998 referendums. Yet Sinn Féin were still using the IRA's guns and explosives as a bargaining tool to defy that popular will.

There is no doubt in my mind that part of Gerry Adams' long game was to use the end of the IRA's campaign to replace us as the party of nationalism. That was part of what he was doing when he used the courtship of prime ministers and taoisigh so cleverly: to put the idea in their minds that Sinn Féin were now the party of the North's nationalists. That's what he was doing in his many visits to Dublin, London and Washington when David Trimble and I were working day and night to get an Executive off the ground in Belfast. Tony Blair in particular was susceptible to finding the challenge of crossing swords with hard-as-steel negotiators like Gerry Adams and Martin McGuinness particularly interesting. And they were very clever in showing their 'soft' side: bringing presents for Blair's children and chocolates and flowers for Cherie Blair.

This business of displacing the more centrist party was also happening on the unionist side. There the divisions and fears among the Ulster Unionists were being exploited by the anti-Good Friday Agreement forces of Ian Paisley, Peter Robinson and the DUP to very damaging effect.

The North/South 'implementation bodies', although limited in powers and scope, were one of the new features in the post-Good Friday Agreement landscape. I was particularly proud on 13 December 1999 when as Deputy First Minister I was able to welcome the whole Irish Cabinet to Armagh to jointly launch the North South Ministerial Council (whose secretariat would be based there) along with the new Executive. There had been a last-minute scare the previous evening when the news came through that John Hume wanted to be present. When Gerry Adams heard that John was coming, he insisted that he too wanted to be there. David Trimble quickly made it clear that if Adams turned up, he would not, and there would be no launch of the North South Ministerial Council at all. A senior Irish official, Tim O'Connor, had to make a late-night phone call to Hume to explain why he could not come. He quickly understood the situation and agreed, with Gerry Adams following suit.

I quoted Victor Hugo on that occasion, saying there was 'one thing stronger than all the armies in the world: that is an idea whose time has come'. I said for us 'partnership' was that idea: partnership between the two traditions in the North of Ireland and partnership between North and South. At the inaugural meeting of the British-Irish Council (bringing together the devolved administrations in the UK with the British and Irish governments) in London the following week, I emphasized the pluralism of these islands, with our mixture of Celtic, Roman, Anglo-Saxon, Viking, Norman and other ancestries. They had all left their legacy, I said, and 'we too will leave a legacy. I am confident it will be a legacy of peace, a deeper, truer peace than ever before.'

Our greatest achievement in those short years of interrupted government led by the Ulster Unionist Party and the SDLP was that we showed that power-sharing government could work, and old enemies could work together for the benefit of the people of Northern Ireland. More specifically, we put together an excellent Programme for Government and it was agreed by the Assembly. We benefited a lot from Colm Larkin and Hugh Logue's experience of EU administration in Brussels, and Colm's superb drafting skills. The Programme for Government set up cross-departmental action programmes to get around the bureaucratic silos that many individual government departments in the North had become after so many years of running things in their own way. We knitted together the completely unprecedented North/South bodies with those departments, who often viewed them with distaste. There was a lot in it about equality and inclusion. We set up an Executive Fund to redistribute underspent monies to strategic projects like new road infrastructure and the Strategic Investment Board. We were assisted by some excellent senior civil servants like Tony McCusker, Rosalie Flanagan, Peter May and Andrew McCormick.

Unfortunately, because of all the stops and starts in that first version of the Executive – it was suspended three times in less than three years – it was difficult to follow through and get the programme fully implemented. Despite this, I believe we achieved more in that short time than later DUP–Sinn Féin governments did over much longer periods. Trimble and I worked well together to arbitrate between ministers from four often very antagonistic parties, one of which, the DUP, boycotted Executive meetings. The DUP were auditioning for a future government role by running their departments but refusing to attend Executive meetings, while Sinn Féin wanted to show they could run government departments effectively while avoiding any commitment on decommissioning. It was not at all easy for the two of us caught in the middle.

My fellow ministers were tolerant in allowing me to smoke – both pipe and cigarettes – in Executive meetings, with the result that they were held in an atmosphere shrouded in tobacco fumes. I was known for being curmudgeonly if I was asked to do something I did not want to do. Apparently someone approached the Sinn Féin health minister, Bairbre de Brún, to suggest that I might be requested to stop smoking for the sake of everybody's health. She responded, 'You must be joking.'

I reported to the Irish government in January 2000 that even at that early stage power-sharing was beginning to work well and confidence in it on the ground was beginning to develop. But I continued that if it were to collapse over the decommissioning issue, 'it would take the guts out of everything. The IRA are putting us all in the position that they are God.'

I do not accept that unionists and nationalists cannot work together with a feeling of mutual respect. Out of my own experience, both during the 1974 power-sharing period and my time with David Trimble from 1999 to 2001, there was a good working relationship between the two sides. During one argument with Trimble about flags, I suggested we follow Westminster's example of flying the Union flag on certain days, and we agreed on this very reasonable compromise.

The great majority of people in Northern Ireland want their politicians to get on with the business of government in an atmosphere of pragmatism and mutual respect. That clearly did not happen in the years of DUP–Sinn Féin government up to its collapse in January 2017 over the Renewable Heat Incentive row. During our time, after the initial teething troubles, a group of politicians with fundamentally opposed ideologies and little experience of running an administration worked effectively alongside civil servants who had never worked with politicians before.

The contrast with recent years is striking. Then we had senior civil servants having ready access to their ministers, as is the norm in democratic governments; in recent years they were blocked by unelected party special advisers. We also had fully minuted meetings (which were available for public scrutiny through Freedom of Information legislation); recently we heard the head of the Northern Ireland Civil Service admitting they did not take minutes of key meetings involving ministers precisely to avoid public scrutiny through Freedom of Information. Then we had a working power-sharing arrangement between four very different parties; in recent years it was more 'sharing out' the benefits, including financial benefits, of office between the DUP and Sinn Féin and their supporters.

I was greatly assisted in my daunting new job by the man who became my private secretary, Billy Gamble. Billy was a gem of a man: knowledgeable, wise, and knew the ropes in the Northern Ireland Civil Service intimately. To mark my arrival in my new office he bought me a little plaque that read 'I come to clear the alligators out of the water.' He was a great civil servant and an even greater friend. I'll give an example of his wisdom and friendship. A cousin of mine in Philadelphia asked me if I would like to go to Rome meet the Pope. When it was arranged I said to Billy, a member of the Church of Ireland, that I would love him to accompany me, but he should feel free to say no. He insisted he was going. It was 5.30 in the morning when we went into Pope John Paul's oratory. Nearly thirty people were there, and a good half of them were doctors and nurses because he was not at all well. The archbishop organizing the Mass told me I would be reading the lesson. Then it was time for Communion. I was heading back from the altar when I was passed by Billy Gamble going up. When we came back to our *pensione* for breakfast I asked Billy why he had gone to Communion in the Pope's oratory. 'It's my God too, you know,' he replied. And I said: 'Thank God there are people like you.'

John Hume had not been well for some time. When the Executive was set up at the end of 1999 would have been the optimum time for him to stand down as leader for several reasons: number one, because of his health; number two, because his continuing leadership of the SDLP made it difficult for me as Deputy First Minister. In that job I had key decisions to make, but out of courtesy to John as party leader I had to go back before I made them to consult with him. I had the power of appointing ministers to the Executive, but John continued to insist that it was his call who should be appointed from the SDLP. I had to tell him that any such decisions by him would be constitutionally invalid.

On one occasion when Tony Blair flew into Belfast for a late-night meeting about the North/South bodies, John was driving back to Derry when he heard about his visit on the radio. He turned his car around and came back to Stormont. Mo Mowlam had to tell him that this was a matter for the two governments, Trimble and myself, and that he had absolutely no role.

It would have been in both Northern Ireland's and the SDLP's interest if the Deputy First Minister and the SDLP leader's posts had been held by the same person. Friends sometimes commiserated with me for having to manage the difficult balancing act of being Deputy First Minister and deputy leader to two difficult and headstrong men, David Trimble and John Hume (some of those friends would add that I could be a difficult and headstrong man myself!). But I was never going to make the SDLP leadership an issue; I had far too much respect for John. Friends who were closer to him knew only too well it was time to step down and should have put the question to him.

Then, by the time he himself decided that he was going to give up the leadership in the autumn of 2001, I was going through a personal crisis because my wife Gertrude was very ill with increasingly serious dementia. That summer she received serious burns in a household accident. She was in Belfast's Royal Victoria Hospital for four weeks getting skin grafts. Then she was in hospital in Dublin with another severe illness for six more weeks, and I was up and down between Belfast and Dublin attending to her. So I had to decide – which was my greater responsibility, to lead the SDLP or to look after my very sick wife? – and I decided it was to look after her. She had made great sacrifices for me during the dog days of the 1970s and early 80s, and now it was time for me to return that love. Obviously as a politician my ambition would have been to lead the party I had been part of for my whole political life, but things rarely work out as you would like. That was not a good time for me and I could make only one decision.

The timing was unfortunate. On 17 September Hume announced that he would step down from the leadership of the SDLP on health grounds. Two days later I announced that I would be resigning as deputy leader and would not be contesting the leadership. At the beginning of November I also said I would not seek re-election as Deputy First Minister (I had been forced to relinquish that position after David Trimble resigned as First Minister over lack of movement on decommissioning). It can't have been easy for the party to lose its two top leaders in the middle of the latest decommissioning crisis.

I had got the feeling even when I was Deputy First Minister that the Irish government was making plans to abandon the SDLP for Sinn Féin and the British government to leave the Ulster Unionists for the DUP. I hope I'm not being paranoid when I say got the first hint of that as early as November 1997. I was attending the inauguration of President Mary McAleese in Dublin Castle and was shown into the room beside the main hall (from which you could not actually see the inauguration ceremony). Martin McGuinness was also in that room at first. But then the head of the Department of Foreign Affairs, Dermot Gallagher, came in and ushered him into the inner room.

Then there was a time during the foot-and-mouth-disease crisis in 2001, when I was Deputy First Minister, and I went to meet somebody in a hotel in Newry on a late Sunday afternoon. I was going to the reception desk and I looked around and saw Dermot Gallagher, Martin Mansergh, the Taoiseach's adviser, Tim Dalton, the head of the Department of Justice, and the senior diplomat Dáithí Ó Ceallaigh, whom I had known for years. I walked past and said 'Good evening, all' – but nobody replied. To his credit Dáithí then came over and spoke to me, but the others cut me dead. Because Dalton, the man in charge of security, was there, I knew they were seeing the Provos.

Senior civil servants in both Belfast and Dublin were certainly convinced that a DUP–Sinn Féin alliance was the way forward as early as 2000. Civil service friends in Belfast have told me that while up to the end of 1999 there was little interchange with the DUP and Sinn Féin, after that there was a lot of dialogue in the background between the Northern Ireland Office and the Department of Foreign Affairs and those two parties. The biggest movement was on the unionist side, with 'the writing on the wall for Trimble from very early on'. Peter Robinson, in particular, had 'his game plan working to make the DUP more acceptable'. It was particularly galling for those of us from the SDLP in government to see how deferential Irish civil servants were to Sinn Féin and the DUP, the very parties who were making their, and our, lives so difficult.

Dublin civil servant friends have put the date when the courting of Sinn Féin began even earlier. They believe it started with the lack of progress in setting up the institutions in the long months after the Good Friday Agreement, when with Trimble and the Ulster Unionists insisting on 'no guns, no government', the Irish government's emphasis shifted to keeping Sinn Féin on board. 'How were we going to break that logjam?' one sympathetic official has asked me. 'This wasn't an argument between David Trimble and Seamus Mallon, but between David Trimble and Gerry Adams. Inevitably the key protagonists became the Ulster Unionists and Sinn Féin, and the SDLP were squeezed out.'

Soon after I stepped down as Deputy First Minister in November 2001, I was aware of regular meetings Tony Blair was having separately with the DUP and Sinn Féin, and we and the Ulster Unionists – still the main parties in the Northern Ireland Executive – were being excluded. SDLP members used to contact me and ask me what the party should do about this. I said Mark Durkan, who succeeded me as Deputy First Minister and John Hume as party leader, should go into Downing Street and tell Blair, 'You don't bloody do this to us, mate.' But that didn't happen.

The problem was that during those years the overriding problem remained decommissioning, and that suited Sinn Féin's long-term ambitions. I accept there were times when Sinn Féin wanted to move forward, but were caught between the IRA's intransigence on decommissioning and the Ulster Unionists' refusal to move on restoring the institutions until that happened. For example, in March 2000 the West Belfast priest Father Alec Reid reported to the Irish government that there was deep resentment in the nationalist community after Secretary of

State Peter Mandelson's suspension of the institutions the previous month to pre-empt David Trimble's resignation as First Minister, and that the view in the republican movement was that 'the Agreement was finished'.

However, in an insightful article the following month, Ed Moloney[4] wrote that during periods when the Executive was suspended, politics was dominated by the decommissioning debate and the need for a deal between the Ulster Unionists (later the DUP) and Sinn Féin. We in the SDLP were completely eclipsed as the two governments worked on the unionists and republicans. In those circum-stances the nationalist electorate drew its own conclusions and began to shift to Sinn Féin; one result was that in the June 2001 general election Sinn Fein's vote exceeded our party's for the first time. Moloney argued that Sinn Féin had no interest in reaching agreement with David Trimble on decommissioning and devolution. There was even a belief that they would like to see his demise, with the intention of using the subsequent turmoil within unionism to advance their electoral ambitions against the SDLP by arguing that an unreformable Northern Ireland needed a much tougher nationalist party.

---

4. 'SDLP could end up playing second fiddle to Sinn Féin', *Sunday Tribune,* 16 April 2000.

10. *Policing and Justice in a Divided Society*

During the turbulent years between the mid-1970s and the late 90s, when I was the SDLP's spokesman on justice, I was faced with the almost impossible task of trying to propose a solution to the problem of policing in the North of Ireland. Impossible because it goes to the heart of why and how the Northern Ireland state was set up nearly a century ago and how it has been maintained ever since. Since the foundation of that state in 1921 the Royal Ulster Constabulary – and until it was disbanded in 1970 its reserve force, the Ulster Special Constabulary (or 'B-Specials') – were for the great majority of Catholics the unacceptable face of that state's oppressive unionism. For their primary role was to defend the Northern Ireland state against its nationalist enemies, those who had opposed the establishment of Northern Ireland in the first place.

Thus from the beginning there was little or no chance of setting up a police service that would operate on the basis of consensus, and which commanded the support and allegiance of all sectors of the community, one of the hallmarks of the police in a properly functioning civil society. There was no cross-community consensus on how the laws of the new state should be enforced, how its towns and villages and countryside should be policed and how its individual citizens should be protected. What we had instead was a largely unionist police force for a unionist people.

My south Armagh born-and-bred SDLP colleague, the late Ben Caraher, described the Catholic view of the RUC as follows: 'The police were the Other – and they were the most visible sign of the Other, of state power. There was no identification with it: it was not ours, it was not us. You either came in conflict with it, if you were unlucky, or you ignored it for most of the time.'[1] This belief by Northern Catholics, and particularly border Catholics, that the RUC were a force expressly formed to oppress their community, goes back to the yeomanry of the eighteenth century.

Of course behind unjust policing is always an unjust legal system. The RUC always had an arsenal of extremely repressive legislation at its call. Foremost was the Civil Authorities (Special Powers) Act of 1922, which gave the Stormont government extraordinarily wide-ranging powers, including in its original mani- festation, the death penalty, flogging, internment, the prohibition of inquests, arrest without warrant and banning newspapers, books and films. Infamously, John Vorster, then South African justice minister, when introducing a new Coercion Bill in the South African parliament in 1963, said he 'would be willing to exchange all the legislation of that sort for one clause of the Northern Ireland Special Powers Act'.

The RUC first came to world attention when its policemen brutally broke up a civil rights march in Duke Street in Derry in October 1968, beating scores of people, including the MP for West Belfast, Gerry Fitt. To its dismay this was filmed and shown by RTÉ, the Irish public service broadcaster, and thus made international headlines. This was the beginning of the slide into wide- scale violence in Derry and Belfast in August 1969, including the killing of five Catholics by the RUC, and the introduction of the British army as the police completely lost control of the situation. The British government was forced to set up the Hunt Committee (headed by the 1953 Everest expedition leader Lord Hunt), whose October 1969 report into the role and structure of the force stated two salient truths: 'The RUC had to perform what is in fact a dual role. In addi- tion to carrying out all those duties normally associated in the public mind with police forces … it is responsible for security duties of a military nature.' Hunt described its military role as having been 'of first importance', playing a signifi- cant part in 'the training and traditions of the force'. He went on:

Policing in a free society depends on a wide measure of public approval and consent. This has never been obtained in the long term by military or paramilitary

---

1. F. O'Connor, *In Search of a State: Catholics in Northern Ireland* (Belfast 1993), 156–7.

means. We believe that any police force, military in appearance and equipment, is less acceptable to minority and moderate opinion than if it is clearly civilian in character.

Welcome as some of the Hunt Report's recommendations were – notably the abolition of the B-Specials – it failed to recognize that the police in Northern Ireland (unlike in normal democratic societies) would not be accepted by the nationalist section of the community until there was a change in the unionist domination at the heart of the Northern Ireland political system. As the years passed, I became more and more convinced that the policing problem could not be solved in isolation from the political process; bad politics and bad policing were interlocked in the old Northern Ireland. And so it proved when we finally found a solution, with the Patten Commission on policing being an essential element emerging from the 1998 Good Friday Agreement.

The report of the New Ireland Forum expressed this interlocking of politics and security cogently in 1984:

> The problem of security is an acute symptom of the crisis in Northern Ireland. Law and order in democratic countries and, in particular, the introduction of emergency measures, depend on a basic consensus about society itself and its institutions. Present security policy has arisen from the absence of polit-ical consensus. In Northern Ireland extraordinary security actions have taken place that call into question the effectiveness of the normal safeguards of the legal process. This has led to harassment of the civilian population by use of abnormally wide powers of arrest and detention, exercised not for the purpose of bringing suspects before a court of justice and making them amenable to a process of law, but for the purpose of gathering information and unjustifiably invading the privacy of a person's life; e.g. between 1978 and 1982 more than 22,000 people were arrested and interrogated, the vast majority being released without charge. This has the consequence that the availability of the legal remedy of *habeas corpus* in Northern Ireland is in practice extremely limited.
>
> It has also at different periods led to the use of internment without trial combined with inhuman interrogation methods that have been found to be in breach of the European Convention on Human Rights; the trial and convic-tion of people on evidence of paid informers; the use of plastic bullets; and killings by some members of the security forces in doubtful circumstances. The various measures were introduced on the basis that they were essential to defeat terrorism and violent subversion, but they have failed to address the causes of violence and have often produced further violence.[2]

2. New Ireland Forum Report, Volume 1 (Dublin 1984), 18–19.

Elsewhere the Forum report noted:

> The framework within which security policies have operated and their often insensitive implementation have, since 1974, deepened the sense of alienation of the nationalist population. Inevitably, as during the 1980–81 hunger strikes when the warnings of constitutional nationalists were ignored by the British government, security issues have been exploited by the paramilitaries in order to intensify alienation and with a view to increasing their support. Such alienation threatens the civilised life and values of entire communities and undermines the belief that democratic policies alone can offer peace, justice and stability.[3]

I have always made it clear that although I sometimes had to publicly criticize RUC officers and their behaviour, that did not mean I was attacking the police in general. What I sought was a fundamental reform of policing in Northern Ireland so that people in nationalist areas could join the police service, become part of it, defend it and create an ethos of support for policing in the communities it would serve. That is the only way policing will work in a deeply divided society like the North.

At the same time, behind fair policing we need a just and even-handed system of law. At its worst the failure of policing and the law during the Northern Troubles was leading to murderous excesses like the involvement of policemen and UDR men in paramilitary killing squads like the Glenanne gang. Martin Luther King once described as a myth the argument that great problems cannot be solved by legislation, because 'You've got to change the heart and you can't change the heart through legislation.' He said this was a half-truth, and continued:

> Certainly if the problem is to be solved in the final sense, hearts must be changed. Religion and education must play a great role in changing the heart. But we must go on to say that while it may be true that morality cannot be legislated, behaviour can be regulated. It may be true that the law cannot change the heart, but it can restrain the heartless. It may be true that the law cannot make a man love me, but it can keep him from lynching me – and I think that is pretty important also.

I remember in a speech in the House of Commons in 1986 supporting Nicholas Scott, one of the more thoughtful Northern Ireland ministers we have had, for saying that 'repressive policies, without regard to moderation, civilization and restraint, could actually feed terrorism'. How right he was. He put his finger

---

3. *Ibid*, 14.

on the classic Northern Irish dilemma. In the ninety years between the state being formed and the return of justice and policing powers to the Stormont Executive in 2010, there was never a period when we did not have derogation from normal standards of justice. We have always had repressive emergency legislation. That gave a potent propaganda weapon to the men of violence, which they used successfully, and it alienated large sections of the community, especially young people. As a result, confidence in and respect for the law diminished to a frightening degree.

I gave the example of internment without trial as the most serious derogation in any democratic society. I pointed out that it had been used in Northern Ireland in every decade since the 1920s, but it had never defeated violence. It had fuelled it, recruited for it and passed on the ethic and subculture of violence to future generations. One former IRA commander, Jim McVeigh, has called it 'among the best recruiting tools the IRA ever had'.

The panoply of new emergency legislation and measures brought in during the Troubles period only exacerbated the problem: the Emergency Provisions Act, which set up the Diplock courts so that terrorist offences would be tried by a single judge without a jury; the Prevention of Terrorism Act, with its power to exclude Northern Irish people from Britain; the RUC 'holding centres' in Castlereagh, Armagh and Derry, whose lack of safeguards to protect those being questioned inevitably led to them being abused and beaten; the use of the 'supergrass' evidence of informers, which led in the 1980s to mass acquittals as judges decided this kind of dubious evidence was undermining the court system itself.

Amazingly, as late as 1994, Secretary of State Sir Patrick Mayhew was proposing to 'identify the policing priorities of the people of Northern Ireland through an expanded network of Police Liaison Committees'. That he should embark on this futile exercise a decade after the dire warnings contained in the New Ireland Forum Report and less than a year after the Downing Street Declaration had publicly launched the Northern Ireland peace process, indicates clearly how far removed he and his government were from the fundamental questions that were at the heart of the policing problem in Northern Ireland.

As we debated the policing issue at SDLP conferences through the late 1970s, 80s and early 90s, it became clear that there were some in our party who did not agree that we should seek deep and fundamental reform, but were open to encouraging young Catholics to join the RUC if there were small cosmetic changes such as giving the weak Police Authority some extra powers.

I tried to persuade them that it was not as simple as that, because for nationalists to support the police, and to encourage young nationalists to join it, would be the granting of allegiance for the first time since the foundation of the unionist state to a system of policing with which they could identify politically and culturally. Given the RUC's treatment of the nationalist community over many decades, the whole ethos, structure, composition and identity of the force needed to be overhauled. This would have to lead to a radically new situation in which for the first time people from the two communities would be joining a police service with an equal sense of pride, and with no censure (or worse) from their own community. It would mean young men and women serving and protecting the whole community in Northern Ireland as a trusted and valued part of it, and in turn being protected by that whole community. It would mean the active involvement of nationalists, alongside unionists, in policing in a way that had not been possible since the foundation of the state.

I recognize that there have been equally daunting challenges facing the unionist community, especially since the replacement of the RUC by the reformed Police Service of Northern Ireland in the early 2000s. The deep emotional bond that was felt by many unionists for a police force they saw as their defenders, and which had been ruthlessly attacked by republican paramilitaries, had to expand generously to include the entire community. The historic and symbolic legacy that had wedded policing almost exclusively to the unionist perspective had to give way to a new human rights-based ethos, with which the entire community could identify. No section of the community in any healthy society can regard policing as its own.

This has been a stern task for all of us. But it has turned out to be – after fierce lobbying by the SDLP, among others, to make sure that the recommendations of the Patten Commission were implemented in full – one of the real success stories of the peace process. As soon as I read the Patten Report I knew this could be the template for the kind of policing system I had been seeking for nearly thirty years. It was a real moment of truth for me after such a long and difficult struggle. In the event, the setting up and performance of the Police Service of Northern Ireland (PSNI) has led to a lasting system of even-handed policing, which can become a template for other places in the world trying to deal with the problem of policing their own divided societies. All through the tough political talks in the late 1990s and early 2000s, I always insisted that such equal and impartial policing was essential for the stability of any political solution in Northern Ireland. It is striking that even with the collapse of the Northern institutions in January 2017, the nationalist community in particular has continued, by and large, to have confidence in the rule of law in a way that was never there before. The radically reformed policing system has helped to stabilize Northern Ireland; I hope at least some unionists can see that.

The Good Friday Agreement had pledged to provide 'the opportunity for a new beginning to policing in Northern Ireland with a police service capable of attracting and sustaining support from the community as a whole'. It set up an independent commission chaired by the former Governor of Hong Kong, Chris Patten, which reported in September 1999. Patten's 175 recommendations were wide-ranging and essentially required the establishment of an entirely new, human rights-based police service accountable to an independent Policing Board, answerable to an independent Police Ombudsman, and with a target of 50 per cent of its recruits coming from the Catholic community. Compare this with the figures for the RUC, which had 21 per cent Catholics in its ranks in 1923, 11 per cent in 1969 and a miserable 7.5 per cent in 1998.

However, when the Police (Northern Ireland) Bill was first published by the British government in the spring of 2000, we identified countless defects in it. The main author of these was the new Secretary of State, Peter Mandelson, who appeared to be trying to put together a compromise between the Patten Report and unionist demands that there should be as little change as possible. I pointed out that Patten was already a compromise: it proposed a policing system that was neither unionist nor nationalist but which served the whole community. I said in the House of Commons during the Bill's Second Reading debate, aiming my remarks at Mandelson, that the 'clever way' to deal with Patten was that 'one espouses it, and then emasculates, diminishes and reduces it from what it was intended to do'. I was like a cracked record repeating that if the crucial policing issue in the North was not properly addressed, there would not be a worthwhile or lasting political settlement here.

I said that if we got this legislation right, I would go into the hardest areas of Northern Ireland – those traditionally most bitterly opposed to the RUC – and ask people to join the new police service; but only if we got the legislation right. I quoted Patten, a former Conservative Cabinet minister, emphasizing his simple message that if you wanted to get young Catholics, as well as young Protestants, to join the new police service, then that service 'can't be identified with the central political argument in Northern Ireland'. Along with my SDLP colleague Alex Attwood and legal adviser Brian Barrington, I worked long hours, in between my responsibilities as Deputy First Minister, to prepare amendments and lobby Peter Mandelson to ensure that this defective Bill would be changed so that it fully and faithfully reflected the Patten Commission's recommendations. For his part

Mandelson, an enormously arrogant man, put great pressure on both me and the SDLP to recognize the new police before the legislation was satisfactory, accusing us of indulging in the 'politics of boycott'.

In the end my SDLP colleagues John Hume, Eddie McGrady and I put down over a hundred amendments as the legislation passed through the House of Commons. We insisted that for all its operational purposes, including all its interactions with the public, the new body's title should be the Police Service of Northern Ireland, with no reference to the old RUC. We safeguarded the independence and wide-ranging powers of the new Policing Board. We strongly supported Patten's recommendation that the new police badge and flag should contain the symbols of neither the British nor the Irish state. When the Policing Board eventually chose that badge, it featured a range of small British, Irish and Northern Irish symbols in perfect symmetry. We equally endorsed Patten's recommendation that the Union flag should no longer be flown from police buildings.

We demanded that the powers of the Secretary of State and the Chief Constable to block inquiries initiated by the Policing Board should be removed, including inquiries into past abuses (although the Secretary of State's continuing powers in this latter area remain a matter of concern). We ensured that the protection of human rights would be at the heart of the new policing dispensation and that community policing would be a core function of the new service. We obtained a guarantee that the new Police Ombudsman could investigate police policies, practices and past abuses as well as individual complaints. We safeguarded the 50/50 Catholic/Protestant recruitment policy proposed by Patten for more than ten years. We pressured the government to make sure that the Special Branch – which had for so long been a law to itself, refusing to share its information with other branches and running informers who were paramilitary killers – should cease to operate as a separate force within a force and would be incorporated into the wider police service. Other amendments covered an indicative date for ending the full-time police reserve; secondments of senior officers from An Garda Síochána; and closing the RUC holding centres in Castlereagh, Derry and Gough Barracks in Armagh.

One could argue that two of the most important elements in this huge programme of police reform were in train even before the legislation to implement the Patten Report was on the statute book. A 1997 report by the distinguished Northern Irish civil servant Maurice Hayes had recommended the setting up of a completely independent Police Ombudsman. In conversations with Hayes I had emphasized the need for this office to have the power to investigate every single complaint against the RUC, big or small.

The first person in this post was the redoubtable Nuala O'Loan, whose fear-lessness and strong sense of morality led to her harsh indictment of the RUC's performance in first failing to prevent and then investigating the 1998 Omagh bombing, which she said showed 'defective leadership, poor judgement and lack of urgency', and was particularly damning of the Special Branch. Her report, published in 2001, was one of the first big signs that policing in Northern Ireland would never be the same again. The appointment of Hugh Orde, the man who had been investigating RUC collusion with loyalist killings, as PSNI Chief Constable in 2002, was another.

The Patten Report's most single important innovation was probably the Oversight Commissioner. This was to be an independent and authoritative outsider, a key figure who would be responsible for supervising the implementation of Patten's recommendations. We fought hard to secure the very significant powers and independence of this new office in law. The first Oversight Commissioner was an American, Tom Constantine, former director of US drug enforcement and chief of police of New York State. In his annual reports Constantine would feature in large type his opinion that the proposed reforms in Northern Ireland policing were the 'most complex and dramatic' ever attempted in a police force in a modern democratic society.

As the Committee stage of the Police Bill proceeded in the House of Commons, the junior minister who was presenting the government's position, Adam Ingram, stated on a number of occasions that some of our key amend-ments would be dealt with when the Bill returned to the Report Stage on the floor of the Commons, as is often the practice in the UK Parliament.

In May 2000 I was worried enough to decide to take matters into my own hands by paying an unannounced visit to Tony Blair at his Chequers residence on a Sunday morning. I'll never forget that visit: it was an astonishingly beautiful place with marvellous gardens. Tony was all smiles and offered me champagne, which I declined. I said: 'I just want to tell you that your man Mandelson is putting the resolution of the policing problem into serious jeopardy. He is scuppering any chance of creating a new and fair policing order in the North of Ireland that everybody could support and defend.' Unless there were wide-ranging changes in the legislation, I told him, the SDLP would not be supporting the new policing service nor taking its place on the new Policing Board.

When the legislation came back to the Commons in July, I got the distinct impression that something was afoot. When I entered the Chamber there were huddles on the government benches as Peter Mandelson rose to speak. There was an uneasy hush about the place as he announced that a 'guillotine motion' would apply at the Report Stage of the Northern Ireland Police Bill because of shortage of time. This meant all our amendments that were referred from the Standing Committee would fall without debate. This, to put it mildly, was sharp practice. I suspected the source of it was a meeting Mandelson and Blair had held with the Ulster Unionists that morning. In my speech that day I denounced Mandelson's 'political chicanery' and said what had happened in the House of Commons had done 'irreparable damage to the prospect of a new policing dispensation'.

My message took some time to hit home. It took the appointment of a new Secretary of State, John Reid, and another crisis conference. In July of the following year the British and Irish governments and all the Northern parties met again at Weston Park, another beautiful period mansion in Shropshire, to try to find a way to resolve the two big obstacles – policing for the nationalists, decommissioning for the unionists – that were blocking progress. It was at Weston Park that much of the Mandelson version of the policing legislation was rolled back so as to remain more faithful to the Patten recommendations. A senior Irish civil servant told me that at a Weston Park breakfast with the two prime ministers, Tony Blair asked him about one particular clause of the Patten Report that the Irish official was insisting should go into the legislation in its original form. When the clause was pointed out to him, Blair turned to the senior Northern Ireland Office man present and said: 'It's in Patten. Just do it.'

Two years later the government finally brought in the Police (Northern Ireland) Act 2003. It was a good if belated experience to see that law go through the Commons because we already had all the amendments ready to go from the previous Bill. If I had to point to one very hard-won achievement in my nineteen years in the House of Commons, I would point to that.

I would also like to pay tribute again to the Ulster Unionist Party. I know they felt deeply hurt at the way the RUC ended, and at the failure of their efforts to keep its name in some form in the title deeds of the new police service. Yet they have conscientiously worked alongside nationalists on the new Policing Board. There were many rows, but they never walked out. They accepted that if you want to build a civilized society, the one thing you do not mess with is the rule of law.

At Weston Park, Blair gave his word to the SDLP that if an international judge appointed by the British government recommended a public inquiry into the killings of the loyalist leader Billy Wright, the nationalist solicitor Rosemary Nelson, the innocent Portadown Catholic Robert Hamill and the nationalist solicitor Pat Finucane, such inquires would be held. That promise was not fully kept. After a report by the distinguished Canadian judge Peter Cory, public inquiries were held in the cases of the first three of these. But there has never been a public inquiry into the savage killing in front of his family of Pat Finucane by the Ulster Freedom Fighters in February 1989. I took a particular interest in the Finucane case, having warned a month earlier in the Commons that an unforgivable statement by Home Office minister Douglas Hogg that some solicitors in Northern Ireland were 'unduly sympathetic' to the IRA meant that they would become targets for assassination and, if that happened, the responsibility would lie with the minister and the British government.

Judge Cory said he had seen 'strong evidence' of collusion by the British army's undercover Force Research Unit (FRU), the RUC Special Branch and MI5 in Finucane's killing, but the question of the security forces having advance knowledge of the attack could only be resolved through a public inquiry. His opinion was supported by former Metropolitan Police commander Sir John Stevens, who in his investigation of the Finucane case said the solicitor's murder could have been prevented if the security forces had not been involved in collusion. He defined collusion as wilful failure to keep records, withholding of evidence and intelligence, and the involvement of intelligence agents in murder. Tony Blair once said to me at a meeting in 10 Downing Street: 'You know we can't have an inquiry into the Finucane case – it stinks.' Some years later his successor David Cameron admitted that there were 'frankly shocking levels of state collusion' in Pat Finucane's murder.

The foul smell from the Finucane killing did not prevent the Blair government changing the law so that the rules governing the very limited inquiry that was held ensured that the Secretary of State would be allowed to decide what information should be provided to it, and that any important evidence would be heard in private. Judge Cory made clear his serious reservations about this inquiry, which was largely a review of the paperwork relating to the case: 'I don't know how any self-respecting Canadian judge would be part of it in light of the restrictions on independence it would impose.' Lord Saville, the Appeal Court judge who headed the public inquiry into the 1972 Bloody Sunday killings by the British army, agreed: 'As a judge, I must tell you that I would not be prepared to be appointed as a member of an inquiry that was subject to a provision of this kind.' The shamefully inadequate inquiry into Pat Finucane's killing was only the latest example of what happens when policing becomes an agent for the protection of the state rather than the primary means of upholding the law.

The nationalist community's lack of confidence in the courts was another huge issue. I believe the single-judge Diplock court system in Northern Ireland was an unacceptable affront to the highest British legal standards and traditions, regardless of the argument that they were needed because juries might be intimidated by paramilitaries and their allies. Yet this serious derogation from normal, democratic legal standards became entirely normal in that abnormal society. I asked the question repeatedly in the House of Commons: In the absence of juries, do Diplock courts give the optimum protection possible to the accused?

Once again the problem was that many people in London and Belfast saw the law and the courts as state law and state courts, whose priority was to defend the state rather than protect the individual, particularly against the backdrop of the various pieces of draconian emergency legislation that had already substantially diminished the rights of the individual. I told the Commons that in a divided society overburdened with prejudice it was vital that the court structures and practices should be above reproach, a beacon of rectitude shining into all sections of society. Three-judge courts on the Irish model were the least that we asked for. On this issue there was unusual cross-party agreement, including the DUP and the government's own largely toothless Standing Advisory Commission on Human Rights. But such unanimity had little or no effect on government policy.

Viscount Colville – a judge whose family has sat in the House of Lords since the seventeenth century – reported to Parliament on the effects of the Emergency Provisions Act and the Prevention of Terrorism Act in 1987 and 1990. He advised us 'not to query the philosophy behind the legislation'. I believe that he was wrong, very wrong indeed. It was imperative that this be done, so that the recurring recourse to repressive legislation to govern Northern Ireland could be seen in its vital historical context, going back to the Special Powers Act and the Irish Coercion Acts of the nineteenth century. The House of Lords was told that there had been eighty-seven Coercion Acts in Ireland between 1801 and 1887, a rate of one per year.

Each and every one of these pieces of legislation is based on a false premise: that if you bend the law to enforce the law, you increase its efficiency. Perhaps the most striking example of this is the way in which the use of uncorroborated 'supergrass' evidence almost destroyed confidence in the judicial process in the 1980s. Equally spurious is the notion that repressive legislation will bring peace. For many years the arbitrary use of powers to stop, search and arrest, forced young people in the North of Ireland into, at best, disillusionment with the justice system and, at worst, membership of violent organizations. The notion that punitive action in the courts, the police station, on the roads or in the home, will create stability, is patently erroneous.

There have been significant improvements since the Good Friday Agreement in the administration of justice in Northern Ireland. Judges are now appointed by an independent Judicial Appointments Commission; until the collapse of the Executive in January 2017, senior judges had to be appointed by the Prime Minister on the recommendation of the First and Deputy First Ministers acting jointly; the courts must have 'due regard' to international human rights conventions; and the Director of Public Prosecutions must refer to the Police Ombudsman any cases of alleged police misconduct discovered in his or her work.

There are now more judges from the Catholic community: for example the Lord Chief Justice, Declan Morgan, is a Catholic from Derry. Seamus Treacy, once a young, left-wing barrister, is a Lord Justice of Appeal and was the judge in the 2017 Glenanne relatives case. He was one of the barristers who successfully challenged a ruling that barristers in Northern Ireland must swear allegiance to the Queen. In the old days Catholic QCs did not want to become judges; they might be killed if they did. Another reason was that they were making too much money, while for many of them it was more about not wanting to be identified with the Northern Ireland state in that way.

Judges in Northern Ireland have now asserted themselves. They do not see themselves as having to protect the backs of rogue policemen in the service of a corrupt state. We saw, for example, High Court judge Bernard McCloskey standing down recently to allow the families of the six men killed by loyalists in Loughinisland, County Down, in 1994 to put their case to a different judge. He had been accused by their lawyers of bias after saying that a Police Ombudsman's report alleging collusion between the killers and the police had gone beyond its statutory powers.

The young Margeret Thatcher said back in 1964: 'Any country or government that wants to proceed towards tyranny starts to undermine legal rights and starts to undermine the law.' Ten years later, she said: 'You cannot have liberty without a just law impartially administered. You will not have political liberty for very long if all power went to the state.' That was the same Margaret Thatcher who was leader of a government that for many years turned a blind eye towards the collusion of some in the British army, the RUC and the UDR with loyalist terrorist organizations who had killed hundreds of people. I hope the British have learned the lessons of thirty years of the Northern Ireland Troubles and several hundred years of trying unsuccessfully to coerce Ireland. It is only through justice that we can create peace, and peace is the only firm foundation upon which a lasting solution can be found.

11. *My Catholicism*

I am sometimes called a Catholic nationalist politician, so perhaps I should explain what my Catholicism means to me. My Catholic faith is something that I go to when I am in difficulty. It is not the main basis of my religious belief, more the manifestation of it. I was reared in the Catholic tradition; I served Mass for years as a youngster. I have had my times of doubt, but those doubts were intellectual doubts: how can you apply logic to various aspects of Catholic doctrine, and above all what comes after life ends.

To put it in its simplest terms, even in my worst times of doubt I could find nothing better. As a human being, I need the concept of a God. To use an almost forgotten word, I still have that 'numinous' sense of awe: a religious or spiritual feeling indicating the presence of God, which many believe the Catholic Church is losing. I also find that the longer I live the more I have a strong need for communal worship. I think there is much more power if you are praying in a chapel or church with other people.

Do I see the Roman Catholic Church as the one true Church? Again, if I had to start from scratch, it would be the one I would choose. That said, I often say to my Protestant friends and neighbours here in Markethill: think about it – we worship the same Christian God. You do it very slightly differently. It is remarkable that some of them still disagree with that statement. A lot of them have a different concept of God as a stern, forbidding Calvinist personage.

My relationship with my God through the Catholic Church was cemented during my wife Gertrude's long and terminal illness. It was then we both came to realize the deep human need for the love and help of the Supreme Being whom we call Jesus Christ.

The difficulties that the Catholic Church is going through now, notably the whole question of clerical child abuse, are simply making clearer things that were going wrong for a long time. People are surprised about it, but I don't know why. Priests and nuns have been running schools for nearly two hundred years in this country, although schools were no place for them. Power and prestige were what motivated many clerical people in positions of authority, and, as the English Catholic historian Lord Acton reminds us, power in human hands is always a major instrument of corruption in human institutions. The great power the Catholic Church had in Ireland for a long time was no way of ensuring that the faith of the people was nurtured.

Then there was the way in which very young men were put into seminaries and kept there away from their peers and the opposite sex. Few priests going into schools as teachers had any vocation, preparation or training. After six or seven years in a seminary they were thrown into a role, willingly or not, for which they had little or no aptitude. From there they progressed into a parish where they had little or no communication with the people – men, women and children – on a human level, and they simply had no idea of how to live in that context. A major part of the problem was the authoritarianism that came from that system, and particularly the authoritarian way they ran education.

My father, who graduated as a teacher from St Patrick's College Drumcondra in 1917, was one of the generation who then came up against what I would call the maladministration of the schools by the Church. The parish priest had absolute control: he hired you and fired you. He might demand that a new young woman teacher took the church choir, whatever her musical ability or lack of it, as a condition for teaching in his school. There was a case where my father and other teachers – who were members of the recently formed local branch of the Irish National Teachers Organization – took up the case of a woman who was sacked from her job in a school outside Newry by the parish priest. The union paid her salary until she died. But all the men involved in that case were refused promotion, including my father. So while he was a very conscientious Catholic, he had that experience burning within him, and did not think much of many clergymen as a result.

So I often say I am a Catholic despite everything; not because of things that happened, but despite things that happened. Thus I am a Catholic despite the lust for power and the exercise of that power by the men who used to run the Church, the likes of the former Archbishop of Dublin John Charles McQuaid and others who were much more subtle about it.

As I get older I often think about the hereafter and I can't impose any logic on it. Yet I cannot think of any other religious creed that could give me a better read than I have, which is no read at all! If I had a blank sheet, I would start again on the same Catholic page.

My Catholicism is also very much part of the Catholicism of the North of Ireland and of County Armagh, which, for want of better words, was defensive and beleagured, with many grievances. This is the strangeness of it: people here were politically disadvantaged because of the religion they had. Catholicism, as the religion of the native Irish, who were driven off their lands and treated as second-class citizens by the incoming Protestants, was part of what welded together a culture here. It was thus a part of the long-standing historical problem at the heart of this place in the sense that in Northern Ireland Catholic usually equals nationalist and Protestant equals unionist.

These clashing religio-political identifications, which must seem so strange to many people in secular Western Europe in the second decade of the twenty-first century, go back at least to the invading English Protestants fighting the native Catholic Irish in the Cromwellian wars of the 1640s. The most notorious incident of those wars in this area was the 1641 massacre by dispossessed Irish Catholic rebels of more than a hundred English Protestant settlers, drowned or shot in the river Bann in Portadown. So for historical reasons my Catholicism is politically orientated: not through any choice of mine, but because that was the way things were here and that's what I grew up knowing. That was particularly so in Armagh. It was a question of clinging together at all times and sometimes at all costs because of the nature of the enmity there was for us in British, Protestant Northern Ireland and of which we would have seen ourselves as the victims.

During the worst days of the Troubles, with the Kingsmill massacre, the murder of innocent people like the Reavey brothers and the deadly activities of the Glenanne gang, you could genuinely say there was a stench of evil about this place. It was there in the contrast between Sadie Reavey's face, the face of hope and goodness, and the 35 bullet marks on the walls of her living room. During those years I did sometimes doubt the existence of a benevolent God in the sense that I wondered why these things were allowed to happen. On the other hand, one of the things I marvelled at – and still do – was the way in which people who were bereaved in such grievous ways were able to be so Christian, so generous and forgiving. The goodness and gentleness of that more than compensated for the evil that was roaming this country.

Jimmy and Sadie Reavey were an example for me of a truly forgiving Christian family. The day after their three innocent young sons were mowed down in their home by a loyalist gang that included RUC men, Jimmy was on the radio pleading for no retaliation. In the bitterest of ironies, at the very moment he was issuing his plea, the Provisional IRA were massacring ten innocent Protestant workmen at Kingsmill, less than a mile away.

Sadie was a great person in the community, involved in every community organization in that area. A rare Catholic member of the overwhelmingly Protestant local Women's Institute, she stopped going only after she felt she was not getting the support of her fellow members following the murder of her sons. That ordinary woman, who had lost her children in appalling circumstances, was able not just to think and say forgiveness but to act it. Alan Black, the sole survivor of the Kingsmill massacre, spoke recently on RTÉ about how Sadie had appeared on his doorstep the following Christmas with gifts for his children. He called her 'a saintly woman'.

Jimmy and Sadie's fourth son, Eugene, is one of my best friends and another example of a genuinely good man who has been through a living hell. Eugene, like the rest of his family, is a devout Catholic. At the time of the murder of his brothers he was a poultry adviser visiting local farms. Among those he visited was James Mitchell's farm at Glenanne. He was always on the go, talking to people; he loved nothing more than a good scrap on a football field, and was always active in the community, as were all his family.

In the weeks after his brothers' funerals, Eugene was harassed horribly by the security forces. On his first day back at work three weeks after the murders, he was stopped by a British army patrol on a bridge across a river two hundred yards from his house. He was pulled out of his car and the car ransacked. The officer demanded again and again: 'Who shot the people at Kingsmill?' When Eugene repeatedly said he did not know, the soldiers dragged him into the river. It was early February, bitterly cold and the river was in spate. He was forced to his knees on the river bed so that the water was up to his chin. The officer put a gun to his head and pulled the trigger five times; five times it clicked on an empty chamber. Eugene believed he was about to die. That terrifying ordeal happened on four mornings of his first week back at work.

Eugene was a lost soul for a while after that. He estimates that his harassment by the security forces went on for twenty years. On another occasion his brand new car was torn apart, with the seats and wheels thrown into a ditch. Once he lost his composure after a UDR man struck him in the side with his rifle and punched the man on the jaw, leading to a serious beating in the Land Rover on the way to the local Bessbrook RUC station. When he complained to the police they just laughed at him. Letters of complaint to the RUC Chief Constable led to further harassment, including death threats, at UDR roadblocks.

A Protestant businessman who Eugene worked with told him there was a 'very bad whispering campaign about your boys'. On the instructions of a named senior RUC officer, he said policemen at roadblocks were telling local Protestants that the Reavey brothers had been in the IRA, but had refused to kill UDR and RUC men, and for that they had been executed by the organization.

In 1999, twenty-three years after the attack on the Reaveys, Ian Paisley used parliamentary privilege and a false RUC dossier to make the horrific accusation in the House of Commons that Eugene had been involved in the Kingsmill massacre. I wasn't in the chamber on that day. I tried to raise it the next day, but the Speaker would not allow it. I demanded in public that Paisley withdraw his outrageous allegation, pointing out that both the RUC Chief Constable and his Protestant neighbours had said unequivocally that Eugene Reavey was an innocent man. He refused to apologize.

Eugene took that very badly. He told me that a few days later he was at a cattle sale and men he had known all his life turned their backs on him. It took a huge toll on him and his family: they believed if it had not been for the fact that the paramilitaries were on ceasefire at the time, their lives would have been in serious danger. Years later, after the Historical Enquiries Team confirmed that no member of the Reavey family had ever had any paramilitary connection, the police issued an apology for the way they had been treated. Yet still there was no apology from Paisley, despite Eugene publicly asking him for one. When Paisley was being lauded as a man of God, and later as a man of peace, I never forgot that particular vile slander of an innocent man who could not answer back.

Eugene and Majella O'Hare's brother Michael were close friends and they certainly had family tragedy and heartbreak in common. I spoke recently at a meeting in the Irish Centre in Hammersmith with Eugene and Michael. Everyone present was inspired by Michael's Christian compassion and forgiveness as he spoke quietly and with great dignity about his family's agony at the loss of 'lovely little Majella'. The meeting was chaired by the leading English TV journalist, Jon Snow, a man who has always cared about what was happening in

Ireland in a most objective yet compassionate way, and who said he had never been so emotionally affected in all his years of covering war and conflict.

In 2014 Eugene, Michael O'Hare and Stephen Travers, who had survived the Miami Showband murders in 1975 (another attack believed to have been carried out by the Glenanne gang), set up the Truth and Reconciliation Platform to work for post-conflict reconciliation and to seek the truth behind the murder of their loved ones. Others who became involved included Alan McBride, whose wife was killed in the IRA's 1993 Shankill Road bombing, and Joe Campbell, who believes his father, a Catholic RUC officer, was killed by the notorious loyalist killer Robin Jackson with security force collusion. Eugene now speaks frequently about his experience at Truth and Reconciliation Platform meetings; organizes meetings between Protestants and Catholics in south Armagh, and takes local farmers from both sides to meet government officials in Dublin. I have chaired a number of the meetings he has addressed, and he speaks with a powerful sense of sorrow and fortitude about the things he has lived through. But there is absolutely no bitterness in him.

I sometimes ask myself rhetorically who was the better Christian: Ian Paisley or Eugene Reavey? The answer is not difficult. On the one side there was the hate-mongering politician and preacher, using parliamentary immunity to make an utterly unsubstantiated, life-threatening and character-destroying accusation against an innocent man, and then refusing to withdraw and apologize for it when the evidence of his innocence was produced. On the other is that deeply wronged man, who now devotes much of his time to actively working for peace and reconciliation between Protestants and Catholics.

Another example of Christian goodness in the midst of evil was the response to the INLA's attack on the Darkley Gospel Hall near Keady in November 1983, when three worshippers were shot dead in the hall's doorway and seven more wounded by machine-gun fire through its thin wooden walls during their Sunday evening service. In the words of the *Irish Times* report: 'The Monaghan border curves less than two miles away. With all its lights blazing the little hall stood out on the hill, the easiest of easy targets.' The leaders of the four main churches described this attack on a sixty-strong congregation largely made up of farming families as 'an act of sectarian slaughter on a worshipping community which goes beyond any previous deed of violence'.

I knew the pastor, Bob Bain. I went up to the house of one of the three men killed. It was like something out of Arthur Miller's *The Crucible*, the hallelujahs, the simple pentecostalist prayers, the old-fashioned costumes, the quaintness of the people. Ultimately it was their way of Christianity that impressed me: we all think we have the best way of worshipping God, but there is no best way. I was attracted by their simple godly worship, utterly without affectation. I was asked by Pastor Bain to say a prayer and I made one up, basing it on the 'Our Father'. It was their utter defencelessness that was the most pitiful thing: they were in their hall praying and singing 'Are you washed in the blood of the Lamb?' when the gunmen came out of the dark and attacked them in their little hall on that winter evening.

When he was walking along the border a few years later, the novelist Colm Tóibín was greatly taken with Bob Bain's charm, resilience and independence of spirit; out of his experience of terrorism had come 'a shining grace'. Tóibín wrote that it was terrible he had not met an old-fashioned, 'born-again' preacher like Pastor Bain before:

> It was one of those moments when the partition of Ireland seemed to me immensely sad: my community in the South had been deprived of the presence of men like Bob Bain as a living, vibrant, fully accepted part of our religious and civic life. We could have been nourished by the sheer difference.

12. *Northern Ireland as Our Shared Home Place*

The new Article Three of the Irish Constitution, incorporated into the Good Friday Agreement and approved overwhelmingly by the Irish electorate in the May 1998 referendum, says:

> It is the firm will of the Irish nation, in harmony and friendship, to unite all the people who share the territory of the island of Ireland, in all the diversity of their identities and traditions, recognizing that a united Ireland shall be brought about only by peaceful means with the consent of the majority of people, democratically expressed, in both jurisdictions in the island.

There is a long and noble tradition of using peaceful, democratic means to bring about progressive change in Ireland: from O'Connell through Parnell to the Good Friday Agreement. In stark contrast, one of the most corrosive consequences of the troubled history of this island has been that the use of violence became legitimized and acceptable as a means of asserting and imposing our different identities, English and Gaelic, Protestant and Catholic, unionist and nationalist. This resort to violence for political ends, whether to achieve Irish national independence or to resist it in the cause of maintaining British supremacy, has been used time and time again over many centuries. Even the

Protestant father of physical force Irish republicanism, Wolfe Tone, recognized that the means to reach the end of breaking the connection with England and achieving Irish independence was 'to unite the whole people of Ireland, to abolish the memory of past dissensions, and to substitute the common name of Irishman in place of the denominations of Protestant, Catholic and Dissenter'. I believe it is time to rediscover the latter part of this much-quoted maxim in order finally to start persuading our Northern brothers and sisters to join us in a truly united Irish nation.

It is a universal lesson that political violence obliterates not only its victims, but all possibility of rational discourse about future political options. It shuts down any possibility of rational debate, in some cases for generations. Whatever political point a person is making before he kills his opponent, that argument is utterly lost once he commits that murderous act. After it the family and friends of the dead person will tell those behind the killing of their loved one that all their arguments have come to naught with that act; if they were not anathema before, they are now. They want nothing to do with those people or their arguments; they want either justice or revenge. And so, with the notable exception of a few noble people like Gordon Wilson, it has been in Northern Ireland.

The reverse also applies: twenty-one years of largely sustained peace in Northern Ireland since the Good Friday Agreement is an enabling element that was not there before. Despite all the problems of the past two years – the Executive collapsing and repeated failures to put it back together – if you asked me whether I thought that major political violence in Northern Ireland has finished, I would say I do, at least for the present and the foreseeable future. I would also caution, however, that violence loves a vacuum. The first key imperative of political leadership today, both nationalist and unionist, is to ensure that whatever else happens, there must never be a return to violence as a political weapon. If violence is now at an end, the second key imperative for nationalists is to address how we accommodate and reach agreement with unionists to live together on this island. That is now the real search for peace, justice and stability in Ireland.

In Northern Ireland there is a fault line running through our society and our politics that is deep and wide and continues to threaten us now and into the future. This fault line is no accident of history. From the 1600s onward the two communities in the North were deliberately set in enmity against each other by the English colonizers. English monarchical and government policies decided whose property would be taken from them, and to whom it would be granted; who would wield the military power, and therefore who would inevitably rise up against that power; who would rule and who would be oppressed. Two groups of people who were different in religion, in culture, in tradition and in political outlook being set against each other was the consequence of British policy right up to the suspension of the Stormont Parliament in 1972.

For the final fifty of those years, the task of ensuring who would have the power and who would be powerless was carried out by the unionist administration at Stormont. The structure and nature of that one-party government ensured that the relationship between the two communities in the North remained both dialectic and toxic, a zero-sum game: if one was up, therefore the other had to be down; if one was supremacist Protestant, the other was rebel Catholic; if one was ruling British, the other was revolutionary Irish.

The first real opportunity to begin to heal this deep fault line was the 1974 power-sharing experiment and the Sunningdale Agreement. Twenty-four years after that collapsed we had another opportunity with the Good Friday Agreement, using an even more complex form of consociational government between ancient enemies, based on the d'Hondt voting system. Consociationalism was developed in the 1960s by a Dutch political scientist, Arend Lijphart, to help stabilize communities that are divided along ethnic or religious lines by developing democracy through power-sharing initiatives.

Unlike Sunningdale, the Good Friday Agreement has proved itself sustainable at many levels, even if much remains to be done. Most importantly, it has been endorsed by the people of Ireland, North and South, and has provided the basis for a long-lasting peace. A key feature of the Agreement is the way it has set out a framework of principles, which can guide the way forward in all circumstances. The cornerstones of this framework are parity of esteem and unity by consent.

While the Agreement set out this framework of principles for the future, this does not mean that it is cast in stone. In the remaining chapters I want to explain why, twenty-one years on from 1998, I believe this is an appropriate moment to look at a further evolution of the Agreement, while remaining absolutely faithful to its core principles.

Why this moment? Firstly I think we are at a key juncture in the history of Ireland. We are marking the centenary of the events between 1914 and 1923, which shaped the creation of two jurisdictions on the island, and as we look back we can only be struck by the extent to which those events continue to have a profound impact on the lives of people in both jurisdictions. Secondly, the changing demographics in Northern Ireland have led to a situation where for the first time the Unionist parties are in a minority in the Stormont Assembly.

Thirdly, and most critically, has been the deeply destabilizing impact of Brexit, which, to reach for an unavoidable cliché, 'changes everything'. Or even if, at the end of the day, it does not change everything, it has certainly triggered an almighty flux in unionist–nationalist, North–South and Irish–British relations. One immediate result has been the suspension of the Northern Ireland institutions, which have not been functioning for over two years, with little sign of their early return. A stalemate has set in and nobody knows how we can begin to move forward again.

Many of the old certainties are now crumbling. A new reality may be beginning to take shape at a pace few of us foresaw even a short while ago: some kind of move towards Irish unity may be a possibility for the first time since partition (certainly a substantial section of Northern nationalists now believe this). For all the reasons just given, it becomes vital that we initiate a dialogue about that much hoped for – and much feared – outcome which is calm and reasoned and which, above all, ensures that we learn the lessons of British–Irish history, and avoid at all costs its traditional regression into violence. We must find an answer to the one fundamental question that all nationalists who care about the future of our country need to be asking: how do we ensure that a future united Ireland is a peaceful and agreed Ireland?

In other words, is it not incumbent on those of us who care about what that longed-for unity will look like to make sure that we do not consign the next century in Northern Ireland to a rerun of the last: with the two sides simply changing positions – nationalists in a majority in a 'united' Ireland and unionists the sullen, alienated and potentially violent minority?

My contribution to this critical conversation is based four-square on the Good Friday Agreement's core principles of parity of esteem and consent. My contention is that twenty-one years after that Agreement it is time to look again, in the very changed context prevailing today, at what these vital concepts mean for our generation and the next. I have always been keen on the idea that it is for each generation to write its own history. I believe it is now time for some new history to be written, building on the foundation stones of the 1998 Agreement while remaining true to its framework principles.

Most fundamentally, I think we need to look again at how we define the principles of consent and parity of esteem in so far as they affect the constitutional status of Northern Ireland. I have come increasingly to the view that the Good Friday Agreement metric of 50 per cent plus one for unity will not give us the kind of agreed Ireland we seek.

Put simply, we have to find some more inclusive and generous way to quantify consent so that it reflects true parity of esteem between the unionist and nationalist communities. In the Good Friday Agreement, the principle of consent had two manifestations. In the Agreement's constitutional section, the principle of consent, which defined whether Northern Ireland would remain part of the United Kingdom or become part of a united Ireland, was to be measured on the basis of a 50 per cent plus one vote of the people of Northern Ireland. The SDLP put a variation of this principle, calling it Parallel Consent, into the section of the Agreement dealing with the Northern Ireland Assembly, requiring that key decisions in that Assembly would require the support of parties representing *both* traditions. This was to protect nationalists from an inbuilt unionist majority, which might vote as a bloc to undermine their rights in a future Northern Ireland. Thus consent would be measured in a different way in the Assembly, where it would require a weighted majority of Members, than in a Border Poll, which would require a simple majority of the Northern electorate.

My question in these pages is whether this clause of the Good Friday Agreement, Parallel Consent in the Northern Ireland Assembly, could be extended across into the constitutional space and thus be used to protect unionists if a future Border Poll were to result in a narrow overall majority for a united Ireland, but without the consent of both traditions in the North. This is definitely an idea worth exploring and I begin to do this in the next chapter.

Sinn Féin would be happy with the barest of majorities. Gerry Adams wrote in 2017 that the Good Friday Agreement 'allows for Irish reunification in the context of a democratic vote: 50 per cent plus one. I believe we can secure a greater margin, but ultimately that will be for the electorate. That's what democracy is about.'[1]

I do not believe in the kind of 'democracy' that leads to conflict. If we have a 50 per cent plus one vote for unity, that is when the real problems for the whole island will begin. I believe there is a serious risk, based on the precedents of Irish history, that it could lead to a major resumption of violence, this time led by the loyalists. I believe Dublin and other Southern cities and towns would not escape that loyalist-led violence, which would be aimed at making the new all-Ireland solution unworkable, in the way the loyalist bombings of Dublin and Monaghan in May 1974 were aimed at making the Sunningdale Agreement unworkable. Will a narrow vote for unity lead to harmony and friendship, as laid down by the

1. Letters to the Editor, *The Irish Times,* 3 August 2017.

new Article Three of the Irish Constitution, between unionists and nationalists? I very much doubt it.

A Border Poll in the wrong circumstances could once again seriously undermine the democratic process. Again we have to learn from Northern Ireland's history. On many occasions in the fifty years of Stormont rule and the thirty years of the Troubles, nationalists boycotted elections and referendums. Led by the SDLP, they boycotted the last Border Poll on unity in 1973, thus rendering it meaningless. What is to stop the unionists doing the same? And what would the point be of a referendum then? It would be about as democratically meaningful as a vote in Stalin's Soviet Union or Mugabe's Zimbabwe.

Even assuming the unionists do not boycott such a Border Poll, and there is a narrow vote for unity, it is only then that the extremely difficult questions begin for nationalists. The complexity of moving towards Irish unity will not be solved by a Border Poll, but will only become evident after it. Is some kind of temporary joint authority between the British and Irish governments feasible to ensure that the government and administration of the North do not break down during a transitional period before unity? Will there be some kind of alternative staged process? What kind of parliamentary and community consultation, public-finance and public-service structures will be put in place both during and after that transitional phase? How will justice, law and order be guaranteed during the inevitable breakdown of law and order that too precipitate a transition will cause, with the danger that revived loyalist paramilitaries would violently resist it and revived republican paramilitaries seek to enforce it? What guarantees will be put in place so that the proud British identity of the unionists will be protected, cherished and incorporated into the institutions, ethos and symbols of the new state? What will be those unifying institutions and symbols? Would they work best on an all-island basis or in a new northern regional context? Will the constitutional arrangements involve some form of federalism or confederalism?

All those options have got to be looked at straight in the eye, honestly and courageously. They must be examined, discussed and negotiated in fine detail before any Border Poll can even be contemplated. Nationalists may decide that, given the huge uncertainties surrounding such a poll and its aftermath, it might be better to opt for something close to but less than the total unity that they ultimately aspire to, but something they can live with, just as Sunningdale could have been and the Good Friday Agreement was until two years ago. Such a compromise may be necessary again if we want to live in a spirit of equality and friendship with our unionist neighbours. I believe that if nationalists cannot over a period of time persuade a significant number of unionists to accept an Irish unitary state, then that kind of unity is not an option, and we would once again have to find another constitutional arrangement short of that ideal.

There are two unionist vetoes in Northern Ireland, one legitimate, the other illegitimate. Unionists have a natural veto because they live on this island, it is their home, and their agreement is essential if unity is ever to be achieved. No matter how many people the Provisional IRA killed, that veto remained, and indeed was reinforced by such killings.

But historically unionists have also had a veto on British policy towards Ireland, and later Northern Ireland, which, for example, they exercised for many years in the second half of the twentieth century to prevent power-sharing between unionists and nationalists and a vital Irish dimension in the government of the North. They had no right to that veto whatsoever. All that was changed forever by the Anglo-Irish Agreement in 1985, which the British and Irish govern-ments negotiated between each other thus bypassing the unionist parties. That was a huge blow to the unionists because it showed for the first time that the British would go over their heads and involve the Irish government in the affairs of Northern Ireland for the common good of both communities. For the first time the British government was effectively taking the Irish government as its main partner in running this region, and largely discarding its previous partner-ship with the unionists. That was a huge break with the past, and the massive protests by the unionists against the Anglo-Irish Agreement, the largest since the Third Home Rule bill in 1912, showed they recognized that.

As the unionist MP for Armagh Harold McCusker said in a memorable speech in the House of Commons, by signing that Agreement, the British government had 'signed away my birthright'. Never again, he said, would he 'listen to people telling me that Northern Ireland is an integral part of the United Kingdom. We shall never hear those words. They will be removed from the political dictionary of Northern Ireland.'

The past has always been binary in Northern Ireland: one side had to be victorious and the other defeated. This mindset continues. Both sides have always believed in some kind of Darwinian struggle in which the strongest will ultimately prevail: whether through the might of British political and military power (much reduced these days); the dogged defensiveness of Ulster unionism; the capacity of Irish republicanism to struggle, endure and inflict; or the demographic reality of a growing Northern Catholic population.

This kind of zero-sum game never ends well. Its various versions have been tried, in Ireland as in other places around the world, and have left nothing behind but grief and suffering. Despite the ending of the 1968–98 Troubles, it has caused the fault line between Northern Irish people to become in some ways even deeper and wider. The sectarian 'sharing out' rather than genuine power-sharing practices of the DUP and Sinn Féin in recent years have only served to exacerbate this division.

True reconciliation, trust and mutual understanding – the only bases for a long-term peace on the island of Ireland – have eluded us in Northern Ireland since the hoped-for new dawn of the Good Friday Agreement. The DUP and Sinn Féin have failed even to start becoming parties of reconciliation; they remain parties of confrontation and triumphalism who believe in victory for their side. With total honesty and realism we now need to put away thoughts of victory and defeat and try, whatever our deep and historic perceptions of difference, to work as one shared community in a way that is fair, balanced and mutually respectful of the other.

The Good Friday Agreement, the miraculous accord that brought to an end thirty years of violence, has not yet bridged the fault line of bitterness, mistrust and suspicion between unionism and nationalism. That delicate political mechanism, so painstakingly conceived, debated and fashioned over seventeen years between 1993 and 2010 so as to be inclusive of all sectors of the community, has been misused to create instead two competing political silos, each looking after their own, with little regard for the concepts of equality, partnership and reconciliation that the 1998 Agreement required.

What we need now is an evolution of the principles of the Agreement. Nationalists need to recognize that for unionists Northern Ireland is their home place, which they share with us. We need to stop using pejorative terms like 'planters' and replace them with warm, meaningful words indicating recognition of our common home. There is a word in Turkish – *komshulak* – meaning 'common neighbourhood, neighbourliness, the spirit of being next door peacefully'. We need more words like that. We need to end the prejudicial nonsense of Northern nationalists talking about 'different kinds of Irish people', as if there were two classes: superior nationalists for whom *tiocfaidh ár lá,* and inferior unionists who are doomed to end up in the dustbin of history.

The Sinn Féin leader Gerry Adams does not appear to understand this. When he said at a Queen's University Belfast conference in April 2018 to mark the twentieth anniversary of the Good Friday Agreement that he would be sorry to be a unionist politician today, that it was 'a terrible position' to be in, he appeared to think he was reaching out to unionists. In fact he came across to unionists as saying: 'I feel sorry for you because your unionist position is illegitimate, with no validity, and would you ever just give up and accept the inevitability of Irish unity.' That is deeply hurtful and only confirms unionists in their certainty that they want nothing to do with any unity project motivated by such a philosophy.

Adams' and the republican leadership's close association with thirty years of IRA violence makes it even worse: it makes unionists believe that Sinn Féin aims to obliterate their tradition in Ireland. Irish republicanism needs a new, more open, more flexible leadership if we are to persuade some significant element of unionism of the merits of unity. We need a nationalism that is the diametric opposite of what Adams espouses: a sensitive and generous philosophy that allows unionists the space and time to put forward their arguments for the continuing union with Britain in a safe and respectful atmosphere. We need nationalist leaders who accept that Northern Ireland is in many ways different to other parts of Ireland and propose an agreed future for the region and for the island that recognizes this difference.

I see that difference. I accept that Armagh and Antrim and Derry are different to Galway and Kerry and Cork. I also recognize that the psyche of the present-day Republic of Ireland has changed considerably. My nationalist friends and neighbours in Armagh have a strong desire for reunification, even while acknowledging that they may have to postpone it for the present. They also have a strong sense of historical grievance because of the alienation of and injustice against their community that does not exist in Kilkenny or Killarney. And I do not see any strong signs of a commitment to Irish reunification in Kilkenny or Killarney.

Irish unity would have to be the genuine wish of not just a majority in Northern Ireland but of a majority of people in the Republic, many of whom will not want the kind of major legislative and social changes in their now settled and prosperous society that would be needed to satisfy unionists. After nearly a hundred years of independence, they have developed their own institutions, systems and ethoses. This may be another argument for some kind of federal or confederal solution in the future, with the North being largely governed by its own laws and traditions. I outline this as a possible option in the next chapter.

The challenge for me as a former nationalist leader is to persuade my fellow nationalists to recognize the differences between North and South and to start thinking about innovative future constitutional solutions that reflect those differences. Because of the rise of Sinn Féin, demographic change and the catastrophe of Brexit, there is a strong sense in the Catholic community in the North these days that nationalism is now on an unstoppable march towards unity. The threat of a post-Brexit hard border in a chaotic post-Brexit United Kingdom, despite 56 per cent of people in Northern Ireland having voted to stay in the EU, has confirmed them in this opinion. I would understand completely if they told me: 'Sorry, Seamus, but at this point we'll just let the clock run down to reunification. It's taken us a very long time to get to this final stretch on the long, hard road to unity, so we're not for moving now.'

So my most challenging conversation will be with Northern nationalism. If we cannot secure the consent of nationalists to put a generous proposition to unionists like the one I outline here, then we have no proposition to put to that community. It was F.W. de Klerk, the leader of the white community in South Africa during the transition to black majority rule, who said that during a peace process the most difficult negotiations are not with your adversary, but with your own side.

The core of the Northern Ireland dilemma is what happens now to the 900,000 Northern unionists for whom this place is home, and the dilemma is the same whether they remain a narrow majority in the North or become a signif-icant minority in the whole island. As John Hewitt, a socialist from a unionist background, wrote in his poem 'The Colony':

> For we have rights drawn from the soil and sky;
> The use, the pace, the patient years of labour,
> The rain against the lips, the changing light,
> The heavy clay-sucked stride have altered us;
> We would be strangers in the Capitol;
> This is our country also, nowhere else;
> And we shall not be outcast on the world.

Unionists have exactly the same right to call Northern Ireland, or the North of Ireland, their home place as nationalists.

Unionism and nationalism are also not homogeneous entities. Some union-ists, including descendants of the Presbyterians who formed the United Irishmen in the late eighteenth century, greatly value cross-community partnership, mutual understanding and reconciliation, and might one day, I believe, be open to the prospect of an 'agreed Ireland'. Remember that Northern Ireland's first Prime Minister, James Craig, said in 1921: 'In this island we cannot live always separated from one another. We are too small to be apart or for the border to be there for all time. The change will not come in my time but it will come.' And Edward

Carson said: 'There is no one in the world who will be more pleased to see an absolute unity in Ireland than I would.'

Unionist people need to be encouraged to find a way of accepting the complexity of their identity: Ulster unionists with British citizenship, but also Irish people for whom most British people do not have any feelings of solidarity or empathy. There are others who, like the fiercest critics of the 1985 Anglo-Irish Agreement, vow that they would rather 'eat grass' than even contemplate any form of relationship with the Republic of Ireland. I believe this absolute determination to have nothing to do with the rest of the people on this island would be weakened if life outside the European Union became fraught with difficulty.

Nationalism is also a broad church. Some cling to a hope of total victory over those who claim British allegiance. Thankfully, most regard unionists as their friends and neighbours, and as an integral part of life on the northern part of this island. Our joint challenge is to find a new definition of our common home place that embraces the two traditions as co-equals. In the words of the nineteenth-century Protestant nationalist Thomas Davis: 'May the time soon come when Irishmen of all creeds and classes, forgetting the bitter memories of the past, or, thinking of these, learn the wisdom of a better course, shall work together for the common good of our beloved land.'

I know that any acceptance of a common home place by people here begs the perennial question: 'Is Northern Ireland British or Irish?' This has always been presented in binary terms: if it is one, it cannot be the other. Or can it? Perhaps the time has come to consider a different way of looking at this question. Maybe Northern Ireland is both British *and* Irish. Maybe, in Taoiseach Leo Varadkar's words, when referring to a possible EU special status for Northern Ireland after Brexit, it can be 'best of British, best of Irish'.

This is the great conundrum of this small patch of earth, a place that two different groups of people love and treasure as their common home, but neither of which have yet found a way to define and describe so that it includes the other as a co-equal partner and thus becomes a truly shared home place. And what misery we have inflicted on each other in our battles to dominate this home place! As the journalist, left-wing activist and former civil rights leader Eamon McCann put it recently: 'What do we have now in this little patch of the world that would justify the cruelty, the misery, the pain, the grief and the bereavement that has attended the Troubles?'[2]

---

2. M. Fitzpatrick, *John Hume in America: from Derry to DC* (Dublin 2017), 198.

In my concluding comments to the Queen's University conference on the Good Friday Agreement, I talked about how to devise a system for living together in the North of Ireland. I posed the question as to whether the region is British or Irish or British–Irish or Irish–Irish or whatever. I said I did not care what it was called as long as we could all call it our shared home place. When I used that phrase 'shared home place', there was a spontaneous round of applause from the assembled politicians, community leaders and other dignitaries. Both David Trimble and Peter Robinson, sitting beside me on the stage, nodded in approval.

The former Ulster Unionist leader Mike Nesbitt was also at that conference. In a follow-up conversation in Markethill he said I had 'hit the nail on the head' when I talked about a shared home place. He went on:

> For hundreds of years we have failed to recognize the fact that nobody in this place is going away: in five or ten or fifty years, there will still be nationalists and republicans, unionists and loyalists and others, on this little piece of planet Earth. We are going to have to learn to share it, to rub along together, maybe even to be ambitious enough to strive to benefit from our diversity. Everybody has a right to be here, it is everybody's home place. If we recognize that, we change everything. For example, I hear lots of talk about a united Ireland. I respect people's right, which is enshrined in the Belfast/Good Friday Agreement, to argue peacefully for that. I hear some people, including Seamus Mallon, saying that if it were to come about, we would have to think very carefully about the rights of unionists, their culture and ethos and symbols. What I haven't really heard from nationalists is that, 'We want you in this new dispensation and here's why.' And I understand how ironic it is to hear this from a former unionist leader, when during the first fifty years of this state's existence unionism spectacularly failed to say to people like Seamus, 'We want you here in Northern Ireland and here's why.'
>
> I am of the generation that grew up with the Troubles, so the chant I heard from republicans and nationalists was 'Brits Out'. Maybe those chanting that meant the British army. But Seamus Mallon knows what I know: that most unionists are Brits, and we took that chant personally. So somebody has to explain to me why we've gone from 'Brits Out' to 'Brits In'. That's not for me to explain. That's for those who want change. My challenge is to redouble my efforts to persuade people that we're all better off within the United Kingdom. But that debate still has to be had. Seamus argues that such a vital debate can't happen quickly, because out of that lengthy and detailed debate we need maximum certainty if we are ever going to change Northern Ireland's constitutional status.
>
> If we go for a hasty Border Poll we are going to repeat the mistake of Brexit. If people vote with their hearts without a proper debate they will not understand

the implications of that monumental change. As Seamus Mallon points out, a Border Poll with a very narrow vote for constitutional change would leave Northern Ireland in a far worse situation. The law as laid down by the Good Friday Agreement says that a Border Poll majority of 50 per cent plus one would mean constitutional change leading to Irish unity. But if it actually happened like that, we all know it would be an utter disaster. I know from private discussions with politicians and their advisers in Dublin that my fears about what would happen in the aftermath of a hair-breadth vote for unity, including fears about loyalist terrorism, are shared there. Seamus has closely analysed the implications of that disastrous outcome and has gone on to propose a way forward that is different, practical and typically – and because it is from Seamus Mallon – generous to unionism.[3]

Mike Nesbitt is an open-minded, liberal unionist who fully understands the concept of the shared home place. Unfortunately our divided history means there are many other people, unionist and nationalist, who simply do not agree with him, although political correctness means they rarely if ever articulate this. Deep down they believe that this region is not actually home for the 'other side' and therefore cannot be shared. When DUP leader Arlene Foster was asked in a recent television programme by the comedian Patrick Kielty (whose father was murdered by loyalists) what she would do in the event of Irish unity, she responded: 'I'm not sure that I would be able to continue to live here, I would feel so strongly about it. I would probably have to move.' This appears to mean that she would feel that Northern Ireland was no longer her home if it was shared with nationalists as part of a united Ireland.

On the other hand is the republican demand to remove the 'British presence in Ireland', including all symbols of Britishness, ignoring the fact that by far the most significant element of this presence is the 900,000 Protestants and unionists for whom Northern Ireland is home. Too many nationalists and republicans still believe that unionists whose ancestors came here hundreds of years ago do not really belong. Both groups insist on believing that their place is home only for themselves, and if the other lot don't like it they can just leave. The attitude – 'this is our place: that lot can feck off if they don't like it' – is part of the victory impulse so prevalent in both communities.

What makes a shared home place? Safety, security, stability, comfort and a sense of belonging. The challenge is to create a society in the North of Ireland where both communities feel a sense of belonging. The writer and *Guardian*

---

3. Interview with Mike Nesbitt, November 2018.

columnist George Monbiot outlines three kinds of belonging: 'belonging with', suggesting symmetry and reciprocity, as in a marriage; 'belonging to', such as a child feels when she or he feels the authority and ownership of its loving parents; and 'belonging in', suggesting

> the ease we feel when we are at peace with our social setting or other elements of our surroundings … from infancy we have a powerful need for all these modes of belonging: to be owned by a family and a society, to own a place within them that allows us to reciprocate, and to feel at ease with that place. It is this need for belonging that an effective politics recognises and recruits.[4]

There are many people in Northern Ireland who certainly do not feel at peace with their place or social setting. We need *both* communities in any future constitutional settlement to feel they belong to their common home place in an equal and mutually respectful way. Only in that way will we ensure a future of peace for the North, rather than a continuation of the fearful and always potentially violent stand-off between two historically antagonistic groups. It can happen. I have lived in my home village of Markethill for my whole life. And despite all the fear and misery, division and terror that have visited Markethill in the period of the Troubles, I feel absolutely that I belong there; it is my home place.

However, it remains a deeply divided community, with many Protestants still feeling that it belongs to them in many ways, and proclaiming this with signs like 'Markethill Protestant Boys'. This is not conducive to Catholics and nationalists feeling it is their shared home. So when I ask nationalists in a place like Markethill if they will allow the unionists the space to express their culture because that might help them get used to the idea of Irish unity, they say: 'Are they still going to march up and down the streets every Friday night in spring and summer with their pipe bands and Lambeg drums and put up their union flags all over the place as if they still own it?' We're going to have to tell them there are no simple, triumphalist answers to this question, and a complex response is needed because of the tangled nature of Irish history. Part of that response is that they are going have to be allowed, even encouraged, to carry on marching and hoisting the British flag that is so dear to them as we move towards some form of Irish unity.

I rather like pipe bands; it's the lashing of the warlike Lambeg drums I object to. It would be good if the Orange marchers could agree not to take over the streets of places like Markethill regularly for six months of the year, but that local

---

4. G. Monbiot, *Out of the Wreckage: A New Politics for an Age of Crisis* (London 2017), 71–2.

bands could occasionally march through the village on the way to some field out in the countryside where they could hold a band festival with the bands and marchers and crowds from other parts. This is what happens on 'the twelfth' in Belfast. If they could concentrate on the music in that way – and above all avoid anti-Catholic songs and chants – it would take a lot of the poison out of it for nationalists. On the other side, we need to stop republicans bedecking majority nationalist towns like Newry with tricolours. If we could make a start on a new joint approach to marching and flags in that way, it would be very helpful.

What applies to marching applies a hundredfold to politics. The huge achievement of the Good Friday Agreement was that, for the present at least, it removed the use of violence as a means of political expression in Ireland. But little or nothing has changed in the underlying attitudes. Ten years of joint DUP–Sinn Féin rule did little to change those. The situation is made much worse by the unionists' acute awareness, rarely voiced, that because of their declining numbers they are losing the long-term struggle for supremacy: every day their sense of themselves as having a home in Ireland is eroding; every day they know they are losing the battle for their future as British people in Ireland. There are two competing senses of the future in Northern Ireland: for most nationalists their day is coming; for many unionists their day is nearly done.

The political scientist Benedict Anderson, himself an Irishman, invented the concept of 'imagined communities' to explain the strength of nations and nationalism in the modern world. Nations are 'imagined' because, 'in the minds of each [citizen] lives the image of their communion'. They are 'communities' because, regardless of the inequality and exploitation that may prevail in each, the nation is always regarded as 'a deep, horizontal comradeship'.[5]

Clearly in Northern Ireland there is no common 'deep horizontal comradeship' that might constitute a nation, whether British or Irish. The challenge for us as nationalists is to work to create some sense of togetherness, a sense of a shared home – while recognizing the deep differences between the two communities – where we can all learn to live together with at least some modicum of an agreed communal image and comradeship. Because of the changing demographic situation, and the consequent likelihood that we are moving in the direction of some form of political reunification on the island, the first thing we have to do is to allow the unionists the space and time to contemplate that probable, and for them deeply threatening, outcome – and to be able to propose alternatives more comfortable for them.

---

5. B. Anderson, *Imagined Communities: Reflections on the Origin and Spread of Nationalism* (London 1983), 48–50.

One thing unionists and nationalists have in common is that they are largely detached from the mother countries with which they identify so strongly. Northern unionists are detached, or at least semi-detached, from the British Parliament and people to whom they declare such loyalty, because that Parliament and people find them an unattractive, archaic bunch and make little secret of their lack of interest in the region. Boris Johnson's contemptuous dismissal of concerns about the Irish border in Brexit negotiations as 'pure millennium bug stuff' is one example of this. Another is the harsh language of former *Times* editor Simon Jenkins, commenting on the DUP's initial vetoing of a Brexit agreement between Theresa May and the EU: 'Decades of Westminster indulging its political primitivism have come home to roost' and 'terrible vengeance should be taken on them'.[6] A year later he said he would 'tear up the Treasury subvention' to Northern Ireland if they voted against May's latest EU package (which they did).[7]

The North's nationalists are perhaps the most detached people in these islands: detached from the Republic of Ireland after nearly a century of partition; utterly detached from Britain (with Sinn Féin political representatives who do not even take their seats in its Parliament) and now about to be detached from Europe. For the eighteen years up to the 2016 Brexit vote we had the luxury of not having to think much about our constitutional future at a time of relative peace, power-sharing, North–South cooperation and the effective disappearance of the border. Now we have to look at the central constitutional issue again in the light of being torn away from the rest of Ireland and the rest of Europe against our will. Sir David Goodall, the senior British official who was one of the architects of the 1985 Anglo-Irish Agreement, once said: 'The long-term aim should be to bring the island as a whole within the framework of the European Community freely back into some closer relationship with England, Scotland and Wales.' Brexit has taken that hopeful possibility away from us.

For most of my life the Social Democratic and Labour Party has tried to put forward solutions to our multiple political problems that are not simple answers but complex challenges. We always insisted that change in a deeply fractured and contested place like Northern Ireland would have to be gradual, participatory and inclusive. We told the British that they had created a system in the North based on a sectarian headcount, and when one tells the majority community that it can protect itself only by remaining a majority, one invites it to maintain sectarian solidarity as the only means of protection; in this way one makes sectarianism

---

6. 'Theresa May must call the DUP's bluff – this EU deal has to happen', *Guardian,* 5 December 2017.

7. 'Our warring MPs should realise all Brexit roads lead to Norway', *Guardian,* 7 December 2018.

the motive force of politics. We warned the unionists that they could not govern Northern Ireland without the consent and participation of the nationalists. We insisted that a future solution would have to be based on a complex system of power-sharing within the North and an Irish dimension involving a significant Irish government involvement in its affairs.

We cautioned that when one systematically removes all means whereby people can air their grievances democratically, one creates a dangerous vacuum, which will be filled by violence. We warned the IRA that a solution based on 'Brits Out' would ignore the rights of up to a million Northern Protestants. We reminded everyone that the huge opportunity for the revitalization of Northern Ireland represented by the Sunningdale Agreement was tragically not taken by the unionists; was bombed out of existence by the IRA; and was strangled by loyalists in the face of a supine British government led by a cowardly Secretary of State. We said that any successful exercise in self-determination in Ireland would only work when it was not the majority telling the minority what to do, but the people of the island deciding how they would live together. We worked long and hard for the Good Friday Agreement, one of the most complex peace and diplomatic agreements anywhere in the world in the late twentieth century, although we noted that Sunningdale, with its much stronger North–South structures, had been a better deal for nationalists. If we had Sunningdale's Council of Ireland with executive powers now, it would be a much fuller expression of the Irish dimension than the Good Friday Agreement.

We always warned that eventual Irish unity would have to be based on uniting people rather than territory. As John Hume put it so eloquently in 1976:

> Ireland is not a romantic dream, it is not a flag, it is not just a piece of earth. It is four and a half million people divided into two powerful traditions and its problems can only be solved, if the solution is to be lasting and permanent, not on the basis of victory for either, but on the basis of agreement and partnership between both. The real division of Ireland is not a line on a map but is in the minds and hearts of its people.[8]

Given that deep division between our people, we always stressed that overcoming it would require extremely nuanced and complicated institutions, with multiple safeguards to protect the interests of the different communities.

To those nationalists who say that because of the growth of the Catholic population, unionists becoming a minority at Stormont and the disaster of Brexit we

---

8. S. Farren, *The SDLP: The struggle for agreement in Northern Ireland, 1970–2000* (Dublin 2010), 118.

are now closer to Irish unity, I would say that unless we define and shape it very carefully, it will be more like Irish *disunity*. What the nationalist community has to start realizing, as many do, is that unionists are Irish people living on Irish soil. This is their home too. Reunification won't happen by putting them like cattle into a pen and adding up the numbers and deciding that because now there are slightly more of us than of them, we will suddenly have Irish unity. It is not enough to claim that most unionists' utter imperviousness to reasoned argument on the unity issue means that force (as the IRA used in the past) or coercion through marginally greater numbers (as Sinn Féin propose to use now) are the only ways forward.

Attachment to an Irish nation is a sense of identity which the unionists do not share. It was the British who gave them their identity by conditioning them to believe they were superior to the Gaelic 'papists' they often displaced; just as the Catholic community was conditioned to be people with grievances who felt they could only respond to those grievances through insurrection. Those of us who want to see Irish unity need to tell our unionist friends what that unity will look like and how they will feel a sense of belonging to it. We have never done that except in the most general terms. Does anybody know what the form of unity will be? It is a fact of life that if you want to persuade somebody to go somewhere with you, you have to tell them where you are going and how you are going to get there. The alternative is to tell them that one day soon the boot will be on the other foot, the nationalist foot, and then we will have many more years of the kind of hatred and violence that we have had in the past.

At this late point in my life I am issuing a difficult new challenge, aimed primarily at the North's nationalists. I am asking them to accept my argument as coming from the pragmatic realist I have always tried to be, and not to seek a premature Border Poll, which may deliver a narrow and completely unwork-able majority in favour of Irish unity. This will only lead to a captured unionist minority inside a state from which they are completely alienated. Does that sound familiar? Are we going to force the unionists into a situation in a united Ireland that John Hume used to articulate on behalf of the nationalists in the North: 'The British government may still prevail over us. But they should bear this in mind: You do not have our consent. You have never had our consent. All your military might cannot force our consent'?[9]

Albert Reynolds told the Oxford Union in 1994 that the lessons of Irish, and especially Northern Irish, history showed that 'stability and well-being will not be found under any political system which is refused allegiance or rejected on grounds of identity by a significant minority of those governed by it'. He said the

---

9. *Guardian,* 26 November 1984.

Irish government 'accept that consent is essential, both morally and legally and as a practical necessity. We are not an enemy to the unionist people, and do not have any wish to coerce the unionist community. Any such idea would be repugnant to the overwhelming majority of the people of the State, which I represent.'

I am asking nationalists to consider a different approach already enshrined in the Good Friday Agreement that will help us to build a greater degree of consent for an 'agreed Ireland', in the hope that significant numbers of unionists will eventually consent to be part of this new state (see next chapter). Many northern nationalists will denounce me from the heavens for making such a suggestion. They will say I am tearing up the Good Friday Agreement, but they will be wrong. I am positioning my proposal four-square within the parameters and framework of that Agreement and in complete consistency with its letter and spirit. I am simply proposing the evolution of its terms to align with a new reality twenty-one years on.

For now, the aversion of each northern community to the political vision of the other continues to be almost absolute. I hope and pray that one day we will have a 32-county state, with sovereignty residing in the Constitution of that state, and that both unionists and nationalists will seek election to and serve in the parliament of that state, but I do not believe there will be such a form of Irish unity in my lifetime or in the near future after my lifetime. The broad level of consent is simply not there to bring it about; particularly among unionists, but also perhaps among people in the South who have not considered the malign consequences of it happening without that broad consensus. In the meantime, wishful thinking must be set aside – and above all coercion must be shunned – and another ingenious solution, building on the Good Friday Agreement, must be found to allow another generation to learn the difficult business of living together peacefully in Northern Ireland.

As Seamus Heaney wrote in his poem 'Squarings xlviii':

> Strange how things in the offing, once they're sensed,
> Convert to things foreknown;
> And how what's come upon is manifest
> Only in light of what has been gone through.

What this means to me is that once we understand how things can work out for the best, however complicated and difficult they are, we will then say, 'I knew that all along.'

13. *Parallel Consent, Generosity and Other Ideas*

I

The only way we can have peace in Ireland as a whole is when a significant number of people in *both* Northern communities give their consent to a constitutional settlement, along with the people of the South. Therefore consent to Irish unity must include a substantial element of support from the unionist community. We must also keep our minds open to the possibility – unlikely at this moment – of a substantial proportion of nationalists continuing to prefer to remain part of the UK.

My proposal combines process and substance as a way of moving towards gaining the consent of both communities for unity in the future. Firstly, in terms of process, the 'Validation, Implementation and Review' section of the Good Friday Agreement should be triggered to enable a fundamental re-examination of how future change in the constitutional status of Northern Ireland might be effected. Some mechanism needs to be devised that would ensure the support of what I will call a 'sufficient plurality' of both communities, unionist and nationalist, for a united Ireland. My goal is to see if a way can be found to measure the support for unity in both communities that is more facilitative and generous than the simple 50 per cent plus one majority vote currently required by that Agreement.

The means I am proposing, Parallel Consent, is a concept already enshrined in the Good Friday Agreement, although in a different context. Parallel Consent as currently outlined in the Agreement relates to the working of the Northern Ireland Assembly, aimed at building safeguards into its procedures so that 'all sections of the community can participate and work together successfully in the operation of these institutions and that all sections of the community are protected'. The Agreement (Strand One, clause five) laid down that 'arrangements to ensure key decisions are taken on a cross-community basis' should be implemented according to one of two mechanisms: 'either (i) parallel consent, i.e. a majority of those members present and voting, including a majority of the unionist and nationalist designations present and voting; or (ii) a weighted majority (60 per cent) of members present and voting, including at least 40 per cent of each of the nationalist and unionist designations present and voting'.

Parallel Consent was a mechanism the SDLP proposed for the new Northern Ireland Assembly as part of the Good Friday Agreement to prevent the unionist parties coming together to form a majority that could block key legislative decisions that would be detrimental to the nationalist community. I believe that the same mechanism could be used in the constitutional area in the future to protect the unionists. Its aim would be to reassure unionists that Irish unity would not come about by a 50 per cent plus one (or a similarly narrow majority) in the North. Nor would it come about by a narrow majority in the North backed by a majority in the Republic in simultaneous referendums (there is no explicit mention of a unity referendum in the South in the 1998 Agreement, but it is clearly required by the clause recognizing the Irish people's 'right of self-determination on the basis of consent, freely and concurrently given, North and South, to bring about a united Ireland, if that is their wish'). It would also require a majority – or at least 40 per cent support – within the unionist community.

I publicly outlined the principle of Parallel Consent at a speech in Belfast's Waterfront Hall in September 1998 in the presence of Bill Clinton and Tony Blair:

> In its essence it is a very simple concept. It means from now on, all key decisions will require the consent of *both* major traditions. That represents both a reassurance and an incentive for us all. But more than anything else, it symbolizes the sense of partnership at the heart of the new dispensation. We are partners in this great project together, in which the interests and concerns of one have to be the interests and concerns of the other. This is a radical departure from the past and the key, I believe, to a better future.

Nobody could seriously argue with Irish unity if 40 to 50 per cent of unionists were supporting it. This would truly be an 'agreed Ireland', as outlined by John Hume as the preferred goal of constitutional nationalists as long ago as the 1960s. This Parallel Consent mechanism may be cumbersome in its working, but it should be seriously considered as a realistic alternative to a bare majority vote in a deeply divided society like Northern Ireland.

The Taoiseach, Leo Varadkar, seemed to be thinking along similar lines in a speech in April 2017 (when he was campaigning for the Fine Gael leadership) and in a BBC interview the following October. In the speech in the Dublin suburb of Goatstown he said Sinn Féin's 'demand for a Border Poll is alarming. It is a return to a mindset in which a simple sectarian majority of 50 per cent plus one is enough to cause a change in the constitutional status of the North. It represents a mindset of "There's one more of us than you, so now we're in charge. It's our turn to dominate."' He continued:

I believe in a united Ireland and would dearly love to see it occur in my lifetime. But before we have territorial unity we must have unity among people. Bouncing Ulster Protestants into a unitary Irish state against their will would be as grievous a wrong as was abandoning a large Catholic minority in the North on partition. It could lead to alienation and even a return to violence. A unitary state formed on this basis would not be a good one … Real lasting workable unity can only come about with a decent measure of support from both communities. It seems odd that those who have advocated for a shared future and cooperation should now seek to throw that away as they would try to ram through unity on a narrow, simple majority basis. A broader approach based on persuasion, not on what birth rates might produce, would recognize that the destiny of the two communities in the North will always be intertwined and will therefore require a shared future.[1]

In his BBC *Spotlight* interview he repeated his view:

I wouldn't like us to get to the point whereby we are changing the constitutional position here in Northern Ireland on a 50 per cent plus one basis. One of the best things about the Good Friday Agreement is that it did get very strong cross-border support – that's why there was a 70 per cent vote for it. I don't think that there would be a 70 per cent vote for a united Ireland in the morning, for example, or anything remotely [like] that.[2]

---

1. '"Sinn Féin's push for border poll alarming," says Varadkar', *Irish Independent*, 2 April 2017.
2. 'Varadkar says more than 50%+1 needed in united Ireland poll – what do you think?' *Belfast Telegraph*, 17 October 2017.

I have put my proposal to the former Ulster Unionist leader Mike Nesbitt and the following was his response:

> This is a way of addressing the deep problems that will arise if there is, sometime in the future, a hair-breadth majority for constitutional change in Northern Ireland. It is practical, based on a precedent laid down in the Belfast/Good Friday Agreement, and a very generous offer from a leader with impeccable nationalist credentials. If Arlene Foster or I were to propose this, it would be shot down and rightly so. Nationalists would say we were being undemocratic, the rules have been set by the Belfast and subsequent agreements, which you signed up to, so you'll just have to suck it up. But the important thing about this proposal is that it is a challenge to nationalism from an icon of nationalism.
>
> It seems to make eminent sense to me: a majority or a very large minority of unionists who would be in favour of such a monumental constitutional change represents a far more solid basis for going forward than 50 per cent plus one or a similarly tight margin. And nationalists should carefully consider it because it comes from a man who is committed to Irish unity, has devoted his whole life to nationalist politics, and to achieving a goal, which is more about unifying the people who live on this island than about its territory.
>
> After twenty years when we did not really have to consider Irish unity because of the arrangements set out in the Belfast Agreement, constitutional change is now back on the agenda because of Brexit. Seamus Mallon warns us that replacing an imposed majority in Northern Ireland with an imposed majority in a future unitary Irish state would only create another large disaffected minority group who feel they have no sense of ownership or belonging in this new state. The logic of it is compelling.
>
> The lengthy period of deliberation and consultation proposed by Mallon also makes sense. I campaigned against Brexit in 2016 on the basis that I did not understand what it would mean for Northern Ireland, and when I challenged colleagues to spell it out, they couldn't. Two and a half years on we are still no clearer. It would be the same, only worse, if a Border Poll came ahead of the necessary and complex debate about constitutional change; a debate, which would be about what that change would mean for our health service, our educational system, our police service, our political structures and, most importantly, our identity.[3]

---

3. Interview with Mike Nesbitt, November 2018.

II

In contrast, Irish High Court judge Richard Humphreys devotes over twenty pages of his recent book on the Good Friday Agreement and Irish unity[4] to debunking criticism of the simple majoritarian clause in the Good Friday Agreement. He argues that if there is to be equal respect between the two traditions in the North (which he says is the key principle of that Agreement), then the support of a bare majority for Irish unity must be treated exactly the same as an equivalent vote for continuing as part of the United Kingdom:

> The test for a United Kingdom is the support of a majority – in a democracy that is 50 per cent + 1 – of those present and validly voting. That consent will remain effective even if it is a bare majority of one. On the principle of equal and reciprocal respect, the test for a united Ireland cannot be any more difficult. 50 per cent + 1 of those present and validly voting in referendums North and South is legally sufficient to trigger Irish unity. Generally, people who say that one cannot coerce hundreds of thousands of unionists into a united Ireland have no real problem with coercing hundreds of thousands of nationalists into a United Kingdom. If one takes equal respect seriously, one has to accept the consequences of a reciprocal test.

This is an entirely valid legal, as opposed to a political, practical or moral argument. However, it also defies common sense in that it both fails to recognize the potentially malign consequences of a narrow vote for unity for the peace and harmony of the island and ignores the lessons of recent Irish history. In 1920–1 a then large unionist majority in the six northern counties for those counties to remain part of the United Kingdom led to a corrupt and discriminatory statelet being established, which kept itself in power for fifty years through a one-party monopoly, discrimination in the electoral franchise and public jobs, and extreme security measures like the Special Powers Act. That unionist majority state led to the effective exclusion of Northern Ireland's nationalist minority, which in return boycotted its institutions for many years and then, after a failed peaceful attempt to gain its civil rights, gave significant support to a ferocious attempt to overthrow them by force.

Do we want to risk setting up a new Ireland built on equally flimsy and divided foundations? Far from creating a new nation based on the Good Friday Agreement principle of equal respect, we would be in serious danger of creating

---

4. R. Humphreys, *Beyond the Border: The Good Friday Agreement and Irish Unity after Brexit* (Dublin 2018), 84–106.

a society deeply divided by mutual disrespect and loathing. Just as Northern Ireland proved ungovernable because of the withdrawal of support by a sizeable proportion of its nationalist inhabitants, so an Ireland 'united' in this way would prove ungovernable if a large proportion of its new unionist inhabitants were opposed to its very existence. It is a powerful political and moral point, rather than a legal and intellectual one. Further on Judge Humphreys himself accepts the limitations of this majority test:

> One can still recognize the crudeness of the simple majority test. The only answers to that are to make Northern Ireland work as a self-contained entity that respects both traditions, so that the constitutional issue does not matter so much and would make virtually no difference in practice; combined with a lengthy period of cooperation between the two governments so that any eventual transition of formal sovereignty would be slow, gradual and imperceptible.[5]

That is effectively what I am arguing. While never giving up our legitimate aspiration for unity, nationalists must first aim for reconciliation within Northern Ireland, working with unionists to build what I have called our 'shared home place'. The current SDLP leader, Colum Eastwood, said much the same thing in 2016: 'For Ireland to be reunited, Northern Ireland has to work. This is the essence of our progressive nationalism.' Of course the constitutional issue will always be paramount in Northern politics. However, despite the current difficulties, the return of a working Executive in the short term and a slow and gradual transition towards unity until it gains 40 to 50 per cent support in the unionist community in the medium term, must remain the interlinked aims of the next phase of the peace process. I believe this is what most of the politicians and diplomats in Dublin, Belfast, London and Washington intended when they painstakingly drew up the Good Friday Agreement.

Mr Justice Humphreys is scathing about Parallel Consent, which he calls 'joint consent'. He writes:

> That notion is without legal or indeed logical basis. The clear and unambiguous language of the Good Friday Agreement firmly rejects all these alternative proposals, which would have the effect of undermining the will of the people of Northern Ireland as expressed in a referendum. The only legally permissible way in which any such alternative solutions could be advanced would be by way of further international agreement between the two sovereign governments.[6]

---

5. Humphreys, 93.

6. *Ibid,* 101.

Judge Humphreys is dealing here with a legal document that was created over twenty years ago and which, in the hands of the current generation of local politicians, has led to deadlock. I am dealing with the realities behind that document, trying to understand how it might evolve in order to help us move forward to bring the people of this island together, and, if necessary, how it might be amended to ensure that.

I position my proposal firmly within the framework of the Good Friday Agreement by suggesting that the negotiations to work out how that document might be amended, if necessary, should take place in the context of the Review section of that Agreement. This section foresaw that difficulties might arise, which would need to be addressed with a view to finding remedies. It is worth reproducing paragraph 7 of the Review section here:

> If difficulties arise which require remedial action across the range of institutions, or otherwise require amendment of the British-Irish Agreement [the agreement between the Irish and British governments accompanying the Good Friday Agreement] or relevant legislation, the process of review will fall to the two Governments in consultation with the parties in the Assembly. Each Government will be responsible for action in its own jurisdiction.

My proposal derives directly from, and aligns with, the Good Friday Agreement. I am proposing a remedy to a difficulty. Amendment of the Agreement to this end is possible.

I disagree with Judge Humphreys that the Good Friday Agreement sets the legal position in stone. The 1998 Agreement makes express provision for review and adjustment. Moreover, a distinguished Irish constitutional lawyer has advised me that what will define the legal position of an eventual Border Poll will be the terms of the question put to the people, North and South, about this fundamental issue. The two governments will have the most important input into deciding that. So in my opinion there is not a definitive legal position at the moment.

The Review of the Agreement, during which I am proposing that my Parallel Consent proposal be examined, should take place well in advance of a Border Poll, in the event that the Secretary of State for Northern Ireland deemed the conditions right to warrant such a poll. I am not calling for such a Review in the immediate future, rather that it be incorporated early into the timetable of planning a Border Poll. While technically a matter for the Secretary of State, this would presumably also centrally involve the Irish government, given that both governments are co-guarantors of the Agreement.

III

A further dimension to my proposal relates to how a civic dialogue might be incorporated into this process to enable a wide range of people in Ireland, North and South, and in Britain, to contribute their ideas about the future shape of the island. An informal public conversation around issues to do with a Border Poll and moves towards Irish unity has already started, particularly among Northern nationalists. This book is my contribution to that conversation. I fully accept that Parallel Consent would be only one proposal among many for consideration in such a civic dialogue and in the formal Good Friday Agreement Review.

Such a citizens' dialogue should be properly structured and entirely independent of government and political parties. It would be a vital precursor to the official Review; an important opportunity for ordinary people's ideas on the future to be aired and debated. It will ensure that the formal Review will be as thorough and comprehensive as possible. During the years of the Troubles we benefited from various such exercises, which were discursive rather than decision-making, involving a wide range of participants and viewpoints. There were the Irish government-established New Ireland Forum in 1983–4 and Forum for Peace and Reconciliation in 1994–6. More relevant in this instance would be the independent Opsahl Commission in 1992–3, set up by a group of 200 citizens in Northern Ireland to canvass public opinion about ideas for ways out of the North's violent deadlock. This international commission, chaired by an eminent Norwegian human rights lawyer, Torkel Opsahl, collected written testimonies and held public hearings, facilitating around 3000 people in Ireland, North and South, and Britain, to contribute their ideas.

Consideration should be given to establishing another Opsahl-type commission, under an international chairperson, thus ensuring an inclusive, respectful and comprehensive public dialogue in the vital period before a formal government-mandated Good Friday Agreement Review. Other public consultation exercises that could be learned from in setting up such a commission would include the Republic's Citizens' Assembly, which gives ordinary citizens an input into debate about forthcoming controversial legislation, and the series of 'town hall' and community group meetings that contributed to the success in 2016 of the potentially sensitive 1916 Centenary Programme.

This Opsahl Commission-type exercise would not be part of the decision-making process, but would play an important role in informing the governments and parties about public opinion on the highly sensitive and potentially dangerous issues surrounding a Border Poll and its aftermath. Its timing would be a matter for discussion. It should take place well before and therefore feed ideas into the formal Review of the Agreement in advance of any Border Poll.

I realize that for many this will be a difficult discussion. Some nationalists will say that the requirement for Parallel Consent or a weighted majority for unity would be unfair to Northern nationalists who have been waiting for nearly a century to achieve that unity, only to have the bar raised so that it is out of their reach just when the demographic balance is shifting in their favour. I would say to such nationalists: if you think persuading a significant number of unionists to come round eventually to accepting Irish unity is an unachievable piece of wishful thinking, consider the alternative. If you insist that the unity question is put in the near future, and you gain the narrowest of majorities for it, what does that achieve? Is it going to lead to genuine unity between the people of this island?

How can we talk about creating unity, while using a method to bring it about that would itself be a hugely potent source of disunity? The last thing we need is another period of violence like the 1968–98 period; we need time to build and consolidate a common belief in Northern Ireland as a home place for everybody who lives here, with the future option of unity by genuine consent somewhere in the middle distance.

After nearly a hundred years of suffering as an often despised and discriminated minority in the unionist-dominated North, and with the census figures now creeping towards a Catholic (and perhaps one day a nationalist) majority here, it will be hard for my fellow Northern nationalists to embrace my proposal. They will point, legitimately, to the clause in the Good Friday Agreement, endorsed by a strong majority of voters, which says that once there is a simple majority for unity in Northern Ireland, the British government has pledged to implement that constitutional change. They will say not to do this until there is some form of weighted majority for unity is a negation of democracy, and some may turn back to violence to counter it.

IV

I would therefore appeal to a virtue sadly absent from British–Irish, unionist–nationalist and Protestant–Catholic relations on this island: *generosity*. For 120 years Irish Catholics and nationalists found that the United Kingdom into which their country had been incorporated was a 'cold house', with little welcome, equality or generosity. The formation of an independent Irish state in 1918–22 caused unionists to demand their own state, fearful that the new state would be a cold house for them. David Trimble, who first used the phrase in his 1998 Nobel Peace Prize speech, admitted that Northern Ireland, with its inbuilt unionist majority, was a cold house for nationalists. In its opening submission to the pre-Good Friday Agreement talks in 1997, the SDLP said 'healing the fractured political relationships between both parts of Ireland will take time and require considerable courage, forbearance and commitment'. We should have added 'generosity'.

Generosity has been in short supply in any of the attempted settlements in Northern Ireland over the past fifty years. Fearful unionists are not naturally generous people. Sinn Féin, with its background in the violent campaign of the IRA, is not a generous party, although individual republicans, notably Martin McGuinness, have reached out in a generous way to unionists. The current main representatives of unionism and nationalism – the DUP and Sinn Féin – feel far more comfortable with the traditional 'zero-sum' game of seamless unity with Britain or rapid movement towards a unitary Irish state, with little or no consideration given to any generous treatment of the other community. The latter now hold out for the 'zero-sum' win of a narrow majority for unity in a Border Poll in the foreseeable future.

The one thing that might now bring the unhappy centuries-old history of disaffection, division and violence to an end at last is for Irish nationalism in both jurisdictions to consciously demonstrate a measure of generosity that would give real meaning to the opening sentence of the new Article Three written into the Irish Constitution after the Good Friday Agreement: 'It is the firm will of the Irish nation, *in harmony and friendship*, to unite all the people who share the territory of the island of Ireland, in all the diversity of their identities and traditions.' [italics added] I do not think this is too much to ask Northern nationalists, although it may be beyond the tolerance of some 'republicans' who have forgotten the real meaning underlying Wolfe Tone's maxim about uniting Protestant, Catholic and dissenter. It is surely time for nationalists to see themselves no longer as victims, but as generous stewards and custodians for the future of the island.

This generosity could be shown in two ways: (a) by not pushing for unity until there is wider and deeper acceptance for it among the unionist community; (b) by a willingness on the part of nationalism to put forward some arrangement more congenial to unionists than a unitary state. After all, as the New Ireland Forum reported, in an excellent section on the need for a new approach to accommodate both unionist and nationalist identities:

So long as the legitimate rights of both unionists and nationalists are not accommodated together in new political structures acceptable to both, the situation will continue to give rise to conflict and instability. The starting point of genuine reconciliation and dialogue is mutual recognition and acceptance of the legitimate rights of both. The Forum is convinced that dialogue which fully respects both traditions can overcome the fears and divisions of the past and create an atmosphere in which peace and stability can be achieved.

My Parallel Consent proposal will also require a generous response from significant sectors of unionism. That community have to accept that the only way for Northern Ireland to work as a peaceful and consensual society is for unionists and their leaders – notably the DUP – to work alongside nationalists and their leaders – notably Sinn Féin – in a spirit of equality, respect and parity of esteem. This did not happen in the final years of the 2007–17 Executive. If that spirit of equality and generosity is not shown by the unionists, both in the day-to-day running of Northern Ireland and in their responses to generous proposals like Parallel Consent, Northern nationalists will simply ignore proposals like mine and let the clock run down to Irish unity, if necessary by the narrowest of margins.

V

The electorate in the Republic will also have to be consulted. Will a majority of voters there want to risk a rerun of the Northern Ireland conflict – which will very probably extend to the South – by coercing a large number of unionists into a united Ireland they have bitterly opposed for well over a century? The Republic is a safe, peaceful and newly wealthy society, now among the ten most prosperous nations in the world, and, according to EU opinion polls, one of the most contented countries in Europe. Will its citizens want to put all that at risk to take over a fractious, potentially violent and economically dependent North? In the *Irish Times* columnist Fintan O'Toole's words:

> To put it bluntly (as no one ever does), Southerners have no interest in inheriting a political wreck, or becoming direct participants in a gory sequel: 'Troubles III, the Orange strikes back.' They will not vote for a form of unity that merely creates an angry and alienated Protestant minority within a bitterly contested new state.[7]

---

7. 'United Ireland will not be based on 50 per cent plus one', *The Irish Times*, 15 August 2017.

In agreement after agreement from the 1970s onward, the governments and people in the South have shown that sense of careful responsibility. They accepted and welcomed the Sunningdale Agreement in 1974 and the Anglo-Irish Agreement in 1985. They voted overwhelmingly in favour of the Good Friday Agreement in 1998. The popular support in the South for these developments shows that the Irish people now approach the issue of unity in a cautious, sensible and realistic manner.

We may have to face up to these challenges sooner than we think. The unpredictability of British politics in the wake of Brexit may lead to a situation where after the next general election a Border Poll in Ireland might get onto the agenda of an incoming government in London. For example, if Scotland, with its strong majority for staying in the EU, obtains a second independence referendum and votes to go it alone, that will certainly see increasing pressure on a future left-wing Labour government for a unity referendum in Ireland.

At the moment the political class in the Republic is not geared up to begin the vital debate needed before we even contemplate a Border Poll. Back in the 1970s, 80s and 90s in Dublin there was a constant and urgent debate in political, civil service, diplomatic and media circles about the North and how to push forward greater Irish–British cooperation based on the unity by consent principle to resolve its deep problems of violence and division. The outcomes were Sunningdale, the Anglo-Irish Agreement and the Good Friday Agreement. We don't have people doing that today; the generation of brilliant diplomats and senior civil servants who negotiated those internationally admired agreements is long gone. Political leaders and their advisers in Dublin, and of course in London, are now consumed by the existential threat of Brexit. The level of debate about the North in Dáil Éireann is woeful. There is little of the intellectual engagement and planning for future action on the island of Ireland that took place in past decades. Until Brexit is dealt with, there is little appetite, for example, for the difficult business of pressuring Sinn Féin and the DUP to go back into a new Northern Executive.

A former Irish attorney general has told me that Southern politicians will be loath even to start thinking about a Border Poll in the foreseeable future. Understandably, Southern political leaders are concerned, first and foremost, with the security of their own state and their own people. They know that within living memory there was a semi-insurrection in that state, a spillover from the Northern Troubles, with a secret army importing and storing huge amounts of sophisticated weaponry for use north of the border, and a police and military that was sometimes barely able to contain it. 'How reluctant will political leaders be to hold a Border Poll with the prospect of a very narrow majority for unity if the security of the citizens of the Irish state is again going to be put in peril as a consequence?' he asked.

A number of people have pointed out that there is one significant practical problem with my Parallel Consent proposal: how are we to measure unionist consent for unity in order to assess whether it has reached the 40 per cent or 50 per cent threshold? Designating as a unionist or nationalist politician in the Northern Ireland Assembly (as required by the Good Friday Agreement) is one thing. It would be totally unacceptable to expect people to identify in that way *before* a Border Poll; that would be at odds with the whole idea of the secret ballot, a fundamental cornerstone of democracy.

In the US Primaries, citizens register as Democrat or Republican to vote for those parties' candidates in initial electoral contests confined to party supporters. Thus they eventually select a candidate for a presidential or other election for office. This might be one system we could explore. This is something that needs to be discussed with those who will be voting in a unity referendum, and particularly with unionists. We have to say to the latter:

> You will be part of this process. We're not asking you to decide now whether you're going to vote for unity. We're only asking you, when the time comes – and it will certainly come some day – *how* we might do this to ascertain fairly and democratically what are the views of your community? How do you propose this should be measured?

I believe it is time to move – both myself and the nationalist community in both jurisdictions – towards a realization that we have two options: one is to hold a premature Border Poll and, in the event of a narrow vote for unity, face into the risk of another period of instability and violence; the other is to move towards an agreed Ireland in a slow, progressive way, and maybe leave the end product to a future time.

The wise words of former Taoiseach Brian Cowen are worth repeating in this context. In 2010 he said:

> The genius of these agreements [Good Friday and St Andrews] is that we are all on a common journey together where we have not decided on the destination. The problem with our ideologies in the past was that we had this idea about where we were going, but we had no idea how anyone was going to come with us on the journey. We have now all decided: let's go on a journey and forget about

the destination – the destination isn't really important in that respect. We can all work for what it is we would like ideally to see, but this is not something that can be forced or imposed upon people on either side of the island. This is about people of different traditions who live on this island who have common interests. We as political leaders must cooperate to best serve the people we represent; we have an obligation to make sure we share this piece of ground in a peaceful and harmonious way, which will bring a good quality of life for all our people.

That's the great challenge for this generation and for the next generation, and it's a legacy we can leave that is a far better one for our children than others who have had to lead their respective generations at times of conflict, and great pain, loss and anguish for people. A commitment to democratic principles and open, mutually respectful dialogue that brings real benefits and opportunities for people to work and live together seems to me to be something that would get the unanimous approval of every right-thinking person, North and South.

The ultimate destination of any political project is a matter of time working itself out. Therefore the destination – where we end up eventually – is not the thing to be talking about. That will be for other people in another time maybe. We have to make the here and now a better place, and we have to do it on the basis that we have devised a political culture that is less suspicious and less fearful than ever before, that is more open to recognizing the common interests that we have whilst respecting that we are in separate jurisdictions. We should be concerned about what it is we can do together.[8]

VI

The British and Irish governments continue to have a key role and a respon-sibility in this matter, whatever their differences over Brexit. Under the Good Friday Agreement they pledged to be the co-guarantors of that Agreement so that it could lead to an agreed, peaceful Ireland. They have committed them-selves to protect and promote the principles of the 1998 Agreement: 'Partnership, equality and mutual respect as the basis of relationships within Northern Ireland, between North and South, and between these islands'; 'Exclusively democratic and peaceful means of resolving differences on political issues'; and 'To strive in every practical way towards reconciliation and rapprochement within the frame-work of democratic and agreed arrangements.'

---

8. 'Making the here and now a better place: Interview on North–South cooperation with the Taoiseach, Brian Cowen TD', *Journal of Cross Border Studies in Ireland* (Spring 2010), 19–20.

The Good Friday Agreement lays down that if a majority of Northern Irish people voting in a Border Poll express the wish that the North 'should cease to be part of the United Kingdom and form part of a united Ireland', the Secretary of State for Northern Ireland will bring legislative proposals before the UK Parliament to give effect to that wish 'as may be agreed' between the British and Irish governments. This appears to me to mean that there is one vital decision to be made by the British government *before* a Border Poll and one vital decision to be made by the Irish government *after* it. The Secretary of State for Northern Ireland can order a Border Poll if she or he believes it likely that a majority of Northern Irish people would vote for a united Ireland. However, any legislation to bring that about after the poll must be agreed with the Irish government.

Will either government want to act in this way if that majority for unity is likely to be an extremely narrow one? 'France does not have friends, only interests,' President de Gaulle famously once said, and that goes for all governments. I do not believe that it would be in the interests of either the British or Irish government that there should be a resumption of major violence, this time initiated by loyalists reacting against a narrow majority in a Border Poll. Will either government take this risk either by deciding to hold a poll in the first place or by endorsing a very narrow majority for unity in such a poll afterwards? What mechanism will the British government use to calculate the likelihood of a majority for unity before announcing such a poll, itself a deeply divisive event? It would be trundling into madness even to announce the date of a Border Poll without extensive prior consultation, negotiation and preparation.

It is sensible to work on the assumption that the two governments would not agree to the holding of a Border Poll unless they were absolutely certain it would lead to a peaceful and stable outcome for the island of Ireland. Anything less than a likely significant majority for unity would lead to them deciding that the time was not right; that a premature poll would lead only to instability and violence, which – as always in Irish history – would spill over into Britain. It is clear that some kind of understanding between the two governments and the major parties in Northern Ireland about the likely outcome of such a poll and the actions to be taken in its aftermath would have to be in place before anybody would even contemplate holding such a vote. That is why I call for the Review mechanism of the Agreement to be activated, preceded by a comprehensive and independent public consultation exercise.

The approach of a future Border Poll may some day be occasioned by electoral results that show a probable nationalist voting majority in Northern Ireland. The

Belfast-based social researcher Paul Nolan is careful to point out that his much cited recent research on demographic trends, using official Northern Ireland Statistics and Research Agency figures, concludes that Catholics, *not* nationalists, of voting age will probably outnumber Protestants of voting age in the foreseeable future. He believes these figures are unlikely to convert any time soon into a majority of people voting for unity, since between the 1998 and 2017 Northern Assembly elections, the combined nationalist vote (i.e. Sinn Féin and the SDLP taken together) had only risen by a tiny 0.1 per cent of a percentage point. Thus the overall nationalist vote is at a standstill, and 'rather than breaking through the fifty per cent barrier, it finds it hard to break the forty per cent ceiling'.[9]

We need to start work on a preparatory plan well before any possible nationalist voting majority appears on the horizon. Former First Minister and DUP leader Peter Robinson said in June 2018 that while he was confident a Border Poll vote would support remaining in the UK, 'processes and timescales' on constitutional change in the North needed to be agreed in advance, rather than having to 'tackle the issue on the fly' if reunification was ever to be backed in a Border Poll. He suggested fixed polls on unification once in a generation in order to stabilize politics in Northern Ireland and to make the prospect of unity less threatening to unionists. He said that in the discordant aftermath of the Brexit vote, the prospect of a simple yes/no vote on 'colossal constitutional change' was a 'recipe for chaos' for the island. Such a poll should not be held 'at the whim of the Secretary of State, or the demand of a political party ... it should be sufficiently far ahead so that we can have stable government in between'.[10]

What is important is that it should be a careful and extended composition. It is sometimes forgotten that the peace process, whose outstanding achievement was the 1998 Good Friday Agreement, actually lasted almost seventeen years: from the Downing Street Declaration in December 1993 to the devolution of policing and justice in April 2010; or twenty-two years if one begins with the Hume–Adams talks in 1988. The next stage could take even longer.

VII

I have recently come across two other significant proposals for the future – both rather less radical from a nationalist viewpoint than Parallel Consent – that might

---

9. 'North's future may well rest with significant "Other" vote', *The Irish Times,* 19 June 2018.
10. *The Irish Times,* 7 June 2018.

also be considered as part of the Good Friday Agreement Review and Opsahl Mark II hearings. The first is from the former senior Irish official Michael Lillis, a close adviser to Garret FitzGerald and one of the architects of the 1985 Anglo-Irish Agreement. According to Lillis, FitzGerald, who was always most anxious to be inclusive to unionists in any solution to the North's divisions,

> took some comfort from the reasonable speculation that if and when in the future sovereignty over Northern Ireland shifted from London to Dublin, as a result of the political decision of a majority in Northern Ireland (and of course a likely though by no means guaranteed majority decision in the South), the structures he had agreed with Mrs Thatcher would, through a variable geometry, necessarily reverse themselves. Northern Ireland under British sovereignty under the [Anglo-Irish] Agreement involved the active role of Dublin as interventionists for the nationalist side. Under Irish sovereignty Britain would, in co-operation with Dublin, be obliged to support the unionists' interests in Anglo-Irish interactions with a sovereign all-Ireland Irish government.[11]

The second, an advanced and updated version of the first, comes from Brian Barrington, the Dublin lawyer who was my legal adviser during my time as Deputy First Minister. He emphasizes that those who are rightly worried about the prospect of an alienated unionist minority in a united Ireland should equally accept that it would be wrong to have an alienated nationalist *majority* in Northern Ireland as a continuing part of the United Kingdom. But he goes on:

> Just as it was important in 1998 to ensure institutions of government in Northern Ireland in which nationalists participated as equals, so it is vital to design institutions of government in which unionists participate as equals in a future united Ireland. Everything that nationalists sought to reflect their identity and ethos in the North as part of the United Kingdom, they must equally afford to unionists in a united Ireland. That makes sense because whether we are in a United Kingdom or a united Ireland, we will have hundreds of thousands of people who are British and unionist and – as of moral and legal right – will continue to be so.
>
> These people are entitled to the reassurance of knowing – now – what a united Ireland would mean for them. The solution is for constitutional nationalists across the island to guarantee to unionists that the institutions of the Good Friday Agreement will continue in a united Ireland unless and until nationalists and unionists by cross-community Parallel Consent agree to change them.

---

11. 'Irish governments' overwhelming duty is to work together', *The Financial Times*, 4 December 2018 [https://www.ft.com/content/144f3152-f705-11e8-8b7c-6fa24bd5409c].

Nationalists must make clear that the institutions of the Good Friday Agreement are a constitutional backstop for unionists that will endure unless and until *they* agree to change them.

This means, says Barrington, that the Northern Ireland Executive, Assembly and East–West arrangements to reflect the British ties and identity of British people on this island will continue as they are (or should be) now. And just as the Irish government has a say in matters that are not devolved to the Executive and Assembly now, so the British government will have a say in such matters in the future. 'In short, Northern Ireland's place in a united Ireland tomorrow would be very much like Northern Ireland's place in the United Kingdom now. That is what unionists on this island must be guaranteed.'

Barrington continues:

It ought not to be up to unionists to seek these reassurances. Rather it is the job of nationalists to provide them unilaterally and without quibble. With some opinion polls suggesting increasing numbers in the North in favour of unity, the urgency of constitutional nationalists making this clear is greater than ever. And it is not just about planning for a united Ireland that may never happen, but also about sending a message to both main communities now: whether in a united Ireland or a United Kingdom, the need for nationalists and unionists to live and govern together as neighbours and partners will remain. So let's get on with it.

It is also urgent that this message comes from constitutional nationalists, and especially the main Southern parties, Fianna Fáil and Fine Gael, and that it comes now. Because uncertainty breeds fear and suspicion, and given the violent history of this island, unionists have reason to be afraid. Moreover promises from Sinn Féin hold no value for unionists; and if a future Irish government with Sinn Féin as part of it makes this commitment, it will be viewed with equal suspicion. Sinn Féin may see that as unfair, but it is the toxic legacy of the armed struggle that they enthusiastically supported for so long. This commitment will only have any value if it is given by the constitutional parties. It is they, not Sinn Féin, who must write the policy for the protection of British people on this island. And they should start doing it now.

A third option that needs to be seriously discussed is some form of federal or confederal arrangement. The Northern business leader Sir George Quigley, a Presbyterian, said shortly before his death in 2013:

If there is ever a new constitutional configuration for the island, my guess is that the model by far the likeliest to secure consent is the confederal model which featured as the most persuasively argued of a range of options in the New Ireland Forum Report in 1984. On this basis the final agreed Ireland would be a joint, equal venture between North and South, with each having its own governance structure, and with policies related to the powers to be specifically delegated to confederal level determined jointly by representatives from North and South.[12]

The relevant section in the New Ireland Forum Report reads:

A two-state federal/confederal Ireland based on the existing identities, North and South, would reflect the political and administrative realities of the past 60 [now nearly 100] years and would entrench a measure of autonomy for both parts of Ireland within an all-Ireland framework. While protecting and fostering the identities and ethos of the two traditions, it would enable them to work together in the common interest.[13]

I am attracted to some kind of confederal arrangement because I believe unionists will find it very difficult to feel any sense of loyalty to a unitary Irish state. Thus if the reassurance that their Britishness will be protected and cherished cannot be guaranteed through all-Ireland laws and institutions, it will have to be provided through new provisions and structures under a separate Northern administration.

We in the North of Ireland have lived under a different political regime from the people of the South for nearly a century, and that experience has changed people here. That is something nationalists and unionists can agree on, and could therefore be a starting point for a new conversation between us. Once the leaders of both communities accept that particular 'third space', which is Northern Ireland, there are all kinds of possibilities (many of which are already there in the Good Friday Agreement): power-sharing, greater North–South and East–West cooperation (including some kind of continuing British dimension), a Bill of Rights, the need for equality and parity of esteem in all things, some form of federalism or confederalism, and (I hope) the eventual slow coming together of the two societies on the island.

---

12. *The Journal of Cross Border Studies in Ireland* (Spring 2013), 27–8.

13. New Ireland Forum Report, Volume 1, 7.1, 34.

VIII

However, the British may not be willing to continue to engage in a constructive way with Ireland, North and South. There is indifference, even hostility, to Northern Ireland in large parts of the British political establishment. The spoiling role of the DUP in the Brexit negotiations, playing its part in the deep constitutional crisis that eventually gripped that nation, will surely not be forgotten nor forgiven by many in the Westminster Parliament. The rise firstly of Scottish and then of English nationalism has done much to unsettle the three-century-old union that is the United Kingdom. Given the febrile political atmosphere in Brexit-bewitched Westminster, the political class in the Republic needs to be awake to the possibility of some unforeseen move to change the constitutional arrangements in the UK that may rebound on Ireland, North and South.

I expect the lengthy journey that will lead eventually towards some form of consensual unity via a mechanism like Parallel Consent will require close oversight and very significant commitment by both governments. If the British are otherwise engaged with major post-Brexit economic and constitutional issues affecting England and Scotland, that will be a major challenge. The 1993–2010 peace process could not have happened without the huge commitment of successive British prime ministers: John Major, Tony Blair and Gordon Brown. That commitment is clearly not there under Theresa May given the present confusion and uncertainty. In the event of a right-wing Brexiteer like Boris Johnson becoming Prime Minister as part of a chaotic Brexit 'no-deal' scenario, the Northern Ireland imbroglio will probably be relegated to the bottom of the British government's priority list, as it struggles with existential problems elsewhere in the UK.

The role of Britain will remain crucial to any new constitutional arrangement for Northern Ireland and Ireland. One of the major challenges to the viability of any 'new Ireland', if any significant element of unionism is to be persuaded to accept it, will be to find a mechanism for involving Britain in its structures. What I am proposing must not exclude Britain. If a solution can be found based on a larger unionist vote for some kind of unity, the cherishing and protection of the British identity and ethos of those unionists will have to be high on the agenda of future Irish governments. It may require the maintenance of a separate northern region with a significant half-British ethos after that unity: a kind of confederation. The British government will have a key role in that. One can only hope that the British can be persuaded to commit to another complex, long drawn-out diplomatic process in Ireland in the interests of the stability of these islands.

14. *Is Ireland Ready for Reunification?*

Increasing numbers of Northern nationalists now vote for Sinn Féin. This is what my former SDLP colleague and friend John Fee used to call the 'hobnailed boot' syndrome, which goes something like this: when the Northern nationalist community sees 'the men with the hobnailed boots', the DUP hardliners, in control on the unionist side, they turn to 'the men with the hobnailed boots on our side', the hard men of Sinn Féin.

The Newry journalist Peter Makem makes the same point slightly differently. What he calls 'Catch 32' operates as follows: the more the DUP proclaim a 'never, never' intransigence to the slightest move towards accommodation with the South, the more nationalism reacts with a fresh and more militant united Ireland assertion. The more Sinn Féin hoists the tricolour on their march towards a united Ireland, the more the DUP dig into their 'no surrender' trenches. This is the essence of politics, past and present, in the North of Ireland. This is what we have to change.

The arrogance of the DUP, shown in recent years by its politicians' contempt for the Irish language, is part of the reason for the resort to hard-line nationalism: whether it was Arlene Foster's comment about Sinn Féin being 'crocodiles' for demanding an Irish Language Act, or Gregory Campbell's 'curry my yoghurt' speech, or the decision by Paul Givan to scrap tiny grants allowing young people to study Irish in the Donegal Gaeltacht.

Another reason is the public perception of the incompetent and corrupt nature of the last power-sharing administration, particularly on the DUP side, whether it was the Renewable Heat Incentive or NAMA sell-off scandals, the Red Sky property scandal in Belfast or Ian Paisley Junior's dubious holidays. It is little wonder that the Executive was so unloved by nationalists at the end: at one meeting of broad nationalist opinion in West Belfast, Sinn Féin could find only two people out of a crowd of over 150 to support them going back into that government. Too many nationalists felt it was not worthwhile, so it was easy for them to give the DUP a black eye at election time by voting Sinn Féin.

Then there is Brexit. Brexit has allowed the most fear-filled and eurosceptic elements in the DUP, led by its Westminster MPs, to take a hard line anti-EU stance that is, while intrinsic to their psychological DNA, entirely at odds with the interests of the economically exposed province they purport to represent. Their paranoia about weakening links with Britain blinded them to the very real benefits that Theresa May's November 2018 deal with the EU would have brought Northern Ireland. One of Ireland's leading economic commentators, Cliff Taylor of *The Irish Times,* called it 'an extraordinary win-win' for the North. Under it, Northern companies would be able to export freely into both the UK and the EU. There would be some checks and controls on goods coming from Britain, but it is clear that the EU was prepared to bend to minimize these. It meant, for example, that the North could market itself as a unique destination for foreign direct investment, allowing a free flow of goods into both the UK and EU. This could also be of huge benefit to indigenous Northern firms, and avoid much of the disruption of Brexit. The North, unlike Britain, could continue to benefit from other trade deals, which the EU has in place with third countries.[1]

In the longer term, if a pro-EU Scotland eventually votes for independence, the DUP's position may also be seen to be at odds with their political interests, as the United Kingdom they are so passionately loyal to begins to disintegrate. And do they not recognize that a hard Irish border following the UK crashing out of the EU is just the kind of development that will force moderate nationalists into the arms of Sinn Féin, and make the dissidents more attractive to disadvantaged young nationalists? It is hard not to conclude that this is a classic example of 'stupid unionism'.

---

1. 'DUP opposition to Brexit agreement crazy as North is big winner from deal', *The Irish Times,* 17 November 2018.

There are other kinds of unionists. Peter Robinson said in 2018 that while he did not think it would happen, in the event of a Border Poll leading to unity every democrat in Northern Ireland would have to accept that decision; he added that to move towards such a scenario without preparation would be 'madness' and compared it to the UK's ill-prepared decision to leave the EU.[2] The columnist and former UUP communications director Alex Kane wrote in April 2017:

> A significant minority of unionists voted to Remain. They like the European Union and regard it as a stabilizing influence in Northern Ireland. They like being Northern Irish, British, partly Irish and European. That multiplicity of identities suits them. But a Northern Ireland outside the European Union will change the nature of their relationship both with the UK generally and the Republic. It will make them reassess their priorities. They may conclude that a bigger, broader union embracing Ireland and the EU is preferable to a smaller, narrower union of a UK out on its own. Which means they will be prepared to listen to a coherent, persuasive argument from those who make the case for Irish unity within the European Union, particularly if that case is also made by Fianna Fáil and Fine Gael.[3]

Meanwhile Sinn Féin has seized on Brexit to push again for a Border Poll; in party chairman Declan Kearney's words 'accelerated reunification post-Brexit'. I have warned sternly against such an early referendum. Does that make me any less a nationalist? I don't believe it does. One of the main differences between the republican movement's vision of national unity and mine is that they have always used their Irishness as a cudgel to beat people with. They see themselves as the only legitimate Irish republicans. They argue that they are only completing the unfinished business of Irish independence and separatism from Britain that was begun in the War of Independence.

For thirty years they did this through violence; they are now relying on the demographic force of numbers to get an eventual voting majority, however narrow, for unity. On the other hand, I argue for a nationalism based on persuading the unionists that it is in their interest to reach a peaceful and consensual accommodation in order to live together with the other people on this island, no matter how long that takes. My nationalism is a version of the old Irish saying: '*Ar scáth a chéile a mhaireann na daoine*' ('In the shelter of each other we live').

Where I also differ from the republican movement, of course, is on its traditional support for violence. I believe passionately that a united Ireland can only

---

2. 'North "should prepare" for possible unity', *The Irish Times*, 28 July 2018.
3. 'Brexit is greatest challenge for unionism since 1912', *The Irish Times,* 14 April 2017.

come about by agreement and persuasion. How do you persuade somebody if you have shot their father dead or bombed their family? Most Northern nationalists have little or no concept of what has been done to the unionist psyche by a whole range of happenings in recent decades: the killing of so many in their community by republican paramilitaries; British government decisions over their heads like the Anglo-Irish Agreement; the drastic reform or abolition of the security forces they were so loyal to, the RUC and the UDR; and a former IRA commander, Martin McGuinness, who had sent out so many men to kill British soldiers and Northern Irish police officers, becoming a Cabinet minister without a single IRA weapon being handed over. We have to be aware of the genuine hurt in that community. Michael Longley put it brilliantly in the final verse of his 1993 poem 'Ceasefire': 'I get down on my knees and do what must be done/And kiss Achilles' hand, the killer of my son.'

There is also a moral issue here. Did the IRA campaign of violence constitute a 'just war', as defined by Catholic theologians? I believe not, because peaceful, democratic alternatives were always available. I have heard Gerry Adams saying that you should not talk about anybody's morality unless you had walked in their shoes. I have walked in the shoes of many a family – nationalist and unionist – who have lost fathers and mothers, husbands and wives, sons and daughters, brothers and sisters to violence. I have no hesitation in saying that what the IRA were doing for thirty years and more was morally wrong; to kill people in Northern Ireland in pursuit of Irish unity was morally wrong. Far too many people have lost their lives at the hands of those who, in the words of that great singer from Strabane, Paul Brady, are 'still trying to carve tomorrow on a tombstone'. Why did so many people have to die; why did such utter misery have to be endured by so many thousands of individuals and families, when finally not a single one of the 'war aims' of the republican movement was achieved and when in 1998 they had to settle for the 1973 Sunningdale terms ('Sunningdale for slow learners' I called it) plus the entrenchment of partition in the changes to the Irish Constitution?

Many traditional republicans continue to believe that violence is a legitimate way to remove the British presence (whatever about the unionists, whom they usually ignore) from Ireland. You find this simplistic view particularly strongly held by left-wing people in Britain and Irish-Americans, none of whom, of course, have ever experienced the actual violence in the North. I have a vivid memory of speaking in the Emerald Club in Detroit one Friday evening in the 1980s. The Irish Consul General, Liam Caniffe, spoke before me. He was treated very badly. There was a guy at the back of the room and I knew when I walked in that he was the Provo plant. He gave Liam such abuse. I'm sitting up there and this voice is away at the back of the hall. So I said to him: 'Would you like to come up here and say that?' He stood up. He was about six feet five inches tall, broad as a ditch. Here was I, shaking in my shoes, and trying not to show it. I had to stand; I could not back off. He walked up to me and said: 'If I had my gun (note: not *a* gun) I would blow the head off you.' And then he left. That only increased my realization of what had to be done. I threw down a challenge that night. 'Many of you are in favour of violence, killing people, trying to solve political problems with the wrong means. I'll tell you what I'll do. I'll get somebody with money to hire a plane to leave Detroit, taking all your young sons and daughters over the age of fifteen to Northern Ireland to do the fighting. That is the test I'll put to you.'[4]

In 2019 we find ourselves once again incapable of sharing the government of Northern Ireland. The core problem is that neither the DUP nor Sinn Féin subscribed to the reconciling philosophy of the Good Friday Agreement. What happened in the years up to the 2017 collapse of the institutions was a deepening of the intercommunal struggle for dominance, and stalemate and corruption as the two parties 'shared out' the spoils of office rather than shared power in any real way. The long-drawn-out years before the IRA finally decommissioned its arms, by leading to the destruction of the middle-ground partnership that David Trimble and I tried so hard to create, has led to the virtual elimination of the ethos of the Good Friday Agreement.

That ethos would have seen unionists and nationalists sharing responsibility in government and this, in the most benign scenario, could have seeped out into wider Northern society, leading to a diminution of intercommunal divisions. This would have been buttressed by the development of strong North–South and East–West institutions, and the combination of all these factors could have started to drain the swamp of much of the mutual suspicion and antipathy so intrinsic to the North. For their part, the governments did not properly work the North–South and East–West institutions so that the latter, in particular, were allowed to lapse to the point where there were no effective structures for dialogue between Dublin and London following Brexit and the collapse of the Executive.

I believe it was a strategic error by the governments to focus so much on Sinn Féin, the IRA and arms decommissioning, rather than doing more to support the Ulster Unionist Party and the SDLP (and the Alliance Party) to strengthen the centre ground. I still believe we can build a shared centre where most people,

---

4. M. Fitzpatrick, *John Hume in America: from Derry to DC* (Dublin 2017), 73.

unionist and nationalist, can feel comfortable and secure and at home. Once we have achieved that, we can then work towards the unification of the people of Ireland, rather than the forced marriage of territorial unity. To this end I propose replacing the 'sword of Damocles' of a 50 per cent plus one Border Poll vote with the doubly protective 'shield' of Parallel Consent.

The SDLP is now in a difficult position, with its diminished electoral support and without an MP at Westminster. As someone who is retired from active politics for many years, I am reluctant to comment in detail on the recent plan for a partnership between the SDLP and Fianna Fáil. I have always believed it is important for the SDLP to retain the support of all the parties in the South, harnessing the power of constitutional nationalism in the interests of everyone on the island.

What about my own role? I keep returning to Enoch Powell's statement that all political lives end in failure. When it comes to the Last Day and the parable of the talents, I hope the judgment will be: 'Could have done better. Could have done things differently. But tried his best.' Have I done anything that helped to move things towards a resolution based on the concept of republicanism outlined in this book? I hope so. Did I hurt too many people in my campaigns to reform or abolish the RUC and the UDR? Probably. Did I add to people's suffering by trying to be as effective a nationalist politician as I could while at the same time trying to live with my unionist neighbours as fellow human beings in an extremely difficult situation? I hope not.

I see Britain eventually leaving Northern Ireland. Their mindset will be that it is no use to them any more, and sometimes it is an embarrassment. One wonders, for example, if it had not been for the difficult people in the DUP, whether Theresa May would have reached a compromise agreement on leaving the EU sooner and on better terms. There is little love among large sections of the UK Parliament for the DUP after its antics on the side of the hard Brexiteers. I believe the British would have absolutely no problem in leaving the North if there was the prospect of peace and stability there on the basis of consent. The vexed question of sovereignty will be key to ensuring that any such departure is as peaceful as possible. When Britain leaves, there has to be some kind of Irish sovereignty by consent. If not, there will be a political vacuum and mayhem.

If Britain is going to leave one day, it will surely become clear sooner or later to the majority of Irish people that the main obstacle to overcoming the deep and ancient divisions on the island is the unionist fear of Irish nationalism. To persuade a significant part of the unionist community that their fears are groundless, and there is no need for them to live apart from the rest of the island, is now the only meaningful programme for nationalism. This is the last major obstacle to be overcome if we are to realize the nationalist aspiration for unity.

We are in the business here of reconciling fundamental contradictions: nationalist and unionist, Irish and British, Catholic and Protestant, native and settler, republican and monarchist, pro-European and anti-European, anti-imperialist and imperialist – the list goes on and on. In terms of logic, this is seemingly impossible. But it is the dilemma history has imposed upon us.

The biggest challenge for nationalists in the foreseeable future is to help our unionist neighbours face an uncertain future with some confidence, even optimism. When they imagine themselves as a future minority in a united Ireland controlled, as they see it, by their ancient enemies, they are filled with fear and foreboding, and try to avoid even thinking about it. In my home village, they even talk about their fear of having their land, which has been in their ownership for hundreds of years, taken away from them in that new state. Former members of the security forces fear retribution for their involvement in the RUC and UDR. How can we help to liberate them from those feelings of dread? How can we assuage their fears about the perceived threat posed by Irish nationalism to their ethos and way of life? One thing I have found in dealing with unionists over the years is that they do not trust anyone: the British government, the Irish government, their own politicians, even themselves.

One point in our favour is that the Republic of Ireland is now utterly transformed and modernized. It is a far cry from the poor, backward, Catholic Church-dominated society that filled unionists with dread for almost the whole of the last century. It is a vibrant democracy and a dynamic small country at the heart of the European project. I may not agree with all the reforms that have taken place there in recent years: on abortion reform, my position that the destruction of a human being, including the unborn, is wrong in all circumstances, is well known. However, I recognize that it is now an open, liberal and multicultural society with laws on sensitive issues like same-sex marriage that are in advance of most other countries.

Economically it is extraordinarily successful, with growth and unemployment rates that are the envy of other European countries. The economic commentator David McWilliams has estimated that since partition the economic strengths of the two Irish jurisdictions have gone in opposite directions. In 1920 80 per cent of Irish industrial output was in and around Belfast, which was the largest city on the island. By stark contrast, the economy of the Republic is now four times larger than that of Northern Ireland, with industrial output ten times larger.[5]

---

5. 'Northern Ireland and the TripAdvisor index of economic vibrancy', *The Irish Times*, 2 December 2017.

All these factors will play a part in the eventual decisions we will have to make about the island's constitutional future, and in particular the decisions made by the people of the South. I have heard it argued that we should not take a majority Border Poll vote for unity in the Republic for granted, particularly if there is a particularly fraught and tight poll in the North. A straight vote for a united Ireland in those circumstances could be rejected by the people of the South. Modern Irish history has shown that every referendum provokes a coalition of opposition forces with often contradictory arguments.

In the event of a referendum on unity, there could be two such opposition arguments there. The first will be simply that people with a peaceful and prosperous life in the present-day republic will not want to incorporate into their rather contented society a deeply divided and economically dependent Northern Ireland, as well as bearing the huge cost of the British subvention. The second, which I sympathize with, is that Northern Ireland was unstable for nearly a hundred years because it incorporated a large minority of people against their will, and surely we are not going to make the same mistake in a united Ireland.

Another way of putting the big question about the country's constitutional future is to ask: 'Is Ireland *ready* for reunification?' Have the political and civil society leaders in Ireland, North and South, done their homework about the likely outcome and impact of a referendum on unity? What are the chances of a peaceful, harmonious, all-Ireland society resulting from such a vote? An Oxford Union debate in November 2018 heard from six speakers on the motion 'The House believes Ireland is ready for reunification'. Micheál Martin of Fianna Fáil, Colum Eastwoood of the SDLP and Joan Burton of the Irish Labour Party were in favour of the motion; Mike Nesbitt of the Ulster Unionist party, the independent unionist Clare Sugden and Irish High Court judge Richard Humphreys were against it. But in reality none of the speakers was arguing that Ireland was ready for such a huge step in the near future. It is like asking your seventeen-year-old daughter if she is ready for marriage. Has she thought through the huge implications for her life and happiness at such an unthinking age? Has she thought about what it will be like moving into her husband's home, when there is such long-standing antipathy between the two families? Has she thought through the practical and economic arrangements for the union? Not surprisingly, the Oxford Union motion was defeated.

We have also to take into account the interests and opinions of two important categories of people who have not figured at all in this book: the immigrant 'new Irish' from countries all over the world, who now comprise more than 17 per cent of the population in the Republic; and the 'Other Religion/No Religion/None Stated' category in the Northern Ireland Statistics and Research Agency's authoritative Pooled Survey, whose numbers grew by an astonishing 38 per cent in the four years between 2011 and 2015.

The nationalist community in the North have the experience of centuries of being beaten down and and excluded. I fervently hope that my community, as we move closer to being a majority in the North, will not now consider doing to the unionists what was done to us. If global warming spares us, in a hundred years' time we will still be living together, we will still be looking across the hedges at each other, we will still be going down the same roads to church or chapel. If we believe that the way the unionist majority used and abused us gives us the right to despise and trample on them, I won't go along with it. Northern Ireland is their home too.

I have mentioned my neighbour 'Jack Adams', a good man who couldn't do enough for you, but who was shot dead by the IRA because he felt he was doing his duty by joining the RUC reserve. That dehumanizing of individuals, of a community, so they could be killed just for wearing a police or UDR uniform – that is what I will not support. That man and his family had their home here for four hundred years, but he had to be killed because the IRA's little Green Book said so. The awfulness and nihilism of that is what I am fundamentally opposed to.

I believe that thirty years of violence has meant the republican movement has shot and bombed itself out of the vital process of persuading people for Irish unity. We in the SDLP, on the other hand, have proudly stood by our core principles of non-violence, unity by genuine consent and refusing to exclude our unionist neighbours from any future solution.

Former IRA leaders have claimed that it was never defeated. Let me make a counterclaim. Perhaps the IRA in its various forms was not defeated by any external military agency such as the British army or the RUC – but it was defeated by its own internal contradictions and demons. Its defeat came with the first bullet fired without democratic mandate; with the first bomb primed without moral justification. In the long run violent organizations such as the IRA – like today's men of violence, Al Qaeda, Islamic State and Boko Haram – will always fall away. Violence interrupts but does not determine history. The slow work of history belongs to the citizens and democratic politicians who pick up the pieces and start over and over again.

A paragraph in Seamus Heaney's 1995 Nobel Prize lecture 'Creating Poetry' reads:

The violence from below was then productive of nothing but a retaliatory violence from above. The dream of justice became subsumed into the callousness of reality and people settled in to a quarter century of life waste and spirit waste, of hardening attitudes and narrowing possibilities that were the natural result of political solidarity, dramatic suffering and sheer emotional self-protectiveness.

I experienced that 'life waste and spirit waste', particularly in the blood-stained 1970s and 80s. The dream of justice though has also led to very significant changes in Northern Ireland, and I am fortunate and honoured to have been an active participant in some of those changes. As I prepare to take my leave of our shared home place, I find comfort in an old Greek proverb: 'A society grows great when old men plant trees in whose shade they know they will never sit.'

Timeline

1920

Government of Ireland Act partitions Ireland into Northern Ireland and what would become the Irish Free State.

1921

Northern Ireland parliament opens.

1936

August   Seamus Mallon born in Armagh.

1968

October   Civil rights marchers, including Gerry Fitt MP, beaten by the RUC in Duke Street in Derry.

1969

August   John Gallagher becomes the first victim of the Troubles outside Belfast and Derry, shot by the B-Specials in Armagh.

1971

August   Internment introduced, with hundreds of arrests and major outbreaks of violence.

1972

January   Fourteen people killed on 'Bloody Sunday', when British paratroopers opened fire on a civil rights march in Derry.

July   Nine people killed on 'Bloody Friday', in a series of Provisional IRA bombs in Belfast.

1973

May   Seamus Mallon elected to Armagh District Council.

June   Mallon elected to the new Northern Ireland Assembly.

November   Agreement reached between the parties to set up a power-sharing Executive to administer Northern Ireland.

December   The Sunningdale Agreement signed, clearing the way for a power-sharing Executive to be formed alongside an all-island Council of Ireland.

1974

May   Thirty-three people and a full-term unborn child killed by loyalist bombs in Dublin and Monaghan, attacks believed to have been carried out by the 'Glenanne gang', based near Markethill. The Ulster Workers' Council strike causes the collapse of the power-sharing Executive.

1975

July   Three members of the Miami Showband killed outside Banbridge, County Down (along with two UVF attackers), an attack believed to have been carried out by the Glenanne gang.

1976

January   The three Reavey brothers killed in Whitecross, County Armagh, an attack believed to have been carried out by the Glenanne gang; on the following day ten Protestant men killed by the IRA on their way back from work at nearby Kingsmill.

1979

November   Gerry Fitt resigns as SDLP leader, to be succeeded by John Hume, with Seamus Mallon as deputy leader.

1981

March– October   The second republican hunger strike in the Maze prison leads to the deaths of ten IRA and INLA prisoners.

1982

February   Seamus Mallon appointed to Seanad Éireann by Charles Haughey (until November).

1983–4

The New Ireland Forum held in Dublin.

1985

November   The Anglo-Irish Agreement signed at Hillsborough by Taoiseach Garret FitzGerald and British Prime Minister Margaret Thatcher; the Maryfield secretariat set up outside Belfast to implement it.

1986

January   Seamus Mallon wins the Newry and Armagh House of Commons seat after by-elections caused by the resignation of unionist MPs in protest at the Anglo-Irish Agreement.

1988

Secret talks begin between SDLP leader John Hume and Sinn Féin leader Gerry Adams.

1993

December   The Downing Street Declaration signed by Taoiseach Albert Reynolds and British Prime Minister John Major.

1994

August   The IRA declares its first ceasefire.

1996

February   The first IRA ceasefire ends with bombing of Canary Wharf in London.

June   All-party talks begin at Stormont without Sinn Féin.

1997

May   The Labour Party, under Tony Blair, wins the British general election.

July   The IRA declares its second ceasefire.

September   Sinn Féin join the all-party talks; the DUP walk out.

1998

10 April   Senator George Mitchell announces that the two governments and all the parties had agreed what would become known as the Belfast or Good Friday Agreement, setting up a new Northern Ireland Assembly and Executive, along with North–South and East–West bodies.

May   The Agreement approved by referendums on both sides of the border. In NI 71.1 per cent vote in favour; in the Republic 94.4 per cent.

July   David Trimble of the Ulster Unionist Party and Seamus Mallon of the SDLP sworn in as First Minister and Deputy First Minister of Northern Ireland. The Drumcree Orange marchers are prevented from walking through the Catholic Garvaghy Road area of Portadown and three small boys are burned to death in a loyalist arson attack in Ballymoney, County Antrim.

August   Twenty-nine people (including a woman pregnant with twins) killed in a car bomb attack in Omagh, County Tyrone, carried out by the 'Real IRA' – the single worst atrocity of the Troubles.

1999

September/ The Patten Report published, proposing radical changes to policing.
December A power-sharing Northern Ireland Executive sworn in, led by Trimble and Mallon and containing ministers from the Ulster Unionist Party, SDLP, Sinn Féin and DUP (the latter functioning as ministers but boycotting Executive meetings).

2000

February Secretary of State Peter Mandelson announces suspension of the Executive and Assembly because of lack of movement on IRA decommissioning.

May The Executive and Assembly restored following an IRA statement that if the Good Friday Agreement was fully implemented it would 'fully and verifiably put IRA weapons beyond use'.

2001

September John Hume and Seamus Mallon announce that they will be standing down as leader and deputy leader of the SDLP.

November Mallon stands down as Deputy First Minister.

2002

October Following a police raid on Sinn Féin's Stormont offices during an investigation into alleged IRA intelligence-gathering, Secretary of State John Reid announces suspension of Northern Ireland institutions and reintroduction of 'direct rule' from London.

2005

May Seamus Mallon retires from politics after deciding not to contest the Newry and Armagh seat in British general election.

September Commission on Decommissioning announces that the IRA has put all its weapons beyond use.

2007

May The power-sharing Executive restored following the 2006 St Andrews Agreement, with Rev. Ian Paisley of the DUP as First Minister and Martin McGuinness of Sinn Féin as Deputy First Minister.

2017

January Martin McGuinness resigns as Deputy First Minister over the Renewable Heat Incentive scandal, collapsing the Northern Ireland Executive and Assembly.

Abbreviations

DFA	(Irish) Department of Foreign Affairs
DUP	Democratic Unionist Party
FRU	Force Research Unit (of the British army)
GAA	Gaelic Athletic Association
HET	Historical Inquiries Team (of the Police Service of Northern Ireland)
INLA	Irish National Liberation Army
IRA	Irish Republican Army
NIO	Northern Ireland Office
NSMC	North South Ministerial Council
OC	Officer Commanding (of the IRA)
Provo	Provisional Republican movement (Provisional IRA and Sinn Féin)
PSNI	Police Service of Northern Ireland
RUC	Royal Ulster Constabulary
SDLP	Social Democratic and Labour Party
SPG	Special Patrol Group (of RUC)
UDA	Ulster Defence Association
UDR	Ulster Defence Regiment
UUP	Ulster Unionist Party
UVF	Ulster Volunteer Force
UWC	Ulster Workers' Council

Index of Names and Places